WISDOM
of the AGES

Wayne W. Dyer

WISDOM
of the AGES

Eternal Truths
for Everyday Lives

Thorsons

Grateful acknowledgement is made to the publishers for permission
to reprint the following works: 'For Anne Gregory' by William
Butler Yeats: Reprinted with the permission of Scribner, a Division
of Simon & Schuster, from *The Collected Works of W B Yeats*, Vol. 1:
The Poems. Revised and edited by Richard J Finneran. Copyright 1933
by Macmillan Publishing Company; copyright renewed © 1961 by Bertha
Georgie Yeats. 'The Road Not Taken' by Robert Frost: From *The Poetry
of Robert Frost*, edited by Edward Connery Lathem. Copyright 1916, ©
1969 by Henry Holt & Co. Reprinted by permission of Henry Holt &
Co. Inc. 'So That's Who I Remind Me Of' by Ogden Nash: From *Good
Intentions* by Ogden Nash. Copyright © 1942 by Ogden Nash. By permission
of Little, Brown and Company. 'On Being a Woman' by Dorothy Parker:
From *The Portable Dorothy Parker*, edited by Brendan Gill. Copyright
1991 by Viking Penguin. Reprinted by permission of Viking Penguin.

Thorsons
An Imprint of HarperCollins*Publishers*
77–85 Fulham Palace Road,
Hammersmith, London W6 8JB

First published by HarperCollins Publishers Inc.,
10 East 53rd Street, New York, NY 10022, USA 1998.
This edition published by Thorsons 1999.

10 9 8 7 6 5 4 3 2

© Wayne Dyer 1998

Wayne Dyer asserts the moral right to
be identified as the author of this work

A catalogue record for this book
is available from the British Library

ISBN 0 7225 3840 5

Printed and bound in Great Britain by
Creative Print and Design (Wales), Ebbw Vale

To Our Son
Sands Jay Dyer
Bodhisattva Extraordinaire

When you are dead,
seek for your resting place
not in the earth,
but in the hearts of men.

RUMI

Lives of great men all remind us
We can make our lives sublime,
And, departing, leave behind us
Footprints on the sands of time.

HENRY WADSWORTH LONGFELLOW

CONTENTS

CONTENTS

CONTENTS

ACKNOWLEDGMENTS

I wish to acknowledge each of these sixty teachers who felt compelled to share their wisdom for the benefit of each of us living here now.

I am also most grateful to my dear friend and literary agent of the past quarter century, Arthur Pine, as well as my editor, proofreader, typist, and dear dear friend, Joanna Pyle, for their enormous contribution to the completion of this book.

Thank you—thank you—

INTRODUCTION

*I*n my mind I can picture what the world was like in other times, and I am fascinated by what those people who lived before us might have felt in their hearts. To imagine that Pythagoras, Buddha, Jesus Christ, Michelangelo, Shelley, Shakespeare, Emerson, and so many of those we revere as our teachers and spiritual leaders actually walked on the same ground, drank the same water, watched the same moon, and were warmed by the same sun as I am today intrigues me considerably. Even more intriguing is what these greatest minds of all time would like us to know.

I have come to the conclusion that in order to effect deep inner spiritual change in our world, we need to know and live in our personal lives the wisdom these eminent teachers from our past have left us. Many of these profound teachers were considered troublemakers, and some were even put to death for their beliefs. Their teachings, however, could never be silenced, as evidenced by the variety of topics from differing historical eras that are in this book. Their words live on and their advice for having a deeper and a richer experience of life is here for you to read and apply. This collection is a compendium of the wisdom from those topics and times, and what I feel those wise and creative thinkers are telling us now about how to create deep inner spiritual change.

In a sense, those of us who now occupy Planet Earth are in many ways connected to all those who lived here before us. We may have new technologies and modern conveniences, but we still share the same heart space, and the same energy or life force that flowed through their bodies now flows through ours. It is to this mind picture and shared energy that this book is dedicated. What do those ancestral scholars, whom we consider the wisest and most spiritually advanced, have to say to us today?

Their observations of life's greatest lessons are in the prose, poetry, and speeches that they left for us to read and listen to. Though they lived in a separate time with quite different living conditions, they still speak to you and to me. In essence, these brilliant minds of our past are still with us through their words.

I have chosen to highlight sixty of our ancestral teachers, all of whom command my admiration and respect. They are a diverse group, representing ancient, medieval, Renaissance, early modern, and modern times, from all around our world. Some lived into their nineties and others died in their early twenties. Male, female; black, white, Native American, Far Eastern, Middle Eastern; scholars, soldiers, scientists, philosophers, poets, and statesmen, they are here, and they have something to say to you personally.

The choice of these sixty people in no way infers that those who are not in this book are any less significant. Each selection and each contributor were simply my choices to illuminate these subjects. It is as simple as that. Had I included all the great teachers of the past, you would need to rent a trailer and a crane just to lift this book, so prodigious are the offerings of our ancestors!

I have written each piece in a way that explains how these noble masters' works might benefit you directly, here and now. Each contribution is designed to speak to you personally, with specific suggestions at the end of each short essay explaining how you can implement the lessons in your life. I want to provide you with insights that you can apply from some of our most esteemed teachers, rather than have you learn their poetry and prose and passively conclude, "Well, that's nice for a literature or humanities class, but that was then and this is now." I recommend that you read each selection with an openness to the idea that these towering minds share the same divinity and life force as you do and are talking to you directly in their own unique language and art form, and that you are going to apply their wisdom to your life beginning today!

As I wrote each of these essays, I looked at a portrait or photograph of the teacher I was highlighting and I would literally ask the individual, "What would you like those of us here today to know?"—and I would listen and surrender. I allowed myself to experience their guidance and my writing became almost automatic. It may sound strange, but I actually felt the presence of those writers and poets with me as I wrote each of these sixty pieces.

Many of the selections in this book are poems. I view poetry as a language of the heart—not just a form of entertainment or a subject to get past in school, but another way to transform our lives by communicating our wisdom to one another. Here are three examples from my own life of how poetry, the language of the heart, has touched me.

Many years ago, when I received my doctorate, I was at a festive celebration where I was given many nice gifts. The gift that touched me most deeply was a poem written by my mother, which still hangs in my office almost thirty years later. I reproduce it here to illustrate how poetry, which doesn't have to originate in the minds of renowned celebrities, can touch us where we live.

> A mother can but guide . . .
> then step aside—I knew
> I could not say, "This is the way
> that you should go."
>
> For I could not foresee
> what paths might beckon you
> to unimagined heights
> that I might never know.
>
> Yet, always in my heart
> I realized
> That you would touch a star . . .
> I'm not surprised!

When my oldest daughter, Tracy, was just a toddler of five or six, she sent me a picture she had drawn in school along with a poem that expressed from her tender heart how she felt. Her mother and I had separated, and she knew the pain that I felt in not living with her every day. This too has been framed and hangs on the wall next to my desk.

> Even if the sun stops shining,
> Even if the sky is never blue
> It won't matter
> Because I'll always love you.

Reading those precious thoughts expressed poetically from my daughter never fails to tug at my heart and produce tears of gratitude in my eyes.

Finally, our daughter Sommer wrote this poem as a Christmas gift for her mother. It sits, framed, beside her bed for her to read every night.

What Your Love Means to Me

> Knowing your smile greets
> Me at the door
> And your kind words leave
> Me with no worries.
>
> Every time I slip a step
> You help me to my feet
> And when you and I laugh
> Together I only feel complete.
>
> Your love for us shines through
> On every cloudy day
> To think you'd ever abandon
> Us isn't possible in any way.
>
> A Mom like you is impossible
> The kind you'll never see

That's why I love you
That's what your love means to me.

As I said, poetry is the language of the heart, and you are
about to have your heart touched by sixty majestic souls who
wrote directly to you from another place and another time. This
book will serve you best if you think of it as a way of reconnect-
ing to those great souls who have left our material world in body
form but are still very much with us in a spiritual sense.

I encourage you to make this book a two-month renovation
project of your soul in which you read *only one* selection each day
and then make a conscious effort to apply the suggestions that
day. When you have completed the sixty days, use this as a reference book. Look at the sixty subjects in the table of contents, and
if you need a boost in patience, mercy, kindness, meditation, forgiveness, humility, leadership, prayer, or anything else covered by
our ancestral masters, then read that contribution. Review the
essay and work on applying the specific recommendations. Let
your life be guided by greatness!

To me, this is the way to teach poetry, prose, and literature; let
it come alive, let it shimmer in your mind and then take that
inner awakening and put it to work. All of us are deeply grateful
to those who make life throb to a swifter, stronger beat. These
great teachers from the past have done that for me, and I encourage you to apply this language of the heart from the wisdom of
the ages to your life.

God bless you,

Wayne W. Dyer

MEDITATION

Learn to be silent.
Let your
quiet mind
listen and absorb.

PYTHAGORAS
(580 B.C.–500 B.C.)

*A Greek philosopher and mathematician, Pythagoras was espe-
cially interested in the study of mathematics in relation to weights
and measures and to musical theory.*

All man's miseries derive from not being
able to sit quietly in a room alone.

BLAISE PASCAL
(1623–1662)

*Blaise Pascal was a French philosopher, scientist, mathematician,
and writer, whose treatises contributed to the fields of hydraulics
and pure geometry.*

*T*his is the one time in this collection of great contributors that
I have elected to highlight two writers on the same subject. I
selected two men whose lives were separated by over two millennia, both of whom in their own times were considered the most
knowledgeable in the rational fields of mathematics and science.

Pythagoras, whose writings influenced the thought of Plato
and Aristotle, was a major contributor to the development of both
mathematics and Western rational philosophy. Blaise Pascal, a famous

French mathematician, physicist, and religious philosopher who lived twenty-two centuries after Pythagoras, is considered one of the original scientific minds. He is responsible for inventing the syringe, the hydraulic press, and the first digital calculator. Pascal's Law of Pressure is still taught in science classes around the world today.

Keeping in mind the left-brained scientific leanings of these two scientists, reread their two quotes. Pascal: "All man's miseries derive from not being able to sit quietly in a room alone." Pythagoras: "Learn to be silent. Let your quiet mind listen and absorb." They both speak to the importance of silence and the value of meditation in your life, whether you are an accountant or an avatar. They send us a valuable message about a way of being in life that is not popularly encouraged in our culture: that there is tremendous value in creating alone time in your life that is spent in silence. If you want to shed your miseries, learn to sit silently in a room alone and meditate.

It has been estimated that the average person has sixty thousand separate thoughts each and every day. The problem with this is that we have the same sixty thousand thoughts today that we had yesterday, and we'll repeat them again tomorrow. Our minds are filled with the same chatter day in and day out. Learning to be quiet and meditate involves figuring out a way to enter the spaces between your thoughts; or the gap, as I call it. In this silent empty space between your thoughts, you can find a sense of total peace in a realm that is ordinarily unknowable. Here, any illusion of your separateness is shattered. However, if you have sixty thousand separate thoughts in a day, there is literally no time available to enter the space between your thoughts, because there is no space!

Most of us have minds that race full-speed day and night. Our thoughts are a hodgepodge of continuous dialogue about schedules, money worries, sexual fantasies, grocery lists, drapery problems, concern about the children, vacation plans, and on and on like a merry-go-round that never stops. Those sixty thousand thoughts are usually about ordinary daily activities and create a mental pattern that leaves no space for silence.

This pattern reinforces our cultural belief that all gaps in conversation (silence) need to be filled quickly. For many, silence represents an embarrassment and a social defect. Therefore we learn to jump in to fill these spaces, whether or not our filler has any substance. Silent periods in a car or at a dinner are perceived as awkward moments, and good conversationalists know how to get those spaces occupied with some kind of noise.

And so it is with ourselves as well; we have no training in silence, and we see it as unwieldy and confusing. Thus we keep the inner dialogue going just like the outer. Yet it is in that silent place, where our ancient teacher Pythagoras tells us to let our quiet mind listen and absorb, that confusion will disappear and enlightened guidance will come to us. But meditation also affects the quality of our nonsilent activities. The daily practice of meditation is the single thing in my life that gives me a greater sense of well-being, increased energy, higher productivity at a more conscious level, more satisfying relationships, and a closer connection to God.

The mind is like a pond. On the surface you see all the disturbances, yet the surface is only a fraction of the pond. It is in the depth below the surface, where there is stillness, that you will come to know the true essence of the pond, as well as your own mind. By going below the surface, you come to the spaces between your thoughts where you are able to enter the gap. The gap is total emptiness or silence, and it is indivisible. No matter how many times you cut silence in half, you still get silence. This is what is meant by *now*. Perhaps it is the essence of God, that which cannot be divided from the oneness.

These two pioneering scientists, who are still quoted today in university courses, were studying the nature of the universe. They struggled with the mysteries of energy, pressure, mathematics, space, time, and universal truths. Their message to all of us here is quite simple. If you want to understand the universe, or your own personal universe, if you want to know how it all works, then be quiet and face your fear of sitting in a room alone and going deep within the layers of your own mind.

It is the space between the notes that makes the music. Without that emptiness, that silence in between, there is no music, only a noise. You too are silent empty space at your center, surrounded by form. To break through that form and discover your very creative nature that is in the center, you must take the time to become silent each day, and enter that rapturous space between your thoughts. No amount of my writing about the value of daily meditation will ever convince you. You will never know the value of this practice unless you make the commitment to do it.

My purpose in writing this brief essay on the value of meditation is not to tell you how to meditate. There are many fine courses of study, manuals, and audio guides to give you instruction. My purpose here is to emphasize that meditation is not something that is exclusively for spiritual seekers who want to wile away the hours and days of their lives in deep contemplation, oblivious to productivity and social responsibility. Meditation is a practice advocated by those who live by their faith in reason, by number crunchers and authors of theorems and believers in Pascal's Law. You may feel much as Blaise Pascal did when he wrote, "The eternal silence of these infinite spaces terrifies me."

Here are some suggestions for overcoming your terror and learning to be silent and able to sit quietly in a room alone:

- Practice noticing your in and out breaths as a way to cultivate turning inward to the silent self. You can do this in the middle of meetings, conversations, even parties. Just notice and follow your breathing for a few moments, many times during your day.

- Give yourself time this day to simply sit in a room alone and observe your mind. Keep track of the various thoughts that enter, exit, and lead to the next thought. Your awareness of the frenetic activity of your mind will help you to transcend the frenzied pace of thoughts.

- Read a book on meditation to learn how the practice can be initiated, or join a meditation group. Many teachers and local organizations can get you started on this path. The Chopra Center for Well-Being in La Jolla, California, headed by my friend and colleague Deepak Chopra, teaches meditation as a part of its large offering of services.

- Many CDs and tapes are available to guide you in meditation. Find one that appeals to you. I have published one entitled *Meditation for Manifesting* in which I teach a specific meditation called JAPA. I guide you through a morning and evening meditation using my voice to assist you in repeating the sounds of the divine. The profits go to charity.

KNOWING

Do not believe what you have heard.
Do not believe in tradition because it is handed down
  many generations.
Do not believe in anything that has been spoken of many times.
Do not believe because the written statements come from
  some old sage.
Do not believe in conjecture.
Do not believe in authority or teachers or elders.
But after careful observation and analysis, when it agrees
  with reason and it will benefit one and all, then accept it
  and live by it.

BUDDHA
(563 B.C.–483 B.C.)

*Founder of Buddhism, one of the world's major religions, the Buddha
was born Prince Siddhartha Gautama in northeast India, near the borders of Nepal. Seeing the unhappiness, sickness, and death that even the
wealthiest and most powerful are subject to in this life, at age twenty-
nine he abandoned the life he was living in search of a higher truth.*

The name Buddha is actually a title that translates to the "awakened one" or the "enlightened one." It is the title given to Siddhartha Gautama, who left behind the princely life at the age of
twenty-nine and went on a lifelong search for religious understanding and a way of release from the human condition. It is said
that he discarded the teachings of his contemporaries and
through meditation achieved enlightenment or ultimate understanding. From then on he assumed the role of teacher, instruct-
ing his followers in the "dharma," or truth.

His teachings became the basis for the religious practice of Buddhism, which has played a major role in the spiritual, cultural, and

social life of the Eastern world, and much of the Western world as well. I have deliberately chosen not to write, in this essay, on the tenets of Buddhist doctrine, but rather to take this often-quoted passage of the Buddha and discuss its significance to you and me today, some twenty-five centuries after the death of the enlightened one.

The key word in the passage is "believe." In fact, the key phrase is "Do not believe." Everything you carry around with you that you call a belief has become your own largely because of the experiences and testimonies of other people. And if it comes to you from a source outside yourself, regardless of how persuasive the conditioning process might be, and of how many people just like you have worked to convince you of the truth of these beliefs, the fact that it is someone else's truth means that you receive it with some question marks or doubts.

If I were to attempt to convince you about the taste of a delectable fish, you would perhaps listen but still have your doubts. Were I to show you pictures of this fish, and have hundreds of people come to testify about the veracity of my statements, you might become more convinced. But the modicum of doubt would still remain because you hadn't tasted it. You might accept the truth of its deliciousness for me; but until your taste buds experience the fish, your truth is only a belief based on my truth, on my experience. And so it is also with all the well-meaning members of your tribes, and their tribal ancestors before them.

Just because you have heard it, and it is a long-surviving tradition, and it is recorded over the centuries, and the world's greatest teachers have endorsed it, those are still not reasons to accept a belief. Remember, "Do not believe it," as Buddha instructs.

Rather than using the term "belief," try shifting to the word "knowing." When you have the direct experience of tasting the fish, you now have a knowing. That is, you have conscious contact and can determine your truth based on your experience. You know how to swim or ride a bicycle not because you have a belief, but because you have had the direct experience.

You are being reminded, directly by the "enlightened one" of twenty-five hundred years ago, to apply this same understanding to your spiritual practice. There is a fundamental difference between knowing something and knowing about something. "Knowing about" is another term for belief. "Knowing" is a term reserved exclusively for direct experience, which means an absence of doubt. I recall a well-known Kahuna healer responding to my questions about how a Kahuna becomes a healer. He said to me, "When a knowing confronts a belief in a disease process, the knowing will always triumph. Kahunas," he explained to me, "were raised to abandon all doubt and to know."

When I think of the parables of Jesus Christ as a great healer, I can't conjure any doubt. When Christ approached a leper he wouldn't say, "We haven't been having a great deal of success with leprosy lately. But if you follow my advice you'll have a thirty percent chance of survival over the next five years." You can see all the doubt that is present in such a stance. Rather, he would say from an absolute state of knowing, "You are healed." This is the same state of conscious contact with knowing from which St. Francis performed his healing miracles as well. In fact, all miracles come from shifting out of doubt and into knowing.

Yet the persuasiveness of tribal influences is exceedingly powerful. You are constantly being reminded of what you should or shouldn't believe, and what all our tribal members have always believed, and what will happen to you if you ignore these beliefs. Fear becomes the constant companion of your beliefs, and despite the doubts that you may be feeling inside, you often adopt these beliefs and make them crutches in your life, while you hobble through your days looking for a way out of the traps that have been carefully set by generations of believers before you.

The Buddha offers you some great advice, and you can see that his conclusion is devoid of the word "believe." He says when it agrees with reason—that is, when you know it to be true based on your own observation and experience—and it is beneficial to one and all, then and only then, live by it!

Throughout this book I offer you a summation of some of the most famous and creative genius minds of all times. They give you advice from another time, and I encourage you to do the same thing with all the words that come to you from beyond this contemporary world that you do with the words that have been handed down many generations. First and foremost, try the advice in this book. Ask yourself how it equates with your own reason and common sense, and if it benefits you and others, then live by it. That is, make it your knowing.

Resisting tribal influence is often perceived as being callous or indifferent to the experience and teachings of others, particularly those who care the most about you. I suggest that you read these words of Buddha again and again if this is your conclusion. He does not speak of rejection, only of being grown-up and mature enough to make up your own mind and live by your knowing, rather than through the experiences and testimony of others.

You cannot learn anything through the efforts of others. The world's greatest teachers can teach you absolutely nothing unless you are willing to apply what they have to offer based on your knowing. Those great teachers only offer you choices on the menu of life. They can make them sound very appealing, and ultimately they may help you to try those items on the menu. They can even write the menu. But the menu can never be the meal.

To put this wisdom to work I offer you these appetizers on my menu:

- Inventory as many of your beliefs as you can think of. Include such things as your attitude toward religion, capital punishment, minority rights, reincarnation, young people, old people, nontraditional medicine, what happens at death, your cultural biases, the ability to perform miracles.

- From this inventory be honest about how many of your firmly held beliefs are the result of your own life experiences, and how many have been handed to you. Make an effort to open your mind to experiencing things directly before proclaiming them as true and living by them.

- Expose yourself to belief systems that are in opposition to those you are familiar with. Experience what it is like to walk in the shoes of those who are different from you. The more of these "contrary" experiences you allow yourself, the more you will know your truth.

- Refuse to be seduced into arguments on the basis of ideas that have been foisted upon you by well-meaning others. In other words, stop giving energy to the things you don't believe in, or know to be inapplicable to you!

 LEADERSHIP

ACTING SIMPLY

True leaders
are hardly known to their followers.
Next after them are the leaders
the people know and admire;
after them, those they fear;
after them, those they despise.

To give no trust
is to get no trust.

When the work's done right,
with no fuss or boasting,
ordinary people say,
"Oh, we did it."

LAO-TZU
(SIXTH CENTURY B.C.)

Chinese philosopher Lao-tzu wrote the Tao Te Ching, *which means* The Way. *It is the basis for the religious practice of Taoism.*

I am frequently amazed at how many contemporary politicians refer to themselves as "leaders" by virtue of the fact that they hold public office. Historically it is clear that public office holders are seldom the true leaders causing change. For instance, who were the leaders of the Renaissance? Were they the public office holders? Were the leaders the mayors, governors, and presidents of the European capitals? No indeed.

The leaders were the artists, writers, and musicians who listened to their hearts and souls and expressed what they heard, leading others to discover a resonating voice within themselves. Ultimately the entire world listened with a new awareness that was responsible for the triumph of human dignity over tyranny. True leaders are rarely the officials who are addressed by a title.

Consider what titles you are known by and how you attempt to live up to them. You may carry the title of mother or father, which is an awesome responsibility. When your advice is sought because the kids see you as a leader in the family, keep in mind that what you truly want them to be able to say is, "I did it myself," rather than give you credit. Seek to enhance your leadership qualities by being constantly alert to the mistake of thinking that your title makes you a leader. True leaders are not known by titles. It is ego that loves titles!

Helping others to become leaders while exercising your own true leadership qualities means having to work hard at suspending ego's influence. True leaders enjoy the trust of others, which is very different from enjoying the perks and flattery and power that ego insists are the signs of being a leader. You need to give trust to others in order to receive that trust.

Notice the times that you are inclined to insist that others do it your way or take the highway. Lao-tzu tells us that the leader with this attitude is the least effective and most despised. Your leadership style may tend to create fear with statements like, "I'll punish you if you don't do it my way." Lao-tzu tells us that fear-based leaders are poorly qualified to genuinely lead. The leader whose motivation is to bask in admiration, according to Lao-tzu, is still not a master at leading. This style might say, "I'll give you a reward if you do it the way I want you to." The true leader acts in such a way as to be hardly known in the entire process. This leader offers trust, encouragement, and congratulations as others find their own way.

When our lawmakers tell us what we need, or use scare tactics to predict dire consequences, or attempt to get us to act out of admiration for their leadership, they are not true leaders. To qualify as true leaders they must silence themselves and hear the populace express, "Yes, we created this great economy ourselves."

And so it is with you also. To be a true leader in your own life, and in the lives of others, practice resisting the need to be recognized. Lead unobtrusively, offering trust whenever possible. Gently smile at your ego's desire to take credit and silently acknowledge your true leadership when you hear others say, "Oh, yes, we did that ourselves." Here are some suggestions for applying the wisdom of Lao-tzu:

- Before acting, stop and ask yourself if what you are about to say is going to create hate, fear, admiration, or self-awareness. Choose to nurture self-awareness.

- Act on your desire to be a true leader by being as quietly effective as possible. Catch someone doing something right!

- Become aware that it is the ego part of you that is suggesting you are a failure. Rather than seeing yourself as a failure when no credit comes your way, remind yourself that you have succeeded as a leader, and good-naturedly let your ego know that this is the way to successful leadership.

PATIENCE

Do not be desirous of having
things done quickly. Do not
look at small advantages.
Desire to have things done
quickly prevents their being
done thoroughly. Looking
at small advantages prevents
great affairs from being
accomplished.

CONFUCIUS
(551 B.C.–479 B.C.)

Confucius was a Chinese teacher and philosopher whose philosophy strongly influenced Chinese life and culture for over two thousand years.

I have this quote from the ancient Chinese teacher and philosopher Confucius pasted above my typewriter as a gentle daily reminder not to do anything that will prevent "great affairs" from being accomplished. It seems to me that we have a great deal to learn from our nature about how we hinder our greatness. Yet it is our nature that we often ignore in favor of what our mind tells us is the way things ought to be.

Patience is a key ingredient in the process of the natural world and in our personal world. For instance, if I scrape my arm or break a bone, the healing process proceeds precisely at its own pace independent of any opinion I may have about it. That is the natural world at work. My desire to have it fixed quickly is of absolutely no consequence. If I apply that impatience to my personal world, I will prevent it from healing thoroughly, as Confucius advised over twenty-five centuries ago. Shakespeare matched the wisdom of this ancient Chinese predecessor when he wrote, "How poor are they that have not patience! What wound did ever heal but by degree?"

When I was a child, I remember planting some radish seeds in springtime. When early summer arrived I noticed green leafy shoots protruding above the ground. I watched them grow a bit taller each day and finally I could stand it no longer and I began to tug at those radish shoots, trying to get them to grow faster. I had not yet learned that nature reveals its secrets on its own time schedule. As I pulled at the little leaves, they emerged from the ground sans radishes, and my childish impatience to have this thing done quickly prevented it from happening at all.

Now, when I am asked if I am disappointed because one of my books did not appear on a best-seller list as my earlier books did, I think of this observation of the wise Chinese sage, "Great things have no fear of time." What a compliment it is to the genius of Confucius that his words are still being quoted and his knowledge still being applied twenty-five hundred years after his departure. I too write for those souls who have yet to materialize, and if that means sacrificing the small advantage of a position of prestige on a list somewhere today, my impatient ego may be puzzled, but I am content!

There is a line in *A Course in Miracles* that perplexes anyone who is imprisoned by ego because it appears to be a contradiction. The line reads, "Infinite patience produces immediate results," and it echoes the twenty-five-hundred-year-old advice that you are reading about here. Infinite patience describes the condition of faith or absolute knowing. If you know with a complete absence of doubt that what you are doing is consistent with your own purpose and that you are involved in accomplishing a great affair, then you are at peace with yourself and in harmony with your own heroic mission. The sense of peace is your immediate result and is a state of enlightened bliss. Thus infinite patience takes you to a level of faith where doing things quickly is of no interest. You shift out of the need to see the results right now, just as when you know that your cuts, scrapes, and injuries will heal as your nature dictates, rather than as your impatient self dictates.

This kind of knowing has aided me immensely in my writing and in all of my life work. With my children, I am not always overly concerned with a test score or a subpar performance as it registers in this moment because I can see the bigger picture in their lives. As the Oriental proverb, perhaps inspired by the words of Confucius, says, "With time and patience the mulberry leaf becomes a silk gown," so do I think of my children as silk gowns in the making. Certainly we savor the small advantages in the here and now. However, I also know that any current setbacks will enhance rather than tarnish their greatness.

Impatience breeds fear, stress, and discouragement. Patience manifests in confidence, decisiveness, and a feeling of peaceful satisfaction. As you look at your own life, examine how frequently you demand an immediate indicator of success for yourself and others and attempt instead to see the larger picture. When you are on purpose and see the larger picture, you are able to let go of an inclination to seek validation in the form of merit badges and immediate applause.

My experience with addictions and overcoming them may parallel some of your life situations. While still being addicted I would think about quitting the addictive substance, such as caffeine or alcohol. Then I would look for a small advantage, such as no drinking for one day, and when that was accomplished, I would let up on my vigilance and go back to a cola or a beer to celebrate. By looking at my small victories I was preventing the job from being done thoroughly. When I developed infinite patience with myself I turned the whole thing over to God and remembered how perfect God had always been with me, even in my lowest moments. By being infinitely patient I could see that toxic substances interfered with my highest purpose and life mission, and I left those addictive ways behind me.

Make no mistake about it, all my thoughts about quitting, all my trials and failures—those "small advantages" as Confucius calls them—were part of the process of purification. By being patient with myself I could stay patient even with those small victories, and thus they did not deter me from my greater accomplishment. I allowed the process to move at its own pace, and today I can see clearly how getting rid of impatience gave me the ability to move to a level that I never imagined when I kept congratulating myself for my little victories and then retreating back to defeat. If you are appreciating the paradox in this situation, you will enjoy these two paradoxical sayings: "Infinite patience produces immediate results" and "One day at a time produces eternal results."

To see the absurdity of impatience in your life, set your watch ahead several hours and tear off several months on your wall calendar. Then see if you have advanced time! The failures and frustrations, along with the immediate successes, are a part and parcel of the perfection of it all. By observing nature—your nature and the natural world around you—you will see that you must allow a wound to progress at its own pace; to eat a fig you must first let it flower, put forth fruit, and ripen. Trust in your nature and let go of your desire to have things done quickly.

To accomplish this:

- Abandon your conditioned means of evaluating yourself as successful or not on the basis of immediate indicators. If you have a knowing within that you are on a much higher mission than what might show up today, you will free yourself from the folly of those current results. To be ahead in the beginning of the game can be a big disadvantage if it obscures your vision for the entire game.

- Think about what you are doing in increments of five centuries rather than five minutes. Produce for those of us who will be here five hundred years from now and your emphasis will shift off of your immediate results to much greater affairs.

- Be as patient with yourself, through all of your successes and disappointments, as you feel God has always been with you. When you can turn a problem over to a higher authority to which you are connected, you immediately shift to that knowing state of infinite patience, and you stop looking for little indicators of success for today only.

INSPIRATION

When you are inspired by some great
purpose, some extraordinary project,
all your thoughts break their bonds;
Your mind transcends limitations,
your consciousness expands in every direction,
and you find yourself in a new, great
and wonderful world.
Dormant forces, faculties and talents
become alive, and you discover yourself
to be a greater person by far
than you ever dreamed
yourself to be.

PATANJALI
(C. FIRST TO THIRD CENTURY B.C.)

The author of Yoga Sutras, *Patanjali lived in India probably one to three centuries before Christ and is considered the person who established the tradition of meditation. He has been described as a mathematician of mysticism and an Einstein in the world of the Buddhas.*

*I*n approximately the second century before Christ a man considered a saint by his people wrote a Hindu classic titled *Yoga Sutras* under the pseudonym Patanjali. In this book he categorized yogic thought in four volumes. His treatises were entitled *Samadhi* (Transcendence), *The Practice of Yoga*, *Psychic Power*, and *Kaivalya* (Liberation).

Many consider the words of this mystic and the sutras, or methods, he offered on how to know God and how to achieve a heightened level of awareness, the original foundation for building a spiritual base and liberating oneself from the limitations of the body and the ego.

I have selected this passage from Patanjali because I believe it expresses a universal truth across the miles and eons of time. I urge you to go through Patanjali's words with me, step by step, and while you do, remind yourself that millions of people, to this day, study the words of this teacher from ancient times who is still considered an avatar offering us his divine wisdom. He explains that when we become truly inspired by something that we consider extraordinary, truly extraordinary things will begin to happen for us, particularly in our thought processes. Somehow, when we become intensely involved in what we truly love to do, our thoughts begin to change and lose that quality of feeling limited in any way.

From my own personal experience I know that I feel most "on purpose" in my life when I am speaking to an audience and when I am writing. I have a deep sense of being used in some way at those moments, as if it isn't really this physical body called Wayne Dyer that is producing the talk or the book. In those moments I notice that my mind does not contemplate the concept of limitation. I know that I am not alone and that divine guidance is with me, and I speak or write effortlessly. It seems to me that the body and the mind are in a state of harmony during those moments. Some have called this state "flow," others call it "peak experience." Patanjali describes it as "your consciousness expands in every direction, and you find yourself in a new, great and wonderful world."

As you read these words, keep in mind the timelessness of this advice. Even those living in pre-pre-premodern times knew the significance of being on purpose in life. At the moments of peak experience, these inspired moments of feeling at one with God and the entire universe, you experience life as truly wonderful. This occurs when you are involved at a level that is called inspirational. Your attention is not on what is wrong or missing, but on the balanced feeling that comes from being in spirit. You are co-creating with spirit. In other words you are having an inspirational moment.

Patanjali then speaks of what I consider the most phenomenal aspect of being in this state of inspirational grace. "Dormant forces, faculties and talents become alive," he tells us. This means that many of the things we thought were outside our power to manifest awaken within us. I have found that when I am truly inspired in some extraordinary project, I forget about fatigue, despite an absence of sleep. I find that I don't think about being hungry, and in fact my body just seems to cease all its incessant demands and shifts into a state of moving me through my work effortlessly. Jet lag disappears when I am centered in my activity, even though I have crossed eight or nine time zones in a single day.

These faculties and talents that Patanjali describes are simply dormant if you are not taking the steps to become inspired in your life. I think the use of the term "dormant forces" is very critical here. When you are in that centered state of purpose, you activate forces in the universe that previously were out of your range. What you need will show up. The right person will be there on time. The phone call will come. The missing pieces will be brought to you. You manage the coincidences of your life, which sounds paradoxical. But when you enlist spirit by being inspired, the ancient Zen proverb applies: "When the student is ready, the teacher will appear."

When I speak or write from a "how may I serve" mindset and lose my ego in the process, the words "stuck" or "blocked" never enter my awareness. I seem to know that the guidance is there, as long as I (my ego) stay out of it completely. That dormant force that Patanjali mentions is activated by a connection to the divine when the focus is on a project that engages soul purpose. This becomes the inspirational project that attracts the outer forces as long as there is no ego interference. Then, as Patanjali suggests, "You discover yourself to be a far greater person than you had ever imagined." Extraordinary! Goethe once wrote, "Man is not born to solve the problems of the universe, but to find out what he has to do." I might add, "And to pursue it with inspiration."

If you doubt your ability to transcend limitations and activate long-dormant forces, then just consider with an open mind this sage advice from one of the world's greatest spiritual masters. Read each thought as if he is speaking directly to you. Inside you is a greater person than you may ever have dreamed of. Patanjali suggests that person emerges when you are inspired by the extraordinary. Your next question is very likely, "But what if I don't know what that project is? How do I go about finding my purpose?"

Keep in mind that your job here is not to ask how, but instead to say yes! Open yourself to the ideas presented in this passage from the *Yoga Sutras* of ancient times, and trust that the how will be provided. Ask yourself, "When do I feel most fulfilled? When do I feel extraordinary and like a great person?" Whatever the answer to those questions, you will find that it has something to do with serving your fellow man, serving your planet or universe, or serving God. As you let the ego diminish and make the commitment to be inspired and involved in an extraordinary project that does not just benefit your ego, you will know what to do.

To put Patanjali's powerful ideas to work for you, try these suggestions:

• Record in some form the activities of your life in which you feel most in-spirit (inspired). Don't judge them as being too insignificant or invaluable. Whether it's playing with babies, or gardening, or tinkering with your automobile, or singing, or meditating, simply keep a log of these activities.

• Use this inventory to see who out there in the world is actually making a living doing these things every day. Whatever you love can be turned into an extraordinary project to expand your consciousness in every direction. Mobilize new forces and talents in yourself that send you the message that you are a much greater person than you ever imagined.

• Listen only to the voice within you that beckons you to that extraordinary activity. Filter out advice from those who are telling you what they think you should be doing with your life. The key is to become inspired from *within*, not from *without*; otherwise the word would be outspired!

• Remember the words of Ralph Waldo Emerson as you break the bondage of your conditioned way of thinking about yourself and your life's purpose. "The measure of mental health is the disposition to find good everywhere." Try it and see how those faculties and talents come alive.

TRIUMPH

THE SIX MISTAKES OF MAN

- The illusion that personal gain is made up of crushing others.

- The tendency to worry about things that cannot be changed or corrected.

- Insisting that a thing is impossible because we cannot accomplish it.

- Refusing to set aside trivial preferences.

- Neglecting development and refinement of the mind, and not acquiring the habit of reading and study.

- Attempting to compel others to believe and live as we do.

MARCUS TULLIUS CICERO
(106 B.C.–43 B.C.)

Roman statesman and man of letters, Cicero was Rome's greatest orator and its most articulate philosopher. The last years of republican Rome are often referred to as the Age of Cicero.

*I*t absolutely amazes me when I consider that over two thousand years ago our brilliant and persuasive ancestors were walking on the same soil we walk on, breathing the air we breathe, watching the same stars we view at night, and being awed by the same sun we see every day, and speaking and writing of the identical concerns we all share today. There is a profoundly wondrous connection to those people that thrills and mystifies me as I read what they were trying to tell their fellow citizens, and me as well, a citizen who just happens to have appeared on the same planet a couple of thousand years later.

Cicero was once called the father of his country. He was a brilliant orator, lawyer, statesman, writer, poet, critic, and philosopher who lived in the century before the birth of Christ and was momentously involved in all the conflicts between Pompey, Caesar, Brutus, and many of the other historical characters and events that make up ancient Roman history. He had a brilliant and long political career and was an established writer whose work was considered the most influential of its time. In those days, however, dissidents were not treated kindly. He was executed in 43 B.C., his head and hands displayed on the speaker's platform at the Forum in Rome.

In one of his most memorable treatises, Cicero outlined the six mistakes of man as he saw them evidenced in ancient Rome. Twenty centuries later I repeat them here, with a brief commentary. We still can learn from our ancestors of antiquity, and I trust my corroboration of Cicero's six mistakes will not lead to my head and hands being displayed at our national speakers forum!

Mistake #1: The illusion that personal gain is made up of crushing others. This is a problem that unfortunately is still with us today. Many people feel they are able to elevate themselves in importance by finding fault with others. I recently watched an internationally successful motivational speaker being interviewed on television. His approach was, "I am better than everyone else, no one else can provide the tools for living that I can. Don't listen to those who are only providing a pep talk, they are all inferior." I couldn't help but think of Cicero's number one mistake.

There are two ways to have the tallest building in town. One way is to go around crushing everyone else's buildings, but this method seldom works for long because those having their buildings razed will eventually come back to haunt the crusher. The second way is to work on your own building and watch it grow. And so it is in politics, business, and our own individual lives.

Mistake #2: The tendency to worry about things that cannot be changed or corrected. Apparently people in the ancient world spent their energies worrying about things they had no control over, and little has changed since. One of my teachers put it to me quite succinctly. He said, "First it makes no sense to worry about the things you have no control over, because if you have no control over them, it makes no sense to worry about them. Second, it makes no sense to worry about the things you do have control over, because if you have control, it makes no sense to worry." And there goes *everything* that it is possible to worry about. Either you have control or you don't, and either way, worry is a huge mistake.

Mistake #3: Insisting that a thing is impossible because we cannot accomplish it. Many of us are still afflicted with this penchant for pessimism. Too often we jump to the conclusion that something is impossible simply because we cannot see the solution. I have heard many people tell me that angels, reincarnation, soul travel, communication with the deceased, travel to distant galaxies, genetic surgery, time machines, travel at the speed of light, miraculous spontaneous healings, and so on are all impossibilities, simply because they cannot conceive of such ideas.

I wonder how many of Cicero's contemporaries could foresee telephones, fax machines, computers, automobiles, airplanes, missiles, electricity, running water, remote controls, walking on the moon, and so many of the things we take for granted today. A good motto is, "No one knows enough to be a pessimist!" What we can't fathom today will be the accepted reality of those who reside here two thousand years into the future.

Mistake #4: Refusing to set aside trivial preferences. So many of us major in minor subjects as our way of life. We allow our precious life energies to be spent on worry about what others think of us, petty concerns about appearance, or what labels we are wearing. We consume our lives in anguish over squabbles with family or coworkers and fill our conversation with drapery talk. Ego becomes the driving force of our lives with our self-importance persistently taking center stage.

We see hunger and starvation on our planet, but become impatient when we must wait five extra minutes for a table in a restaurant, where half the food will be discarded as garbage. We hear about children maimed and killed by guns and gunmen by the thousands, yet we accept it as a condition that we can do nothing about. In our own personal lives, too many of us believe that we are unable to make a difference on the larger issues, so we immerse ourselves in our game of ego-sponsored trivial pursuit.

Mistake #5: Neglecting development and refinement of the mind, and not acquiring the habit of reading and study. It seems that when we finish our formal schooling, we have completed our development of the mind. We have adopted the credo of reading and studying for the purpose of taking the examination and earning our merit badge in the form of a diploma or an advanced degree. Once the certificate is in hand, the need to study and refine the mind is terminated. Cicero must have noticed this same tendency among his fellow Roman citizens and warned them that it could be a prelude to the downfall of their empire. And so it came to pass.

Our lives are greatly enriched when we immerse ourselves in literature and spiritual writing, not because we are going to be tested, but purely for the sake of personal enrichment. You will find that daily reading and study provide you with a deeper and richer experience of life in all ways. This is particularly gratifying when you know that you are doing it out of choice rather than as an assignment.

Mistake #6: Attempting to compel others to believe and live as we do. Obviously we are still guilty of this sixth mistake. Too often we feel victimized by those who are imposing on us their views of what we should be doing and how we should be living. The result is a high state of tension and resentment. No one wants to be told how to live or what to do. One of the specific traits of highly functioning people is that they have no desire or investment in controlling other people. We need to remind ourselves of this truth, and take the advice of Voltaire in his last line of *Candide*, "Learn to cultivate your own garden."

If others want to grow cabbage and you choose to grow corn, then so be it. Yet there is this propensity to peer into the lives of others and insist that they believe and care in the same way as we do. It is a common mistake of families to impose their will on everyone else in the unit. It is also a common mistake of government officials who are determining what is best for everyone. If Cicero's six mistakes are an unwelcome part of your life, consider the following six suggestions:

• Put your attention on your own life and how to improve it. Catch yourself when you are engaged in the habit of verbally crushing others, and stop instantly. The more you become aware of tearing down the buildings of others, the sooner you will shift to constructing your own tall building.

- Ask yourself as you experience worry, "Can I do anything about this?" If it is out of your control, then let it go. If there is anything you can do, then shift gears and work on that strategy. These two questions will get you out of the worry habit.

- Any time you confront a problem that you feel is impossible to solve, remind yourself that this is nothing more than a *solution* waiting for the right response. If you can't see the solution, begin the process of investigating who can. There is always someone who can see it from a possibility rather than an impossibility perspective. Remove "impossible" from your vocabulary entirely.

- Give yourself assignments to work on what you consider the most significant issues facing all of us. Give up some of your self-indulgent activities in favor of these greater tasks, and remind yourself that in some small way your contribution to the resolution of major social problems is making an impact.

- Give yourself time every day to read spiritual books, or listen to tapes in your spare time, maybe while driving. Make a habit of attending self-improvement seminars or lectures in your community on all sorts of mind-refining subjects.

- Cultivate your own garden and let go of your tendency to examine and judge how others cultivate theirs. Catch yourself in moments of gossip about how others ought to be living and rid yourself of thoughts about how they should be doing it this way, or how they have no right to live and think as they do. Stay busy and involved in your own life projects and pursuits and you will be far too busy to care, much less compel others to believe and live as you do.

From ancient Rome Cicero, the great statesman, orator, writer, and philosopher gives us all a lesson in living. Don't make these same mistakes that mankind has been making throughout the centuries. Instead, vow to eliminate them from your life one day at a time.

BEING CHILDLIKE

Except ye be converted and become as little children, ye shall not enter into the Kingdom of Heaven.

JESUS OF NAZARETH
(C. 6 B.C.–A.D. 30)

Jesus Christ is one of the world's major religious figures, regarded by Christians as the Messiah predicted by the Old Testament prophets.

*R*ecently, while preparing to give a lecture in a town far from home, I had the strange experience of looking directly into a wall mirror while sitting at a desk. The entire wall was one gigantic mirror, and every time I looked up, there was this body looking back at me while I was writing in a notepad. Finally I just stopped and stared back. I couldn't grasp the fact that this was actually me reflected in the mirror. I remember saying to myself, "That's an old man who is renting my face."

As I stared back I thought of the invisible being living inside each of us. This being is without boundaries or form, thus no beginning or end. This is the silent invisible witness that is ageless and unchanging. This is the eternal child inside each of us. It is as ageless children that we become synonymous with heaven, which represents that eternity where forms and boundaries, beginning and ends, ups and downs are all meaningless.

Heaven is not a place with borders, perimeters, edges, and precincts. Rather, it represents that which transcends demarcations. It is the same as that little child Jesus speaks of in this telling observation. In there, always with us, never aging, yet watching, always watching. Noticing the drooping of the eyelids, the wrinkling of the skin, the silvering of the hair. Indeed, it is an old man who is renting my face these days!

The ageless child in me, my eternal unchanging observer, knows nothing of judgment and hatred. There is nothing to judge, no one to hate. Why? Because it doesn't see appearances, it only knows how to look with love on everything and everyone. It is what I call the absolute "allower." It simply allows everything to be as it is and only notices the unfolding of God in everyone it encounters. Being without shape, size, color, or personality, this ageless child inside fails to notice such trivial distinctions. Not living on either side of any manmade border, it cannot indulge in ethnic or cultural identification, and thus warfare over these artificial terminus points is impossible. Consequently that invisible ageless child is always at peace, just witnessing, just observing, but most important, just allowing.

Recently I had the experience of running early one morning and feeling so exhilarated that I hurdled over a three-and-a-half-foot fence as I came back to the hotel at the completion of my run. My wife, who was observing me, let out a scream and said to me, "You can't do that! You don't jump over fences when you're fifty-six years old. You could kill yourself." My immediate response to her was "Oh, I forgot." That invisible, ageless me who is my eternal observer forgot for an instant that it was living in a body that has been here for over half a century!

To me, this passage of Jesus' from the New Testament speaks to the process of forgetting about our bodies as our primary identity—forgetting about our ethnic identity, our spoken language, our cultural label, the shape of our eyes, or what side of the border we grew up on, then making the conversion to become as little children, who are impervious to such compartmentalizing. Jesus was not saying we should be childish and become immature, undisciplined, and uneducated. Instead he was referring to being childlike, which is nonjudgmental, loving, accepting, and incapable of placing labels on anyone or anything.

When we are able to be as little children we realize that in *every* adult there is a child who desperately wants to be known. It is the child who is full and the adult who is usually empty. The fullness of the child is evident in peace, love, nonjudgment, and allowing. The emptiness of the adult reveals itself in fear, anxiety, prejudgment, and fighting. Enlightenment can be seen as a process of remembering that in the heart of a little child there is purity, and it is this pure divine love and acceptance that is the ticket to the kingdom of heaven. Make it one of your goals in life to be more childlike in everything you do.

The quality that we see in geniuses is equivalent to the inquisitiveness of children. Geniuses and children share a willingness to explore without thoughts of failure or worries about criticism. I think the key word in this passage of Jesus' is "converted." We are being told to become something that is perfect, kind, loving, and above all eternal. It resides in each of us, and it cannot age or die. The gentle, silent witness is what we want to convert to. That naive but imaginative mystic who is naturally spiritual is the child we want to convert to. When we do, we become *childlike* and leave behind our *childish* adult ways, which are the ways that prevent us from entering the eternal kingdom of heaven.

That kingdom is available to you here now on earth, as it is in heaven. All you have to do is make that conversion. To do so:

- Spend as much time as you can manage observing little children. As you do, recall the child in you who would love to play with them. The ancient thinker Heraclitus once said, "Man is most nearly himself when he achieves the seriousness of a child at play." Be more childlike, playful, loving, and inquisitive as you make your conversion to the kingdom of heaven.

- When you find yourself acting serious and stodgy, remind yourself of the invisible observer inside you that is noticing your somber side. Is that observer grim as well? You'll quickly see that your childlike witness cannot be at all like what it is witnessing. Then vow to make the immediate conversion.

- Make the decision that "I am never going to let an old person inhabit my body." Your body may indeed be rented by an aging being, but that eternal, invisible observer who is noticing it all will stay childlike, innocent, and ready to enter the kingdom of heaven at the appointed time with such an attitude firmly in place.

You are a distinct portion of the essence of God in yourself. Why, then, are you ignorant of your noble birth? Why do you not consider whence you came? Why do you not remember when you are eating, who you are who eat; and whom you feed: do you not know that it is the divine you feed; the divine you exercise? You carry a God about with you.

> Men are disturbed not by things
> that happen,
> but by their opinions of the things
> that happen.

EPICTETUS
(55—135)

Epictetus, an emancipated slave, was a Greek Stoic philosopher. No written works survive, but his pupil Arrian preserved his essential doctrines in a manual.

When I was training in the field of counseling psychology many years ago, Epictetus was a source of inspiration to me. His name surfaced repeatedly in the study of how the mind impacts our emotions and our behavior, and he was consistently referenced in the literature on rational emotive therapy. I am still impressed by the wisdom of this man who was born a slave in the first century after the Crucifixion, became a freedman in A.D. 90, and was expelled from Rome by the despotic emperor whose tyrannical rule Epictetus criticized. Years later I dug into the primary works of this Stoic philosopher, read his *Discourses*, and learned more about his philosophy.

The two selections I have cited here are valuable spiritual and philosophical insights that are almost two thousand years old. I have included them in this book because I believe they can enrich your life as they have mine.

In the longer selection, which begins, "You are a distinct portion of the essence of God," Epictetus reminds us that we often forget that we contain the divine spark, a "part of God." This powerful idea is so difficult to grasp, yet Epictetus insists, from a background of slavery, that it is simply the truth. Imagine being fully aware that you carry God about with you.

If God is everywhere, then there is no place that God is not. And this includes you. Once you connect to this understanding, you regain the power of your very source. Rather than seeing yourself as separate from the miraculous power of God, you claim your divinity and reclaim all the potency that God is. When you are eating you are ingesting God and replenishing God. When you sleep you breathe in God and allow God to rest. When you exercise, you move about on God and strengthen God at the same time.

This may make sense right now as you read these words, but you are probably like many of us who did not grow up with this concept. A more popular image is something like this: God as a giant vending machine in the sky in the form of a white-bearded male on a throne. Deposit tokens, in the form of prayers, and God sometimes delivers the goods, and other times not. This is the idea of God as separate and distinct from ourselves. Epictetus suggests shifting from this concept of "the universe as a monarchy" to an understanding that you are a principal work, a fragment of God Himself.

Sai Baba is a contemporary avatar living in India who knows and practices being the divine spark of God, which he is a part of and which is a part of him. He publicly demonstrates his godliness in many ways, one of which is a variation of the divine ability to manifest fish and loaves. When a Western journalist asked Sai Baba, "Are you God?" he gently responded, "Yes I am, and so are you. The only difference between you and me is that I *know* it, and you don't." When you know that you are a divine manifestation of God, you have made conscious contact with God and you treat yourself and others as expressions of the divine. In Rome and in Greece, this is what Epictetus was telling us two thousand years ago. Trust in your divine nature, never dispute the nobility of your true self, and treat yourself with the same reverence that you have for God.

Epictetus' second observation, as simple as it sounds, has been perhaps the most useful information I have ever processed in my life. It is our *opinions* of things and not the things themselves that cause the disturbances of our lives. What a great source of liberation to know that no one can upset us, that nothing out there can make us miserable, that we control how we feel by how we decide to process things, events, and other people, and their opinions.

As a school counselor many years ago I frequently invoked the wisdom of this observation. When a student was upset by something someone else had said or done, I would ask, "Suppose you didn't know what they had said about you, would you still be upset?" The student would respond with something like, "Of course not. How could I be upset about something if I didn't know about it?" I would then gently offer, "So it isn't what they said or did. That happened and you weren't upset at all, until you learned of it, and then decided to react by being disturbed." The realization that *no one can make us upset without our consent* began to be a part of the student's awareness.

These two gems from Epictetus have influenced my life and writing, and I enjoy reminding myself of their value each and every day. I share them with you because they have been so valuable to me. The spiritual insights from Epictetus are combined in this ancient Sanskrit saying: "God sleeps in the minerals, awakens in the plants, walks in the animals, and thinks in you." In other words, there is no place that God is not sleeping, awakening, or walking about. God is the universal source of all life, a presence rather than a person, and this presence thinks in you.

And how shall you think? Use this presence of God to realize the enormity of your thinking capacity. It is not the things, events, circumstances, and opinions of others that cause you to feel uneasy and unsettled, it is how you use the God within, your invisible source, to process those extremes that determines your happiness—and nothing more! Realize that God is in you, with you, behind you, before you, and all around you, and can be felt everywhere, particularly in your opinions of the things that hap-

pen to you. To put these two ancient yet very up-to-date observations to work for you, begin to:

- Remind yourself daily that you are a divine creation and entitled to be treated lovingly by others, as well as by yourself. By
  seeing yourself as connected to rather than separated from
  God you will feel a greater reverence for yourself.

- Practice regular rituals to affirm the presence of God in you
  and all that you do. Bless your food and give thanks and, as
  you do, remind yourself that you are feeding the divine. Similarly, during your exercise activities, visualize the energy of
  God in your every cell.

- Give thanks for everything that you receive, including the
  rain, air, sun, and storms, however they manifest. Gratitude is
  one way of recognizing the God in all things.

- Let go of any inclination you have to blame external circumstances for your unhappiness. When you feel disturbed ask
  yourself, "How can I change my opinion of these things to
  remove my discomfort?" Then work at it until the blame is
  gone. This can be accomplished quite readily if you are willing
  to shift off blame and on to God realization as Epictetus
  encouraged us two millennia ago.

❀ ENLIGHTENMENT ❀

Before enlightenment
chopping wood
carrying water.

After enlightenment
chopping wood
carrying water.

ZEN PROVERB

Founded in China in the sixth century and widespread in Japan by the twelfth century, Zen Buddhism emphasizes achieving enlightenment by the most direct possible means.

As I study the phenomena of higher states of awareness and what is generally referred to as being enlightened, this simple Zen proverb is always a great source of pleasure for me. When we think of the elusive thing called enlightenment, generally we are referring to a state of consciousness that we will someday achieve if we adopt the right spiritual practices and work diligently toward becoming enlightened. The expectation is that when we are once fully awakened all our problems will disappear and we will live a life of pure bliss.

But the message of this famous proverb is that enlightenment is not an attainment, it is a realization. Once you reach this realization, everything appears to have changed, yet no change has taken place. It is as if you had been going through life with your eyes closed and suddenly opened them. Now you can see, but the world hasn't changed; you simply see it with new eyes. This proverb about chopping wood and carrying water says to me that enlightenment does not begin in a lotus position in a cave high atop the Himalayas. It is not something that you will get from a guru or a book or a course of study. Enlightenment is an attitude toward everything that you do.

The state of being enlightened, for me, involves a very basic idea of being immersed in and surrounded by peace at all moments in my life. If I am anxious, stressed, fearful, or tense, I am not realizing the potential I have for enlightenment right in that moment. I believe that becoming aware of these nonpeaceful moments is one of the ways to being an enlightened person. I have heard it said that the difference between an enlightened person and an ignorant one is that one realizes he is ignorant, while the other is unaware of his ignorance.

I have felt a deeper sense of inner peace and enlightenment in recent years, and still I chop wood and carry water as I did when I was a teenager. Every day I still do the work that will pay the bills, even though the work has changed. Each day I exercise to stay healthy, eat properly, brush my teeth, and wipe my own behind. In the past thirty years since my first child was born and right until now with seven more children to raise, I have the same basic concerns: how to protect, feed, advise, and deal with them. I continue to chop wood and carry water as a family member concerned with their lives. Enlightenment is not a means to eliminate life's daily tasks. So what does an enlightened outlook on life do for you if it doesn't eliminate daily chores and lead you to a contemplative, problem-free life?

In general enlightenment will not change your outer world, but you will change your way of processing the world. For instance, as I go about the business of parenting, I see my children with an absence of ownership and attachment, whereas previously their behavior could rule my emotional life. Now I see my eight-year-old's tantrum as what she has to do right now to get attention. I don't feel compelled to join her in her emotionally juvenile conduct. I also see the successes that all my children experience from this more detached perspective.

My realization of detachment is not an attitude of indifference. It is one of knowing that I have the power to choose peace for myself in all moments, and that I will still have all the same activities, problems, and events cropping up each day. As long as I am in a physical body I will have some chopping and carrying to do. But the way of approaching it is what constitutes enlightenment.

I can recall the horror that I once experienced when having to change a particularly messy dirty diaper or, heaven forbid, having to clean up the floor after one of the children decorated it with throw-up. I would say, "I simply can't do those things. They'll make me sick," and either I avoided them or, if that was impossible, I literally responded to the olfactory insult by getting sick myself. It is amazing how such an attitude affects your physical reactions as well as making the tougher duties of parenting unpleasant.

Today I can approach a dirty diaper or a pile of noxious throw-up with a completely different attitude. And the most amazing thing is that I no longer have the same physical reactions as I once did, strictly because I changed my thoughts. The diapers are there before and after enlightenment, as is the barf. But in post-enlightenment times, you can bring to the task an air of detachment, and peace is your result. I love this affirmation from *A Course in Miracles*: "I can choose peace rather than this!" To me, that one affirmation sums up this whole business of enlightenment: being able to choose peace while carrying, chopping, cleaning, delivering, hammering, or any of a zillion "ings" you could add to this list.

Enlightenment is not something that will set you free, rather you become freedom itself. You do not become an eagle in the sky; you become the sky itself. You no longer define yourself by the boundaries of your body; the universe itself becomes your body. You are connected in a profoundly spiritual way to all that you see and do. You begin to treat all your tasks, even the most mundane, as opportunities to know God. You bring peace to everything since in your own mind, you are everything and everyone. You become less preoccupied with labeling the flowers and trees and more involved in experiencing them.

This simple little Zen proverb, which has been handed down to seekers of enlightenment for thousands of years, is a great gift. Inside or outside yourself you never have to change what you see, only the way you see it. That is enlightenment!

To put this simple Zen proverb to work in your life here are a few equally simple strategies to practice:

- Become aware of your "ignorance" as it reveals itself each day when you have allowed yourself to slip away from being at peace. Note who you blamed for your moments of despair, what the occasion was, and how frequently you fell into this trap. The recognition of your unenlightened moments is the way to begin turning them around. Remember that those who are ignorant are generally unaware of their ignorance. Become aware.

- Let go of your inclination to see enlightenment as something that you will achieve at some future time when your life circumstances change for the better. You will always have some form of chopping and carrying to do. Your choice is in how you elect to see it.

- Practice making specific changes in your personal approach to things that take you away from your peace. For example, if you find yourself being excessively annoyed in heavy traffic, or in long lines, use these ordinary circumstances of modern life to shift around your inner world. Reserve a space within yourself for enlightenment to appear in the moments when you typically opt for anguish.

- And finally, never make announcements about being enlightened. The person who says, "I'm enlightened" is definitely not. Choose not to engage in conversation about your enlightenment. One Zen teaching says that only after a sincere seeker has asked you more than three times should you respond. The sages are silent on the subject of their own level of God realization.

THE NOW

from *The Rubaiyat of Omar Khayyám*

The Moving Finger writes; and, having writ,
Moves on: nor all thy Piety nor Wit
Shall lure it back to cancel half a Line,
Nor all thy Tears wash out a Word of it.

OMAR KHAYYÁM
(1048?–1122)

Omar Khayyám was a scholar and astronomer who lived in Iran. His poetry reflects his thoughts about the deity, good and evil, spirit, matter, and destiny.

Almost a thousand years have passed since the birth of Omar, the world's most famous tent-maker, poet, and astronomer all rolled into one brilliant philosophical storyteller. This particular quatrain from the *Rubaiyat* contains a lesson that has not diminished at all in the passing of a millennium. These famous words embrace a subtle truth that escapes many people.

One way to understand the wisdom of this quatrain is to imagine your body is a speedboat that is cruising through the water at forty knots per hour. You stand on the stern of that boat and peer down at the water. What you would see in this imaginary scene is the wake. Now I ask you to philosophize about the following three questions.

Question #1: What is the wake? You probably will conclude that the wake is the trail that is left behind, and nothing more.

Question #2: What is driving the boat? (The boat represents you "cruising" through your life.) The answer is "The present moment energy being generated by the engine, and nothing more, is responsible for making the boat go forward." Or, in the

39

case of your life, the present moment thoughts that propel your body to move forward, and nothing more!

Question #3: Is it possible for the wake to drive the boat? The answer is obvious. A trail that is left behind can never make a boat go forward. It is just a trail and nothing more. "The Moving Finger writes; and having writ, moves on . . ."

One of life's greatest illusions is the belief that the past is responsible for the current conditions of our lives. Often we assign this reason to explain why we cannot get out of our ruts. We insist it is because of all the problems that we faced in our past. We take wounds that we experienced in our youth, bond ourselves to them, and continue to blame those unfortunate experiences for our current miserable circumstances. These, we insist, are the reasons we can't move forward. In other words, we are living the illusion that our wake is driving our lives.

Think of when you have had a physical injury, such as a cut on your hand. Your body's nature takes over immediately and begins to close up the wound. Of course, it has to be cleansed to heal, as do emotional wounds as well. Healing takes place rather quickly then because your nature says, "Close up all those wounds and you will be healed." Yet when your nature also says, "Close up all those wounds in your past," you often ignore your nature and instead create a bonding to those wounds, living in your memories and using those ripples out of your past to live the illusion that this is the source of your immobility or failure to move on.

The moving finger that Omar Khayyám refers to is your body. Once it writes it is complete, and there is absolutely nothing that you can do to unwrite it. None of your tears will erase a single word of your written story. No amount of wit, prayer, and piety can change a single drop of your wake. It is a trail that you have left behind. While you may benefit by reviewing that trail, you must come to a knowing within you that only your present moment thoughts of how you process the wake are responsible for your life today.

It has been said many times that circumstances do not make a man, they reveal him. The tendency to blame our past for our current shortcomings is tempting. It is the easy road, in that we have a ready excuse for refusing to take the risks involved in driving the boat ourselves. *Everyone,* and I emphasize *everyone,* has conditions and experiences in the past that can be used as excuses for inaction. The wake of all our lives overflows with the debris of our past history. Parental shortcomings, addictions, phobias, abandonment issues, dysfunctional family members, missed opportunities, bad luck, lousy economic conditions, and even birth order are all glaring at us just below the surface in the wake of our lives. And yet the moving finger has written the story and nothing can be done to unwrite it.

Omar Khayyám reminds us from another place, another time, and another language of the simple common sense that the past is over, and not only is it over, but it is not subject to rewind or recall. Furthermore, it is an illusion to believe that the past is what drives or fails to drive your life today. That finger is still attached to your heart, and can write anything it chooses, regardless of what it wrote yesterday. Wake up and get out of the wake, and listen to the wisdom of Omar the tent-maker!

The essential lessons of this quatrain include:

- Live today. Let go of all your attachment to your past as an excuse for your life conditions today. You are the product of the choices you are making right now, and nothing in your wake can affect you today if you heed this common sense.

- Remove all blame from your vocabulary. Catch yourself when you find yourself using your past history as a reason for your failure to act today, and instead say, "I am free now to detach myself from what used to be."

- Let go of your tears that have been a symbol of your attachment to the past. The sadness and self-pity will not wash away one tiny fragment of your past. Gently remind the wounded part of yourself that that was then and this is now. Learn from those experiences. Bless them as great teachers, and then come rushing back to the working unit of your life, *now!* There is a past, but not now. There is a future, but not now. From a thousand years ago grasp this simple truth and write your life with it!

PRAYER

Lord, make me an instrument of Your Peace.
Where there is hatred, let me sow love;
Where there is injury, pardon;
Where there is doubt, faith;
Where there is despair, hope;
Where there is darkness, light;
And where there is sadness, joy.
O Divine Master, grant that I may not so much seek
To be consoled as to console;
To be understood as to understand;
To be loved as to love;
For it is in giving that we receive;
It is in pardoning that we are pardoned;
And it is in dying that we are born to eternal light.

ST. FRANCIS OF ASSISI
(1182–1226)

The Italian founder of the Franciscan order of monks, St. Francis approached religion with joyousness and a love of nature, calling all living beings his brothers and sisters.

This simple prayer is one of the most famous and enduring of all prayers in recorded history. It expresses the deep yearning within all humans to be the spiritual being who inhabits our physical form. In the words of this prayer, St. Francis describes the essential content of our highest self. I love to silently recite this prayer and also at times to say it out loud.

I believe you make direct contact with St. Francis when you recite this prayer, which was written by one of the most divinely spiritual people who has ever walked among us. The same invisible God force that flowed through this man in the twelfth and thirteenth centuries also flows through you and me. If you feel a connection to the man who wrote this prayer, you may want to read his biographies and watch a movie titled *Brother Sun, Sister Moon*. His life has been such an inspiration to me that, as I mention elsewhere in this book, I have visited Assisi to walk in the same woods and pray in the very chapel where he performed so many of his authenticated miracles.

This long-surviving prayer speaks to the very meaning of prayer. For many people, praying is a means of beseeching God to grant special favors. St. Teresa of Avila speaks of prayer in a far different light. She instructs us to "Direct all your prayers to one thing only, that is, to conform your will directly to the Divine will." This is precisely what the enduring prayer of St. Francis provides. This prayer expresses a wish to be the vehicle for God's desires rather than a request for favors from an entity outside ourselves. That is a radical shift for most of us, and it is a beginning step toward spiritual enlightenment.

To ask for the strength to sow love where there is hatred, hope where there is despair, and light where there is darkness is to ask to be free from the pettiness and judgment that imprisons us. It is a request to be an expression of the powerful love that we attribute to the Creator and that is part of our being. Recently I recognized an opportunity to do just that.

I had played in a doubles tennis match with three other men. One of the men on the losing side was annoyingly obnoxious as the match progressed. He slammed his racquet and swore frequently during the match. When we finished playing he stormed off the court, refusing to shake hands. As the remaining threesome, including me, walked off the court, I heard my two fellow players condemning the actions and attitude of the now-absent man. The temptation to join in talking about what a jerk he had been almost overwhelmed the words, "Where there is despair, [let me sow] hope; . . . where there is sadness, joy . . ." which have become a part of me since I often recite the prayer.

When we got off the courts, we saw the angry, hurt man. I went over and put my arm around him and simply said, "We all have our bad moments." It was not any verbal superiority that caused me to act this way. The words of a simple man of God, who lived more than eight hundred years before me, on another continent, spoke to and through me that day on the tennis court.

When we know that we are never alone, we change our strategy for prayer and pray to that which we are already connected to; the highest, most sacred aspect of our own being. If God is everywhere, then there is no place that God is not, including within ourselves. Armed with this awareness, we can pray and ask for nothing but our own moral strength. Instead of asking to be sheltered from danger, we ask for the strength to be fearless. Rather than asking for the removal of pain, we seek the ability to transcend and conquer it. We no longer assume that we know what we need and what will help us in this moment. Yet our experience teaches us that many of the things that we would never have requested have turned out to be the most beneficial. As William Shakespeare once put it, "We, ignorant of ourselves, beg often our own harms, which the wise powers deny us for our own good."

This prayer of St. Francis is a way of seeking to practice in everyday life consoling, understanding, pardoning, and giving actions. We all have these capacities within us, and frequently we are moved to act in these ways. However, we are *most often* asking others, including that entity we think is outside us called God, to console *us*, understand *us*, forgive *us*, and provide for *us*.

By reciting this simple prayer we are taking steps to true spiritual growth. We are leaving ego behind and allowing our sacred self to be a dominant force in our lives. The very private, almost universal, awareness or practice of prayer is an incredibly powerful force for transformation in our lives when we place the emphasis of this activity on a kind of communion with the infinite in which we ask for the strength and courage to operate our daily lives from the principles laid out by St. Francis.

I've always loved the story of the teacher who told a spiritually advanced young avatar, "I'll give you an orange if you can tell me where God is!" The young person replied, "I'll give you two oranges if you can tell me where God is not!" The moral: God is everywhere. When you pray to God, you pray to a silent and powerful eternal presence that is a part of yourself. Commune with this presence without any idea of being separate. Then practice the divine words of St. Francis, and begin to put them to work in as many places as you can each day. Ralph Waldo Emerson wrote the following words on the subject of prayer. I will close this essay with his insights.

"Prayer as a means to effect a private end is theft and meanness. It supposes dualism in nature and consciousness. As soon as the man is one with God he will not beg. He will then see prayer in all action."

I suggest you practice the words of St. Francis by incorporating the following ideas into your daily life:

- Make a daily practice of privately reciting the words of this prayer. Just by saying the words, you will find yourself beginning to act on them throughout the day.

- If you find yourself in a confrontation of any kind with anyone, be it a family member or a stranger, before reacting ask yourself, "Is what I am about to say motivated by my need to be right, or my desire to be kind?" Then pick a response that stems from kindness, regardless of how your ego objects.

- Practice sending love where you previously radiated hate, particularly when reading newspapers or watching the news on television. By sowing love in the face of hatred, regardless of how difficult it may seem, you will become part of the solution to hatred in our world. This will require strong vigilance on your part to overcome your cultural conditioning of an eye-for-an-eye mentality.

- Look into your heart and be honest about all the people in your past who have harmed you in any way. Where there is pain, practice pardon. Forgiveness is the very foundation of spiritual awakening, and it is what St. Francis is speaking of in this divine prayer.

GRIEF AS A BLESSING

I saw grief drinking a cup of sorrow and called out, "It tastes sweet, does it not?" "You've caught me," grief answered, "and you've ruined my business, how can I sell sorrow when you know it's a blessing?"

JALALUDDIN RUMI
(1207–1273)

Persian mystical poet and Sufi saint Jalaluddin Rumi writes about the pure love we can achieve, beyond ego, in the soul's divine longing and ecstasy of union with God.

Oh how we love to grieve. We even read books about how important the grieving process is to our recovery, and then we go so far as to identify grief as a necessary stage of sorrow that we have to experience to overcome our losses and regain our sanity. But Jalaluddin Rumi, a thirteenth-century mystical poet, writing in the area known today as Afghanistan, sends a message from the Middle Ages. He suggests that grief is a blessing, rather than something to tolerate as a necessary evil on the way to recovery. It is not sorrowful at all, but instead it is an opportunity to drink the sweet nectar that is available in the dark moments of our lives.

For most of us, grieving is how we react to a loss or a tragic event, and it seems to be a natural way of reacting to the experience of pain in our lives. But if we knew the wisdom of Rumi's words, we might be able to shift right in the middle of this grieving process and turn our sorrow into something sweet-tasting.

One of the great teachings of my life came from my exploration of the *Kabbalah*, a mystical text of Judaism that goes back many centuries, as do Rumi's teachings. The simple lesson for me was "The falls of our life provide us with the energy to propel ourselves to a higher level." I read and reread this ancient wisdom. As I allowed it to soothe the sharp anguish of life's painful moments, I began to incorporate this wisdom during times of sadness and grief. I discovered the truth of this idea that every fall provides us the opportunity to generate the necessary energy to move to higher consciousness. Every sinking into despair has within it an energy to move us higher.

How many times in your life have dark times of despair, such as some kind of an accident, an illness, a financial disaster, a breakup in a relationship, a fire or flood, a loss of property, or a death, propelled you into the stages of anguish, anger, denial, and then grief? Like most of us, you sink into sorrow and feel the need to tell everyone about your misfortune. Ultimately, after a long period of time, you begin to rise above it and reach the state of acceptance.

Now suppose you knew that what had taken place in your life which you termed a loss or a fall was exactly what was supposed to happen? Suppose you knew instantly that you *had* to experience the event that triggered your grief and sorrow? Then suppose you could choose to act in accordance with this new awareness? Undoubtedly this "supposing" conflicts with all you have been taught about how you're supposed to react to catastrophe and death. I am not suggesting you *not* respect your genuine feelings. I am suggesting that the truth of Rumi's observations offer you another way of responding to these kinds of circumstances. I am encouraging you to open to the gift or sweetness that is *also* in the sorrow.

This is an intelligent system that we are all an inseparable part of, and there are no accidents. There is something to learn right here, right now in the middle of sorrow. You can take this lesson and taste the sweet certainty in the mystery. You do not have to pretend to like the tragedy, only to vow to use it to generate the energy to move to a higher place in your life. You could call out to your sorrow just as Rumi did over eight hundred years ago and say to yourself, "It tastes sweet, does it not?" That is, there is something to learn right here, right now in the middle of this sweet sorrow, and I am going to drink it in this manner, and ruin the business of the grief peddlers.

In what we refer to as primitive societies death is an occasion for celebration. There is a basic knowing, even in times of grief and mourning, that does not question the divine timing of each person's arrival here on earth, or the divine timing of one's departure either. It is all in order! Perhaps the comfort is the sweetness of seeing that it is all part of the perfection of our universe, which has an invisible organizing intelligence flowing through every cell of creation, including the many painful experiences over a lifetime—then celebrating it all.

As a high school student I was a high jumper on the track team. I won't discuss the heights I ascended to, but we know from the movies that white men can't jump! Nevertheless, I used to set the bar on the stands, take a position thirty to fifty feet back, sprint fast toward the bar, and get down as low as possible to generate the added energy to propel my entire body over the bar. By getting down low I could ascend higher. My high school track days provide me with an image that is analogous with the message of Rumi. It is the message of the *Kabbalah*, and it is my message to you.

Grief, when it is only an inner experience of sadness and sorrow, will keep you down in the very depths of the plunge itself. It will immobilize you and weigh you down with guilt and anguish. But when you know that this despair has within it some sweet blessing, you disrupt the grief/sorrow partnership, and the fall helps you regain your footing and soar above the devastating potholes of life on earth.

Here are some alternatives to the grief/sorrow dilemma:

- Stop yourself in the middle of a sorrowful moment and very deliberately say, "Do I have to suffer now, inside as well as outside, over this loss, which I will ultimately come to see as a blessing?" Listen and follow your response. No matter what, you are introducing to yourself the possibility of an improved response to despair.

- Practice being able to honestly express your feelings of loss without believing that you must be filled with sorrow as well. It is possible to feel the loss, express it, and still know within the blessing in all of this. Do not demand instant change. Allow what is there to be there at the same time that you allow the possibility of different behavior.

- You may have accepted grief and sorrow as inseparable because you have been taught that it is cold and inhuman to be otherwise. When you know that all falls are blessings and all losses are in divine order, you will gradually sweeten the sorrow and you will gain the energy to soar to a higher altitude in all areas of your life.

Every now and then go away,
   have a little relaxation,
   for when you come back
   to your work
   your judgement will be surer;
   since to remain constantly at work
   will cause you to lose power
   of judgement . . .

Go some distance away
   because the work appears smaller
   and more of it
   can be taken in at a glance,
   and a lack of harmony
   or proportion
   is more readily seen.

LEONARDO DA VINCI
(1452–1519)

Italian painter, sculptor, architect, musician, engineer, mathematician, and scientist, Leonardo da Vinci was one of the greatest intellects in the history of mankind.

When a man such as Leonardo da Vinci gives advice, I for one am willing to listen with fixed attention. He has been called by many historians the man with the most inquiring mind of all time. Now that's quite a compliment! His accomplishments were prodigious, and he is often credited with being the initiator of the Renaissance, which moved man out of the Dark Ages.

Leonardo saw mystery everywhere and delved deep to understand it. He studied the earth, the sky, and the heavens. He recorded the movement of stars and drew up plans for flying machines four hundred years before the first airplane. He was an architect and a consummate artist who plunged into the study of nature and human personality. His portraits of faces were more skillful than had ever been seen before or since, embodying a reality that captured every essence of his subjects. Volumes of books have been written on the magnificence of just his painting *The Last Supper*. No subject escaped Leonardo's inquiry, and in this piece of advice quoted above, he offers you a tool for your own creative outlets as well.

When you consider the sheer amount of creative work that Leonardo da Vinci amassed in his lifetime, you might conjure up a picture of a workaholic, Type A person who never did anything but paint, sculpt, and invent, every waking moment of his life. Yet his advice is quite to the contrary, and it is my conclusion as well. This original Renaissance man is advising us to escape from the daily routine and go some distance away to become more efficient and productive.

It seems to me that highly productive people have a great sense of balance and harmony in their lives. They are thoroughly familiar with pacing and knowing when to retreat and clear their heads of the immediate concerns. The key word here is "balance." To avoid being consumed by anything, you must be able to walk away from it. In the process of walking away, you begin to see your work, or family, or project from a perspective that "appears smaller," according to Leonardo.

Leaving a fixed point and then glancing back at it does indeed cause the point to appear smaller. But from a distance you can actually take in more of that point, in one swift glance. Thus any weaknesses or flaws can be spotted in an instant. Even though Leonardo may be speaking as an artist, his advice is applicable today, irrespective of what your life work might be.

I have found Leonardo's advice to be applicable to me in my work of writing and speaking, as well as in other projects. When I leave my research and the yellow legal pads that I write on to go for a long-distance run, or simply go away for several days, almost magically everything seems clearer on my return. I am amazed by the insights I receive when I let go of my work. They seem to pop into my head in the moments when I am least connected to or attached to the outcome. The great Renaissance master is telling us to let go, relax, don't try so hard, remove the struggle and allow our natural divine guidance to assist us. He says, "have a little relaxation, for when you come back to your work your judgement will be surer." One way to do this in today's world is to learn to meditate before you undertake any serious pursuit, be it a plan for conducting a business meeting, going on a job interview, giving a lecture, or painting a portrait. The very act of allowing yourself to go into a meditative state will improve your efficiency enormously. In the past ten years I have never gone before an audience without first spending a minimum of an hour (usually more) alone, in a state of meditation. When I emerge from my relaxing meditation, I find that I can walk on stage or pick up my pen with a sense of confidence that I am connected to a higher part of myself that knows no fear. I become an observer of myself doing the work, and everything seems to flow as if the hand of God is guiding my tongue or my pen.

In the process of getting some distance between yourself and your work, and relaxing into that space, you are inviting divine intervention into your activity. The less stress you place on yourself to accomplish or complete a task, ironically you seem to gain the power to do just that. When you are detached from the outcome you are in process, and you are allowing the outcome to take care of itself. You can see this principle at work in activities of pleasure.

For example, on a dance floor your objective is not to end up at a particular place on the floor. In dancing the object is to enjoy the dance, and where you end up is left to the process of dancing. Similarly, at a concert, your purpose is not to get to the end of the music, but to enjoy each moment of the concert. Getting to the end is of no concern when you are in process. Think of eating a banana. What is the purpose? To get from one end to the other? Or to enjoy each bite? This is true with virtually anything. When we relax and let go, we can get naturally lost in the process, and magically the end result appears.

Leonardo da Vinci encourages us to have balance in our lives, regardless of our pursuits. By all means get involved in your activities, but try to enjoy them for what they are, rather than the final outcome. Moreover, be willing to walk away from an activity when you feel your judgment is out of harmony or proportion. By doing so you gain perspective, and paradoxically you sharpen rather than lose your creative power.

To put this advice of the original Renaissance man to work in your life:

- Practice detaching from outcome in your work and projects. Be in the moment enjoying your activities for the sheer joy of the action, rather than how they will turn out.

- Walk away from your work from time to time to do nothing. No time restraints, no deadlines, no alarm clocks, in fact no clocks at all. Just let yourself be and notice how free you feel. This kind of distancing without restraints will bring you back to your work with new vigor and much sharper judgment.

- Do what I do frequently if I ever feel stuck. I simply turn the entire thing over to God. I say, "I don't know what to do at this point and I feel stuck for answers, I am asking you to guide me in resolving this problem." It may sound simplistic but it always seems to work. The answers come and clarity is restored when I ask God to help me.

- Remember that one of the greatest achievers of all time, in a myriad of endeavors, advises you to "Every now and then go away, have a little relaxation." If there is anyone whose advice I would follow, it is the original Renaissance man.

HOPE

The greater danger
for most of us
is not that our aim is
too high
and we miss it,
but that it is
too low
and we reach it.

MICHELANGELO
(1475–1564)

Italian painter, sculptor, architect, and poet, Renaissance artist Michelangelo Buonarroti is an outstanding figure in the history of the visual arts.

Over the past twenty-five or so years, I have appeared regularly on radio and television talk shows, conversing with listeners who call in and join the discussion. One of the most frequent criticisms I have received from the hosts of these shows is that I offer far too much hope for people in dire circumstances and that this could be a dangerous thing. Despite this kind of fault-finding, I am still at a loss to understand how having too much hope could be a dangerous thing.

When people tell me of a medical diagnosis that implies no cure being possible, I encourage them to shift their aim to a completely opposite outcome. I talk frequently about the law that has allowed any miracle that has ever occurred, since the inception of time, to take place. I explain that that law has never been repealed and is still on the books. I cite cases of people who were told to go home and wait to die, who were given six months to live and who freed themselves of their illnesses and their diagnosis. I receive mail every day from people who refused to listen to the low aims and the low hopes that others have had for them, describing how grateful they were for a message of hope in difficult times.

I believe that Michelangelo, who lived a few days shy of eighty-nine years, still sculpting, painting, writing, and designing in an age when ninety was about sixty years beyond normal life expectancy, was speaking to this idea of having very high hopes and aims in this famous quotation of his. The danger is not in false hope, rather it is in no hope or low hope, and consequently our objectives and aims are diminished by our beliefs before they can be worked on and materialized.

This not only concerns the overcoming of physical maladies, it includes virtually everything in our lives. The world is full of people who have aimed low and thought small who want to impose this diminutive thinking on any who will listen. The real danger is the act of giving up or setting standards of smallness for ourselves with low expectations. Listen carefully to Michelangelo, the man whom many consider the greatest artist of all time.

I recall standing in front of the statue of *David* in Florence and being transfixed. The size, the majesty, the spirit that seemed to jump right out of the marble was Michelangelo saying to all of us, "Aim high." When he was asked how he could create such a masterpiece, he responded that David was already in the marble, he simply had to chip away the excess to allow him to escape. High aim indeed. And speaking of high, take a look sometime at the Sistine Chapel where Michelangelo painted the ceiling by lying on his back and working every day for four years between 1508 and 1512. It was a project that lesser artists would have considered impossible, yet Michelangelo took it on and many more in a lifetime crammed full of high energy, high talent, and, yes, high aim.

Virtually all of Michelangelo's artistry gave expression to the idea that love helps human beings in their struggles to ascend to the divine. This was true in some three hundred sonnets that he wrote, and it showed itself in his depiction of spiritual themes in his painting, sculpting, and architectural design. From a humble beginning as a banker's son in Italy, this man, because of his high hopes, big dreams, and intolerance for low expectations, emerged as one of the most respected leaders of the Renaissance, and in all of human history.

A few years ago, while I was walking with my wife through a rural village on Bali, we were told that the job of an old man who sat at the entrance to the gate was to be a cloud maker. I listened intently as I was told how the villagers believed that a man could produce clouds that would bring rain in times of drought merely by his own consciousness. Yet I must admit to some skepticism because of my own tribal conditioning that says that such events as cloud formations are beyond the scope of human consciousness. Today, though, I know one truth only regarding such conditioning: *No one knows enough to be a pessimist.*

I have on occasion lain on the grass with my own small children making clouds, and while neighbors might mutter about those crazy Dyer kids thinking they can make clouds, I simply ignore such pessimism as I hear one or the other shout, "Look Daddy, I'm making my cloud bump yours right out of the picture!" I see no danger in such thinking. Indeed, I agree with Michelangelo. The far greater danger is in reaching the low expectations that we hold for ourselves.

Michelangelo's advice is just as applicable today in your life as it was in his, over five hundred years ago. Never listen to those who try to influence you with their pessimism. Have complete faith in your own capacity to feel that love that shines through *David, Madonna and Child,* and the heavenly frescoes on the ceiling of the Sistine Chapel. The love is your conscious contact with this artist who shared the same universal spirit of oneness with you and every human being who has ever lived.

His accomplishments arose from the message he offers all of us at the beginning of this piece. Aim high, refuse to choose small thinking and low expectations, and above all, do not be seduced by the absurd idea that there is danger in having too much hope. In fact, your high hope will guide you to heal your life and to produce your own masterpieces, whether they be frescoes or fruit baskets.

To put Michelangelo's advice to work in your own life, follow these simple guidelines:

- Refuse to listen to or internalize the proclamations of those who point to your limitations. You must always remember: *When you argue for your limitations, the only thing you get are limitations.*

- Above all else, never aim low or think small. You are a divine manifestation of God, and in that regard you are connected to that which causes and creates miracles.

- Keep hope alive in you by remembering that famous remark of Albert Einstein's: "Great spirits have always encountered violent opposition from mediocre minds."

- When you consider what you would love to accomplish in your life but feel ill-prepared to bring it about, picture the eighty-nine-year-old Michelangelo living five centuries ago, painting, sculpting, and writing. Imagine he is telling you that you can create whatever you desire, and the great danger is not in having too much hope, but in reaching what you have perceived as hopeless.

MY MIND TO ME A KINGDOM IS

My mind to me a kingdom is,
    Such present joys therein I find,
That it excels all other bliss
    That world affords or grows by kind.
Though much I want which most would have,
Yet still my mind forbids to crave.

No princely pomp, no wealthy store,
    No force to win the victory,
No wily wit to salve a sore,
    No shape to feed a loving eye;
To none of these I yield as thrall,
For why my mind doth serve for all.

I see how plenty suffers oft,
    And hasty climbers soon do fall;
I see that those which are aloft
    Mishap doth threaten most of all;
They get with toil, they keep with fear:
Such cares my mind could never bear.

Content I live, this is my stay,
    I seek no more than may suffice;
I press to bear no haughty sway;
    Look, what I lack my mind supplies.
Lo! thus I triumph like a king,
Content with that my mind doth bring.

Some have too much, yet still do crave;
   I little have, and seek no more.
They are but poor, though much they have,
   And I am rich with little store.
They poor, I rich; they beg, I give;
They lack, I leave; they pine, I live.

I laugh not at another's loss;
   I grudge not at another's gain;
No worldly waves my mind can toss;
   My state at one doth still remain.
I fear no foe, I fawn no friend;
I loathe not life, nor dread my end.

Some weigh their pleasure by their lust,
   Their wisdom by their rage of will;
Their treasure is their only trust,
   A cloaked craft their store of skill:
But all the pleasure that I find
Is to maintain a quiet mind.

My wealth is health and perfect ease,
   My conscience clear my choice defence;
I neither seek by bribes to please,
   Nor by deceit to breed offence.
Thus do I live; thus will I die;
Would all did so as well as I!

SIR EDWARD DYER
(1543–1607)

English poet of the Elizabethan period, Sir Edward Dyer is best known for his lyric beginning "My mind to me a kingdom is."

Sir Edward Dyer, a sixteenth-century courtier and poet, was extremely popular in his time, yet only a small number of his poems have survived. This poem is his best-known surviving contribution, a treasure that I offer to you from half a millennium ago. This poem on the potency of the mind has long been a special favorite of mine. I find its rhythm sweet and easy to read, and it seems to speak directly to me.

I can assure you that my love for this particular poem is not based on the fact that I share the same name with the poet. I have received hundreds of copies of this poem from people all over the world asking if I am related to Edward Dyer. Though the theme of my books seems to match perfectly with the title "My Mind to Me a Kingdom Is," I do not believe Sir Edward and I are biologically related. Nevertheless, every time I read this poem I sit back in wonder and attempt to contemplate this kingdom, my mind.

The poet describes the comfort of detaching from everything, including your body, and being in the kingdom of a quiet mind. Have you ever contemplated what an awesome part of you your mind truly is? You can't see it or touch it. It has no substance, no boundaries, no placement in time or space, and yet it is always with you, guiding and directing virtually everything about your life. This is your kingdom, and you and only you can use it in any and all circumstances to create a dynasty of delight for yourself. The mind represents your corner of freedom, the place that cannot be invaded by others, a refuge of sanity when all around you is tumult. This is the wondering invisible mind. I am inviting you to recognize its powers with awe and appreciation for the magnitude of its vast dominion.

If you crave that which might cause you harm, recall the poet's words, "Yet still my mind forbids to crave." Dyer is referring to the ability to choose. Understand that you possess the power of choice. There is nothing outside yourself to blame for your cravings or unhealthy addictions. Go to your inner kingdom, where your mind is capable of making choices that are more powerful than your cravings. When you get lost in the need to be a victor at all costs, you can either blame the pressures of society or go to this powerful kingdom within yourself and ask your mind to serve the highest good for all concerned rather than your self-important ego.

The need to acquire more than is necessary, to chase after success at all costs, to consistently pursue approval from others is not imposed on us, it is a function of how we choose to use that invisible mystery within us, our mind. Edward Dyer is telling us that there are many around us who have too much, yet crave more. "They are but poor, though much they have, and I am rich with little store." He watches others living in agony, never seeming to be satisfied and always in pursuit of the elusive *More*. "They lack, I leave; they pine, I live."

As the poet gently suggests, there is the choice to become consumed with greed and acquisition, to toil and be a victim of mishap and live with fear, or to decide that "Such cares my mind could never bear." Know that it is your mind that makes these choices. Nothing more. Unlimited happiness and fulfillment is available to you as the poet intimates in this line: "Content I live, this is my stay, I seek no more than may suffice."

Your mind is willing and able to give you a lifetime of peace and tranquility. By deciding to change your mind you can start living. By referring to that inner kingdom you create a life of giving rather than lacking. In your mind, you always have the freedom to be at peace.

Every fear you experience comes not from outside, but from how you choose to use your mind. When you sweep your inner kingdom free of the remnants of lifelong conditioning, you can eliminate even fear of death. This is a state of grace, described by Sir Edward Dyer as "I loathe not life, nor dread my end."

Your kingdom is how you use your mind in the face of any and all circumstances. You are the king, the ultimate ruler. No one can make you upset without the consent of your royal mind. No one can depress you without your permission. No one can hurt your feelings without your decree.

This poem tells you to stop weighing your pleasure by what you lust after; stop the endless need to conquer and prove yourself; stop measuring your success on all those worldly activities and turn inward, to a place where peace and serenity are only a thought away. You are only a thought away from Dyer's conclusion to this famous poem: "My wealth is health and perfect ease."

There is one final thing to consider in your inner kingdom. Your mind is in charge of your health as well as your peacefulness. Change your thoughts about healing and you change your body's reactions to illness. In your inner kingdom, with a quiet mind free of the need to win, acquire, conquer, toil, and lust, you produce molecules of health. You lower your blood pressure, remove the potential for ulcers, strengthen your immune system, and lessen your susceptibility to all manner of invasive disease, and it is all in the kingdom of your mind.

Adopt these words of wisdom poetically describing this idea of your mind being a kingdom with an invisible you reigning within. Put this beautiful piece of sweet poetry to work in your life by following these suggestions:

- Practice mind control to eliminate self-destructive behaviors. Ask yourself why you are choosing to allow yourself to be upset rather than using your mind to create tranquility and peace. Catch yourself in the midst of a depressing or angry reaction and try a new way of thinking.

- Spend some time in awe of your mind and what it is capable of creating for you. Contemplate your inner kingdom and refuse to allow thoughts into that sacred inner space that might pollute it in any way.

- Repeatedly remind yourself that nothing or no one outside you can make you unhappy without your consent. Remember that you are the sum total of the choices you make in your mind. Why choose to use your mind as a pigpen instead of a kingdom? You have the same opportunity as Sir Edward Dyer, to know "My mind to me a kingdom is."

- Memorize his conclusion: "Thus do I live; thus will I die; would all did so well as I," and remember—you are the king of your inner domain.

MERCY

from *The Merchant of Venice*

The quality of mercy is not strained;
It droppeth as the gentle rain from heaven
Upon the place beneath: it is twice blest,—
It blesseth him that gives and him that takes:
'Tis mightiest in the mightiest; it becomes
The throned monarch better than his crown:
His sceptre shows the force of temporal power,
The attribute to awe and majesty,
Wherein doth sit the dread and fear of kings;
But mercy is above this sceptred sway,—
It is enthroned in the hearts of kings,
It is an attribute to God himself;
And earthly power doth then show likest God's
When mercy seasons justice.

WILLIAM SHAKESPEARE
(1564–1616)

English poet and dramatist of the Elizabethan and early Jacobean period, William Shakespeare is the most widely known author in all English literature.

*H*ow do I choose one contribution from the man many consider the greatest dramatist and sonneteer of all time? To read William Shakespeare is to become lost in his unprecedentedly rich and inventive use of the English language. My first selection was the masterful soliloquy from *Hamlet* in which he asks the question that haunts all seekers of truth and higher awareness. "To be or not to be" is certainly *the* question. Yet I felt that I had covered the subject of dealing with the conflict of suffering the slings and arrows of outrageous fortune versus taking arms against a sea of troubles, and thus by opposing, ending them, in several places in this book.

I finally decided to present this selection on the quality of mercy, from *The Merchant of Venice*, because I feel these are the most profound and practical fourteen lines ever written on this human attribute.

Living with a spirit of mercy and putting it to use each day is the way to tame our more base and primitive instincts while nurturing love and compassion. When we are hurt by others, our first impulse is usually to get even. Revenge rather than mercy is what our more savage side urges. Yet Shakespeare says about this quality of mercy, which he calls an attribute of God, that "It droppeth as the gentle rain from Heaven, upon the place beneath: it is twice blest." The first blessing of mercy or compassion is on you, the giver. This message summarizes much of the wisdom that the psychological literature has to offer. That is, be compassionate with yourself, do not judge yourself harshly when you make a mistake or fail to live up to some standard. Be of such a mind that you can detach from the misconduct or failure and be gentle and loving with yourself. Forgive yourself for being so human as to have wandered around in your darker corners and emerged embarrassed or disappointed with your behavior. Give *yourself* mercy, a quality that Shakespeare says "becomes the throned monarch better than his crown." And so it becomes you as well. When you take the first blessing of mercy and apply it to yourself, you open to the potential of offering this quality to "him that takes."

If you are unable to give yourself authentic compassion you will never be able to give it to another, any more than you can give love to another if you do not love yourself, or give money to the poor if you have none. Developing compassion for yourself can be achieved by following the shrewd and wise advice of my teacher Sri Nisargadatta Maharaj. He tells me, "The sinner and the saint are merely exchanging notes. The saint had sinned, the sinner will be sanctified." All of us have sinned, even those we call saints. When you consider these words, compassion for yourself is easier to acquire. Now you can give it away. And this is what Shakespeare means by the double blessing of mercy.

While we all fear those who have the force of temporal power, symbolized poetically by the king's scepter, mercy, as the bard reminds us, is above the "sceptred sway." It takes a godly quality to look into the eyes of those who have behaved badly or harmed us in some way, to remove our inclination to brandish our wands of imperial power. When we instead show compassion toward those offenders we arrive at the point where "earthly power doth then show likest God's."

As parents, or even adults in positions of authority by virtue of our age and size advantage, we often have the option of displaying our symbols of regal power. It is quite tempting to dole out punishments and to exact revenge when we are disobeyed. Compassion is generally the last thing on our minds. In such moments I have learned to remind myself how patient and merciful God has always been with me in my darkest and most frightening times. I've never ever felt abandoned by God, even when many seemed to be anything but compassionate for the errors of my ways. This godlike quality is most helpful when mercy seasons justice, rather than replaces it.

When I am being parental with my children who have broken a rule or failed to live up to an agreement or just generally screwed up in some way, I remember Shakespeare's advice to season justice with mercy. I tell them I have great love for them and I know what it is like to have screwed up, and I season the consequences with mercy and compassion, so they always feel loved when the issue is behind us.

This notion of giving mercy away applies to all your relationships in all areas of your life. Offering compassion to those who have harmed or disappointed you does not mean being a victim. It is instead a way of saying, "I understand, I care, I forgive, but I still do not like it, and I will not tolerate being treated this way or having you think it is acceptable." The difference is not needing to exact revenge or to prove one's superiority. With mercy in your heart you will find yourself much less distracted and disheartened by the evil behaviors that you see and read about almost every day. You will be able to send the offenders love and not become obsessed with anger, hatred, and eventually the desire for revenge.

The quality of having mercy in your heart to give away keeps you focused on what you are for, rather than what you are against. For example, rather than becoming immobilized by your anger at what you are against, such as starvation, you put your attention on what you are for, which is to educate and feed people, thus your compassion leads you to a loving solution rather than an angry reaction. The mercy you feel in your heart toward those you love in your own circle or family will similarly keep you focused on compassion rather than reprisal, on rectifying the affront rather than exacting a retribution.

As Shakespeare says in this inspiring piece, mercy is "mightiest in the mightiest." That is, the more powerful you are as a person, the more power you will display through your mercy, and the less need you will have to display your symbols of authority.

Put the ideas of this passage by one of the world's greatest wordsmiths into your life by practicing the following:

• When you find yourself facing a situation in which you are going to apportion justice, see the two sides of your own personality very clearly. The one side is the king who has the power of retribution, the other side is the mercy merchant who sends love and compassion first and foremost. By all means seek justice, but season it well with mercy.

• Give yourself the compassion you deserve for any and all past actions. Stop judging yourself harshly. All those errors and wrong actions were necessary for you to get beyond that place in your life. Be kind to yourself and eliminate any ill feelings you harbor toward yourself.

• Once you have stated how you feel, and justice has been done, then let go. I mean let go *now*! Don't hold on to grudges and use constant reminders to keep others in a state of guilt while maintaining your own dissonance as well. Let it go.

• Turn your most troublesome disturbances over to God. Simply say, "Dear God, I find it so extremely difficult to give mercy in this situation, and I am turning it over to you completely. I know you will guide me in acting in the most merciful and humane way." This action will free you from your own immobilization and anger and help you to see the saint in the sinner, who have just been exchanging notes with each other.

ONENESS

from *Devotions upon Emergent Occasions*

MEDITATION XVII

No man is an island, entire of itself; every man is a piece of
the continent, a part of the main; if a clod be washed away
by the sea, Europe is the less, as well as if a promontory
were, as well as if a manor of thy friends or thine own
were; any man's death diminishes me, because I am
involved in mankind; and therefore never send to know for
whom the bell tolls; it tolls for thee.

JOHN DONNE
(1572–1631)

*John Donne was an English poet, noted as the first and one of the
finest metaphysical poets. The paradoxical human union of spirit
and matter was a recurring theme.*

*P*erhaps the single quality that defines mysticism is the idea of oneness that John Donne expresses so poignantly in this passage written
in the early years of the seventeenth century. This idea of unity consciousness and the oneness of humanity is omnipresent in all the
sacred literature as far back as the ancient Upanishads. Ancient mystical wisdom tells us that in the garden of the mystics, distinctions
such as I, you, he, she, and they do not exist. John Donne is expressing essentially the same thought, "No man is an island," in the first
line of this very famous poem. To reach a higher state of awareness
and bliss in our lives, we must understand the truth of that first
line. That can only happen when our ego mind gets the message.

Our ego mind insists that we are separate from others and
defined by where our boundaries stop and others start. Similarly,

these ego minds tell us that we are separate from our environment and that we are here to sort of push it around as we desire. Yet mystical teachers and poets are always reminding us of our connectedness and the oneness of everything and everyone. We must look beneath the surface and beyond appearances to grasp the unity consciousness they speak of.

As we look at our body, it does appear to be a separate organism. But a closer look reveals a multitude of organs and rivers of fluids containing zillions of life forms, with even more zillions of invisible bacteria, all working together to form this body. To rephrase John Donne's enduring contribution, "No cell is an island, entire of itself, every cell is a piece of the body, a part of the main; if a life form be contaminated, the whole is the less. Any cell's illness or death diminishes me, because I am involved in the whole body."

Even though the cells of your liver never make contact with the cells of your mouth, they are connected and vital to the entire body, so any cell that is diminished diminishes the whole. And so it is with all of humanity. We are all cells in this body called humanity, and to the extent that we think of ourselves as separate and therefore in competition with one another, we diminish the whole of humanity. Native Americans expressed this idea of oneness with all by saying, "No tree has branches so foolish as to fight among themselves." Obviously any cell that goes to war against the neighboring cells in the same body will end up destroying the whole and itself in the process. This is what a cancer cell does. Failing to cooperate with adjacent cells, it destroys them and eventually, unless checked, it destroys the body and itself in the process. A very stupid organism indeed.

In *Devotions upon Emergent Occasions* John Donne speaks to each of us. He advises us that we are all members of one body, and no one of us can survive alone. Virtually everything about our existence depends on the other cells in this larger body working with and for us. Your solitary existence would be like a heart beating outside your body, independent of all the promontory arteries, veins, and organs that must work in harmony with the heart to keep you alive.

Imagine a wave or a drop of water considering itself apart from the ocean. It is weak when separate from the ocean, but returned to its source it is as powerful as the ocean. The poetic words of John Donne remind us of this truth. When we are as islands, entire of ourselves, we lose the power of our source and diminish the whole of humanity. But in the garden of the mystics, where "we" and "us" supplant "I" and "you," warfare is impossible because on a round planet, choosing up sides is impossible. In our individual lives, seeing ourselves as islands that are not part of the whole is the cause of our inability to find the highest, the fullest, and the richest experience of life.

When you see yourself as connected to everyone, you immediately cease your judgment of the other and see that person connected via invisible threads, just as your ankles and your elbows share the same unseen silent life force. Therefore compassion becomes an automatic reaction to everyone. You see all of humanity as one undivided and indivisible family. Once you can view all others as family members rather than competitors or traitors, you will reach out with love, rather than with a weapon of defense or destruction.

This orientation of oneness is a radical shift from the separateness we learn in the tribes, families, and countries we inhabit. Our identification moves away from what is different about us to what we share in common. Our fixation is no longer on appearance but on how vital we are to one another. Thus hatred is replaced with a desire to resolve anything that divides us, just as an oncologist works to have the entire organism eradicate the troublemaking cancer cell so that it can't be a force of disharmony in the body.

I have found that I am much less troubled and stressful when I remember the opening five words of this sensitive passage. There was a time when I tended to view panhandlers, holding up cardboard signs pleading for money, with contempt, often saying to myself or anyone within earshot, "Why don't they go out and work for their money like I do?" Now I remind myself that in some mysterious and, yes, mystical way I am connected to those people. Their poverty, uncleanness, and ill health diminishes all of us, myself included. I send them a silent blessing and vow to do more to end such conditions on the planet, and most important, I feel more compassionate and loving in my heart. I am reminded how we all need each other, and that our connections are much greater than the mere tribal connections of our immediate genetic families.

When you hear bells ringing out in sadness indicating someone has been victimized by violence, listen carefully and remind yourself of what John Donne wrote over four centuries ago. That bell tolls for all of us, including thee!

To apply these unity consciousness ideas in your life begin to:

- Stop viewing yourself as distant and apart on the basis of your geography, or your isolation from those who are struggling elsewhere. When you become aware of someone suffering on another shore, say a silent prayer for that person, and see if you can experience in your heart your oneness with that person.

- See God in everyone and everything and behave each day as if the God in all things truly mattered. Try to suspend your judgments of those who are less ambitious, less peaceful, and less loving, and instead know that hatred and judgment are the problems in the first place. When you judge the haters and hate the judgers, you are a part of the cancer rather than the treatment.

- Use fewer labels that distinguish you from "them." You are not an American, Californian, Italian, Jew, middle-aged, stocky, female, athletic, or any other label. You are a citizen of the world, and when you stop the labeling process you will begin to see God in every garden, every forest, every home, every creature, and every person, and inner peace will be your reward.

TIME

ON TIME

Fly envious Time, till thou run out thy race,
Call on the lazy leaden-stepping hours,
Whose speed is but the heavy plummet's pace;
And glut thy self with what thy womb devours,
Which is no more than what is false and vain,
And merely mortal dross;
So little is our loss,
So little is thy gain.
For when as each thing bad thou hast entombed,
And last of all, thy greedy self consumed,
Then long Eternity shall greet our bliss
With an individual kiss;
And Joy shall overtake us as a flood,
When every thing that is sincerely good
And perfectly divine,
With Truth, and Peace, and Love shall ever shine
About the supreme Throne
Of him, t'whose happy-making sight alone,
When once our heav'nly guided soul shall climb,
Then all this earthy grossness quit,
Attired with stars, we shall for ever sit,
Triumphing over Death, and Chance, and thee, O Time.

JOHN MILTON
(1608–1674)

John Milton's poetry and prose have helped make him one of the best-known and most respected figures of English literature.

*I*n putting this book together I have had the opportunity to read thousands of poems written by hundreds of great thinkers throughout history. The theme of "time as an enemy" is quite popular with those who record the human drama, particularly among the poets. John Milton is considered one of the greatest of those poets, and many who lived long after Milton have referred to this seventeenth-century literary genius and author of *Paradise Lost* as the most influential poet in their lives.

The human dilemma in regard to time is understandably an ongoing theme or topic because we blame the passage of time for weakening and destroying our bodies. The basic truth of our fleshly human reality can be summed up in one sentence. *In the end, we all grow older and die.* This applies whether you are a seventeenth-century blind poet, a famous actress today, a person of enormous power, or a housewife in Athens. Like it or not, this is our reality. John Milton recognized this fundamental truth as he wrote his poem on time.

However, he was also striving to go beyond the seemingly superior power of time. He writes of the one thing that can defeat the passage of time. Enter eternity. And a warm reception, please, for soul, the eternal friend of the poet and also our key to bliss, grace, and salvation. Milton describes time as going about the business of "glutting itself with what thy womb devours," but poetically explains that everything that it gets to eat is false, vain, and nothing but mortal dross. "So little is our loss" (we humans). "So little is thy gain" (time's).

He describes eternity greeting us with a kiss, and the joy of escaping the clutches of time. Eternity takes over and introduces us to the timelessness of truth, peace, and love. Milton says it beautifully in his conclusion, "Attired with stars, we shall for ever sit, triumphing over Death, and Chance, and thee, O Time."

I love the way he sums it all up. This poet knows this is all we need to be free from our fear of the inevitable process of aging and death.

Milton lost his eyesight in his early forties and had to dictate his poetry when this was a far greater hardship than it would be today. He felt the inroads that "time" was making on his life. I think of John Milton, perhaps sitting in a cold, stone room, blind and dictating, listening as an assistant records his observations, and feeling a deep sense of satisfaction in knowing that he is describing the only means of triumph over his earthly fate. Carefully read his words. You will faintly hear the whisper of time saying, "In the end, you'll simply grow old and die."

But it seems to me that since everything in our physical world is in a constant state of change, and all that we experience with our senses is in the firm grip of time, and being "consumed by its greedy self," that it is possible to know joy and "quit this earthly grossness" now, without having to wait for that individual kiss of eternity to occur at death. I believe we can make a decision to begin living each day in truth, peace, and love, and smile rather than shudder at the passage of time. By doing so, we can thumb our collective noses at time. Our primary identification is not with time, but with the timelessness of love, truth, and peace. Your timeless self does not age and has no fear of death.

I enjoy knowing that I can speak to time with the truth, love, and peace of my eternal self and don't feel that I have to wait for death to enjoy eternity. I celebrate my triumph each and every day of my life by living from the perspective of truth, peace, and love as much as I possibly can right now, and the joy that Milton speaks of is mine. Not in some future moment, but now!

Contemplate your physical self and all its possessions, and practice laughing peacefully at it all. Time has only leased them to you. As you read the poetry of the greats who preceded you here, this theme will crop up repeatedly. The battle is often perceived as being between death and life, chance and choice. And yes, time and eternity. Yet you are here now and you can stop perceiving it as a battleground. Instead make peace with time. Laugh at its work, and know your laughter does not make you a victim. Observe from your eternal perspective that the observer is immune to time.

Feel what Milton is conveying to us through his sightless, aging body many centuries ago. A sense of triumph. A sense of knowing that soul is where our bliss resides. "Attired with stars, we shall for ever sit." Forever includes now!

To transcend the time/eternity duality, practice each day the trilogy that Milton offers in his poem:

• *Truth*. Live the truth that resonates with you, regardless of how you have been conditioned or what the good opinions of others might be.

- *Peace.* Decide to always choose that which brings you and others a sense of both inner and outer peace.

- *Love.* Be a force of love as often as you can and subdue thoughts of hatred, judgment, and anger whenever you feel them surface.

The timelessness of truth, peace, and love give you the tools for looking time right in the eye and saying with conviction, "I have no fear of you for I am eternal and you can't touch me."

SOLITUDE

Happy the man, whose wish and care
A few paternal acres bound,
Content to breathe his native air
  In his own ground.

Whose herds with milk, whose fields with bread,
Whose flocks supply him with attire;
Whose trees in summer yield him shade,
  In winter, fire.

Blest, who can unconcernedly find
Hours, days, and years slide soft away
In health of body, peace of mind;
  Quiet by day,

Sound sleep by night; study and ease
Together mixed, sweet recreation,
And innocence, which most does please
  With meditation.

Thus let me live, unseen, unknown;
Thus unlamented let me die,
Steal from the world, and not a stone
  Tell where I lie.

ALEXANDER POPE
(1688–1744)

*English poet and satirist Alexander Pope was the literary dictator
of his age, and regarded as the epitome of English neoclassicism.*

$\mathcal{A}$t first reading, this very famous poem by Alexander Pope,
appears to be exclusively about the importance of finding peace
and quiet as a prerequisite to happiness. And, indeed, this is a
theme not only of this poem, but of much of the work of this
early eighteenth-century poet who lived in Windsor Forest outside London. He had a curvature of the spine and a tubercular
infection that limited his height to four feet, six inches, and he
suffered severe headaches throughout his life. His deformity and
illness made him particularly sensitive to physical and mental
pain, and therefore the solitude of nature, and the ability to be
self-sufficient away from the noise and mayhem of the crowds,
was a subject of his poetry.

Our late twentieth-century natural world is vastly different
from the one Pope was born in three hundred years ago, making
his poetic advice even more significant for us today. "Content to
breathe his native air in his own ground" in today's world often
means eyes burning from the smog of our cities, inhaling noxious
fumes, and breathing in pollutants. Those of us who can feel self-
sufficient by milking our herds and fleecing our sheep and warm-
ing our bodies from the trees on our property when they are not
providing shade, are few and far between. Furthermore, mighty
few of us are "blest, who can unconcernedly find hours, days and
years sliding soft away, with health of body, peace of mind; quiet
by day."

Instead we experience increasing levels of physical deterioration because of environmental illnesses, higher and higher levels
of stress, and a noisy world of all manner of landscaping power
motors, portable leaf blowers, bulldozers, jackhammers, trucks,
and sirens bombarding our senses. Pope's nearly three-hundred-
year-old poetic advice is certainly pertinent in today's world.

The first three verses of this poem refer to the need to breathe
clean air, find self-sufficiency in nature, and enjoy some solitude
and quiet during the day. I encourage you to do all that you can

to bring these elements into your life, regardless of where you reside. Take the time to get out of the city and be in nature where bliss awaits you in quiet places.

In the fourth stanza, Pope poetically describes how to enjoy sound sleep by mixing together recreation with innocence and meditation. I have written elsewhere in this book on the importance of daily meditation, so I will not repeat that here. But some of the remaining ingredients for a happy life—study, ease, recreation, and innocence—are a mix of perennially good advice for any era. When I give myself the freedom to study subjects of interest, time to ease myself out of pressure, play tennis, swim, or run during the day, I know the childlike innocence that "does most please," particularly as it melds with meditation.

These four stanzas of "Solitude," Alexander Pope's most famous early poem, before "The Rape of the Lock," provide a smorgasbord of ingredients for happiness. They represent a call to commune in as natural and stress-free an environment as possible. I encourage you to heed his poetic counsel, no matter how urban, crowded, or noisy your daily life might be. I personally find myself repeatedly drawn to the final stanza of this poem, "Thus let me live unseen, unknown."

I have had the rare privilege to be in the presence of some divine beings and avatars. My most lasting impression of these highly evolved people is that they have subdued their egos and live as silent sages, unwilling to bask in the halo light of their own divinity. They have literally chosen to disappear as physical beings. They seek no credit for their great gifts, in fact they attribute them all to God. When St. Francis of Assisi, the great healer of the thirteenth century, was asked why he didn't heal his own sickly body, he responded that he wanted everyone to know that it was not he who was doing the healing.

For me, the measure of greatness and happiness is the ability to subjugate ego to the point of needing no credit for accomplishments, to be beyond needing gratitude or applause, to be independent of the good opinion of others, to just be doing what I do, because it is my purpose to do so. The spirit of what it truly means to be impeccable or magnificent, to learn to give anonymously and resist the temptation to be praised, is beautifully expressed in the film classic *Magnificent Obsession*. Once we stop needing glory, we experience a new kind of freedom. As the poet says, "Thus, unlamented, let me die. Steal from the world, and not a stone tell where I lie."

I have felt this in the presence of true greatness. It is a kind of humility that I imagine Jesus of Nazareth, Buddha, and Lao-tzu exuded. When I sat before Mother Meera, a divine teacher from India who resides in Germany, and gazed into her divine eyes she was so ego-less as to reach me without words, and I truly felt as if she needed no recognition now or ever for her incredible spirituality. When Carlos Castaneda wrote of his association with the Naguals, the great spiritual teachers, he was intrigued by their anonymity and humility. These were ordinary-appearing beings, possessing extraordinary awareness, living profoundly yet humbly, ever present but almost invisible. These are the paradoxical qualities that I read into the concluding stanza of Alexander Pope's poem. Learn to live unseen and unknown, free of the need to be noticed. Do what you do because you feel guided, and retreat in dignity and peace.

My first physical contact with my contemporary teacher Guruji involved complete silence that lasted for almost an hour. Words were unnecessary. I was given a manifesting meditation to teach, yet he has never mentioned wanting credit for it. The greatest teachers are aware of the need to maintain anonymity and humility.

No one summed this idea up better than the ancient Chinese teacher Lao-tzu, who has a chapter dedicated to him in this book. He reminds us: "All streams flow to the ocean because it is lower than they are. Humility gives it its power."

To apply the wisdom of Alexander Pope's poem "Solitude," I suggest you consider these ideas:

- Take time out of your day for periods of solitude to do nothing more than be silent. Subdue the strident noises of your life by playing soft classical music in the background of your home or business if possible. The "Mozart effect" creates a sense of balance and peace that literally increases productivity and decreases stress.

- Give yourself extended time to be in nature listening to the sounds of animals and birds, wind and surf, and to breathe in the nonpolluted air slowly and deeply. Wilderness time is great therapy for rejuvenating yourself.

- Take a yoga class or use a video that teaches you the beginning exercises for bringing your body into harmony. Make yoga a regular part of your day.

- Practice giving anonymously to anyone in need, not asking for praise. Make this your magnificent obsession. I encourage you to see both *Magnificent Obsession* and *Brother Sun, Sister Moon,* which is the story of St. Francis and his transformation into a humble giving spirit in the thirteenth century.

- Remember Henry David Thoreau's metaphysical description, which sums up the essential message of "Solitude": "Humility, like darkness, reveals the heavenly lights."

TRUTH/BEAUTY

ODE ON A GRECIAN URN

O Attic shape! Fair attitude! With brede
Of marble men and maidens overwrought,
With forest branches and the trodden weed;
Thou, silent form, dost tease us out of thought
As doth eternity: cold pastoral!
When old age shall this generation waste,
Thou shalt remain, in midst of other woe
Than ours, a friend to man, to whom thou say'st,
"Beauty is truth, truth beauty,"—that is all
Ye know on earth, and all ye need to know.

JOHN KEATS
(1795–1821)

Probably the most talented of the English Romantic poets, John Keats gave up the practice of medicine to write poetry.

$\mathcal{T}$here is something in the universe that outlasts our individual mortal life. Whatever that something is perplexes all of us, and young John Keats wrote about it poetically in his famous *Ode on a Grecian Urn*. As the poet contemplated the figures of the lovers on the Greek urn, he himself was grappling with mortality. His brother had recently died in his early twenties, and he struggled with his own ill health, which claimed his life the following year at the age of twenty-six. This poetic selection is the fifth and final stanza of *Ode on a Grecian Urn*. It concludes with two lines that summarize an approach to living that is transcendent and speaks to your own source of true happiness.

I think about the message in Keats's poem every day when I look outside the window of my office. Two months ago my son and I cleaned out a wooded area in front of the townhouse where I do my writing. We clipped bushes and chopped down dead trees and gave quite a drastic haircut to my entranceway. Right in front of my window we left what appeared to be a dead thin tree trunk with discolored bark, standing about three feet high. We decided to dig it out the following day, since we didn't have a shovel handy. One thing led to another and I had to leave town on a lecture tour, and we ignored the dead stick in the ground. When I returned, I noticed some green leaves sprouting from this dried-up protrusion and I decided to forgo the shovel.

Today, as I look out my window, there are thousands of buds, green branches, and leaves covering the top of the "dead stick in the ground." It is a beautiful sight to see. The life force, invisible to my eye, is the eternity that Keats refers to when he writes, "when old age shall this generation waste, thou shalt remain, in midst of other woe . . ." And yes, this "thou" is a friend to all of us who says, " 'Beauty is truth, truth beauty,'—that is all ye know on earth, and all ye need to know."

The life force that seemed to bring that dead stick to life is what we can call truth. It simply is. Now each of us can view this truth and all the truths that eternity manages to manifest for us, in any way we choose. What John Keats suggests is that we elect to identify beauty with truth and truth with beauty . . . period! Beauty is in that silent form which is eternal and which is our truth. To recognize this "thou" as a gift of beauty is to make peace with one's entire life.

Throughout history, poets, philosophers, and scientists have equated beauty with the peacefulness of a fully realized life. The ability to appreciate beauty is a high-level characteristic in the fully functioning people Dr. Abraham Maslow studied. Maslow was the original pioneer in studying man's potential for greatness; he identified specific traits that were unique to these highly functioning people he called self-actualizers.

Maslow called this peaceful state of awareness "self-actualization." Perhaps what he was describing was a unique kinship with truth. Emerson described beauty as "God's handwriting—a wayside sacrament," and urged us all to "never lose an opportunity of seeing anything that is beautiful." Keats seems to go a step beyond merely appreciating beauty; he speaks of equating beauty with truth.

So what is your truth? First and most important, your truth is what is real for you. And what is real is what you experience with emotion or feeling. Thus, if you feel it, know it, and experience it, it is more than true, it is beauty made manifest. Your feelings of accomplishment are true and beautiful. Your appreciation of a loved one is true and beautiful. Your inspirations are true, and thus beautiful. This invisible eternal spark of life that Keats says is a friend to man is providing you with your truth, and therefore with beauty as well, should you choose to process it in this manner.

Every time I look at what I thought was a dead stump outside my office window and I see that life force expressing itself with beautiful green shoots, branches, leaves, and new growth, I think of the same life force that flows through me. It is my truth. I am sharing this eternal life force with that stick in the ground, and when my generation is turned to waste, the life force remains in the midst of those who will take my place. It is such a divine mystery, yet it is our truth, and consequently I choose to call it beautiful.

In my heart I know that if we paved the entire surface of the planet, that "thou" that Keats refers to would cause a blade of grass to shoot up through the pavement. The eternal "thou" would spring up once again in bloom and beauty. It cannot be stopped. And that is the truth. It is also your truth. To paraphrase Keats, that on earth is all ye need to know.

When a heart opens to the experience of truth as beauty, one of mankind's most troublesome enigmas—death—is solved. Here is John Keats, racked with tuberculosis in his early twenties, facing the fact that his body will soon give up, yet opening to the beauty of the truth of life. See beauty in every place that you feel truth. That beauty/truth will imbue you. Know yourself, and live your truth and you will have beauty.

It seems to me that in these enduring lines of poetry, John Keats was telling each of us to know our truth, to follow our hearts, and we will see beauty everywhere. To do otherwise is to lose our ability to appreciate and experience the ecstasy of life, that same invisible ecstasy that somehow manages to put life into a seed, a root, a blossom, even you.

Make this poetic observation bloom beautifully in your life by practicing the following suggestions:

- Examine what is most true for you. Where does your own personal truth reside? When do you most feel inspired and fulfilled? What provides you with the most inner satisfaction? Your answers are the "thou" that is the eternal life space within you, and the beauty that it engenders is the authentic you.

- Trust in your own assessment of what is beauty and truth. Practice your own truth by being independent of the opinions of others. If you feel inspired and it resonates as your inner ecstasy, then it is true and therefore beautiful as well.

- Let go of judgments that classify the pursuits and interests of others as ugly, inappropriate, or inauthentic. Stay with your truth and allow others the right to be free of your acrimonious judgments.

- Practice beauty appreciation in as many places as possible. Nature provides a virtual smorgasbord of miracles. See the beauty in all of it. Look for the divine invisible "thou" that you know to be eternal, springing up everywhere. Capture it with your heart. If it is true, it is beauty. Keep this thought in mind and refuse to use your mental energy to see it otherwise.

PASSION

LOVE'S PHILOSOPHY

I

The fountains mingle with the river
And the rivers with the Ocean,
The winds of Heaven mix for ever
With a sweet emotion;
Nothing in the world is single;
All things by a law divine
In one spirit meet and mingle.
Why not I with thine?

II

See the mountains kiss high Heaven
And the waves clasp one another;
No sister-flower would be forgiven
If it disdained its brother;
And the sunlight clasps the earth
And the moonbeams kiss the sea:
What is all this sweet work worth
If thou kiss not me?

PERCY BYSSHE SHELLEY
(1792–1822)

English philosophical poet Percy Bysshe Shelley rejected all conventions that he believed stifled love and human freedom and rebelled against the strictures of English politics and religion.

*P*ercy Bysshe Shelley's poetry was his legacy to all of us on the importance of passionately living our daily lives. No less an authority than the *Encyclopedia Britannica* said about this English Romantic poet, "His passionate search for personal love and social justice was gradually channeled from overt actions into poems that rank with the greatest in the English language." Living life passionately has its own tremendous rewards, which are intensified when one is aware that death, in its arbitrary way, can come unexpectedly, as it did for Shelley.

Just think of this. Here was a man living at the beginning of the nineteenth century in England who risked his life distributing pamphlets advocating political rights and autonomy for Catholics in Ireland. He eloped at age nineteen, betraying both families; he lost his first wife to suicide when he was twenty-four; and two of his children died when he was in his mid-twenties. He then married his lover, Mary Wollstonecraft, fulfilling his desire for a life partner who "can feel poetry and understand philosophy." Shelley traveled all over Europe supporting himself by writing and publishing his poetry. He met with Lord Byron in various European cities for joint poetic endeavors, and proclaimed that poets are the unacknowledged legislators of the world because they create human values and the forms that shape the social order.

This man was a fervent idealist who wrote of his love for love and his passion for passion. He completed his enormous treasury of poetry and prose by the age of twenty-nine, when he died in a boating accident during a storm. Not only does his poetry speak to all of us of his enormous passion, but so does his life as well. He took up causes, risked his fame and his life, and drank up every moment of his life. The poem quoted here, "Love's Philosophy," conveys a glimmer of the passion that Shelley felt in his idealistic heart, and it says to me, as does so much of his romantic poetry: *Feel the love for those you adore, and express it with fervor; otherwise live your life in frustration.*

Love, the passionate variety, is that inner sense of longing that pervades every thought, every waking moment. It is a state of bliss that we usually equate with sexual or romantic feelings when they are ecstatically shared with one's lover. All of that mingling, mixing, clasping, and kissing between the rivers, winds, mountains, flowers, and moonbeams are Shelley's metaphors for that shared state of bliss. Why, he implies, would you choose the frustration of not expressing these feelings? I can recall the aching I have felt at various times in my life for a love that I was unable to share with someone. I think I felt as though I'd died and gone to heaven when that love was made manifest by long embraces and kisses and union.

But there is also passion in other circumstances, like the ecstasy of creation. When we consider the matter of having passion in our lives, it is important to pay attention to the things that we feel passionate about. Personally, I know the ecstasy of creation through my writing, and in delivering a talk to an audience. I feel a state of bliss in many situations, which is the same kind of union that Shelley describes in his poetry.

I have felt the ecstasy of being at one with my body in running a long-distance marathon and competing in a hotly contested tennis match. I experience ecstasy in deep meditation and on long walks with my wife, or while watching my children perform. Shelley speaks of a love and a joyful heart that is able to appreciate the beauty of our world and all those to whom we feel connected. His is not exclusively a passion that keeps us enslaved to our sexual ecstasies. What he is describing is living your life not as if today were the first day of the rest of your life, but as if this were the *only* day of your life—which of course it is—and sharing your passion because a shared joy is a doubled joy.

Too often we find ourselves bogged down in a serious approach to life, using our minds to keep us in a state of angst or, even worse, indifference. Joy and ecstasy come from within; they cannot be purchased at any price. We are all seeking joy and happiness, and often feeling it is not a proper state of mind when it arrives. The key to knowing this state is to put passion into your life. In your love and sex life to be sure, but also in your recreation, your vocation, and all your observations of yourself intermingling with this glorious universe. There is so much to be passionate about.

I have found that people who have a passion or a strong will for what they want to achieve, and who do not allow others to smear or sully their inner pictures of what they want to manifest, always seem to get what they desire in their lives. Shelley lived out of his passionate idealism with every breath and heartbeat. His passion is reflected in his magnificent poetry. Reread "Love's Philosophy" and ask yourself, "Why not?"

To put this passion into you life:

- Know that you are a part of a joyful universe. Allow your romantic, ecstatic, blissful emotions to appear more frequently in your daily life. When you feel joy, experience it and express it. As the New Testament says, "Joy is the fruit of the spirit." Don't deny yourself that fruit.

- Write your own poetry. Take the time to record your feelings of passion. Whether your passion is pottery or antique furniture, mathematics or music, express it in your own words.

- Give yourself permission to be a passionate person. Be passionate about anything or anyone you choose, without interference from your inner critic. When that inner critic tries to make you feel foolish, gently but firmly tell it to wait for you in the lobby and invite it to rejoin you later if you want to.

- Tell those you love how you feel about them as often as possible. This will give you the opportunity to share your joy, and by doing so, to double it.

- Read, read, read, and reread the poetry of passionate people like Shelley. Try to feel their hearts beating with yours. Imagine yourself seeing and feeling what they saw before you even arrived on this planet.

A POISON TREE

I was angry with my friend:
I told my wrath, my wrath did end.
I was angry with my foe:
I told it not, my wrath did grow.

And I water'd it in fears,
Night and morning with my tears;
And I sunned it with smiles,
And with soft deceitful wiles.

And it grew both day and night,
Till it bore an apple bright;
And my foe beheld it shine,
And he knew that it was mine,

And into my garden stole
When the night had veil'd the pole:
In the morning glad I see
My foe outstretch'd beneath the tree.

WILLIAM BLAKE
(1757–1827)

William Blake was an English poet, engraver, painter, and mystic.
His poetry is best known for its mysticism and complex symbolism.

William Blake is one of my heroes. In his lifetime he was a consummate poet, painter, and artist, and a visionary mystic who was largely ignored by his contemporaries and considered mad. He lived his entire life on the edge of poverty and died in neglect. Yet today this man is regarded as one of the most original and greatest figures in literary history, and his original engravings are rare treasures worth millions of dollars.

I have devoured his epic poems and quoted him extensively in my lifetime, and deciding what contribution of his to include in this book has been a considerable challenge. His most famous words are the opening lines in "Allegories of Innocence" written in 1803. "To see a world in a grain of sand, and a Heaven in a wild flower, hold infinity in the palm of your hand and eternity in an hour" speaks to Blake's preoccupation with the power of the mind to perceive God or the infinite, the value of our imagination and the oneness of the universe. I have written elsewhere in this book on these themes, and so I have chosen "A Poison Tree" as another great example of what this "madman genius" offers you and me today, from his creative pen some two hundred plus years ago while writing in the midst of the French Revolution, which was transpiring only a hundred or so miles from where Blake was writing.

"A Poison Tree" is a very basic message for maintaining loving relationships through communication. The key thought here is to communicate. "I was angry with my friend: I told my wrath, my wrath did end." Such a simple way to express a profound truth. When you feel something and you have the common sense or the courage to express that feeling to your loved ones, the rage and the fury disappear, almost as if by magic.

My inclination in the past has often been to stay silent when I feel angry. I admit to wanting to stew about it, play it over and over in my mind, where I have extended dialogues with the person I feel angry toward. As long as I take this position of freezing out my loved ones or friends, the wrath persists. Yet when it finally does come out and we are able to communicate about it, expressing our authentic feelings, regardless of how absurd they may sound to the other person, magically and almost instantaneously the fury subsides. "I was angry with my foe: I told it not, my wrath did grow." This is precisely the lesson that I have had to learn, and I admit to still working on it each day.

In past relationships I created foes out of those I loved the most. The moment I made them foes, I kept my wrath inside, playing intellectual games with myself, and creating an unbelievably complex scenario that only I was privy to. Thus the inclination to keep my wrath within, unexpressed, allowed me to create what Blake calls a poison tree. I would water it with my tears and sun it with deceitful smiles. And the result? It would continue to grow and bear fruit. And the fruit is definitely poison—so much so that it would eventually destroy those to whom I had given the tag of foe. There they were, "outstretched beneath the tree."

The message of this poem is profound. It applies not only in personal relationships, but in dealing with everyone in your life. Anytime you feel that spark go off inside you, and your wrath begins to grow, you are headed for a potential morass. The way out of that potential morass is to stop and make that person a friend rather than a foe. Tell that person, "I feel that you are attempting to manipulate me right now, and I would prefer that to stop!" This kind of honest, no-nonsense statement will put the wrath aside and inhibit the growth of a poison tree that will ultimately destroy you or whomever has become your foe.

Similarly, in close family relationships, when you feel something like anger, practice mustering up the courage to say how you feel without being abusive or loud. I have found with my children that when I give the silent treatment, the anger doesn't subside. In fact, it grows worse because both of us are growing our own poison tree inside because we have made foes of each other. When we sit down and I express how I am feeling and what my disappointments are, it generally leads to an open discussion in which we both express ourselves and ends with a hug and an "I love you, too, Dad." Amazingly, "I told my wrath, my wrath did end." These are eight words that you might want to memorize as you think about ways to make your relationships work at a blissful level more frequently.

It is inevitable in any partnership for two people to have conflict. I often express my feeling that in any relationship in which two people agree on everything, one of them is unnecessary. Your soulmate is often the person who is most unlike you, the one who can push the buttons that send you into a frenzy. That person is your soulmate precisely because of this power. When you find yourself in a fury, the person you perceive as causing it is your greatest teacher at that moment. That person is teaching you that you have not yet mastered yourself, that you still do not know how to choose peace as that button is being pushed.

The way to that peace is to tell your friend or your lover or your child or your parent or your mother-in-law exactly how you feel. Do this from a position of being detached and honest, and watch how your wrath disappears. You will have removed entirely the possibility of nurturing and producing a poison tree.

To put the ideas of William Blake's famous poem into your life, begin by following these simple suggestions:

- When you find yourself in the midst of a freeze-out, either self-imposed or otherwise, break the silent treatment with a simple opener. Say something like, "Can we both agree to state how we are feeling right now without any judgment about it?"

- Use your opener to state directly how you feel by prefacing your statements with, "I feel . . ." Emphasize that, at this moment, what you most need is a loving response to the way you are feeling. Own your feeling and feel your feeling as you would with a friend whom you can count on sharing your feelings with. At issue here is not the problem but communicating your feelings. Then listen and hear the feelings of the other person with love and without defensiveness about the issue. Befriend the feelings.

- Give yourself a self-imposed time limit for how long you will stay in a period of no-talking. If you say one hour, then no matter how embarrassed or hurt you might feel, open the lines of communication. You will see that communicating rather than stifling yourself will end the rage almost immediately.

- Don't ever go to bed still holding on to your wrath. This will literally impact the field of energy that you both share and intensify the growth of a poison tree. Before going to sleep, simply state your feelings and make an effort to show a sign of affection, even if it means losing face and subduing your ego.

The more you can create an atmosphere of open honesty, particularly regarding areas of disagreement, the less likely disagreements will become disagreeable. It is in the time of being disagreeable that a seedling sprouts and eventually nourishes a poison tree.

from *Faust*

LOSE THIS DAY LOITERING

Lose this day loitering—'twill be the same story
To-morrow—and the next more dilatory;
Each indecision brings its own delays,
And days are lost lamenting o'er lost days.
Are you in earnest? seize this very minute—
Boldness has genius, power and magic in it.
Only engage, and then the mind grows heated—
Begin it, and then the work will be completed!

JOHANN WOLFGANG VON GOETHE
(1749–1832)
JOHN ANSTER, TRANSLATOR

*German poet, playwright, and novelist Johann Wolfgang von Goethe
expressed his interest in the natural, organic development of things,
rather than an idealistic characterization, and in man's need to believe
in himself.*

Johann Wolfgang von Goethe is universally acknowledged as
one of the true giants of creativity in an amazing array of pursuits. He was the epitome of what we think of as a Renaissance
personality. He not only pursued but achieved world-class sta-
tus in his lifetime as a dramatist, novelist, poet, journalist,
painter, statesman, educator, and naturalist philosopher. In his
eighty-two years of living his achievements are considered
Olympian and include one hundred thirty-three huge volumes,
fourteen of which were on science. He wrote prodigiously on
varied themes in fairy tales, novels, and historical plays, and cul-

minated his life work with *Faust*, one of the masterpieces of modern literature.

Goethe's message to us today is not so much in the voluminous body of his creative endeavors, but in the way he lived his life. He demonstrated a willingness to live a full and resplendent life, to be adept in a multiplicity of pursuits, and to permit a spirit of ecstasy to permeate his activities. Goethe was gloriously alive, a man of enormous creative energy. There is much that we can learn if we allow his greatness to guide us in today's world.

This selection from *Faust* is one of the most frequently quoted passages in all of the literature on self-improvement. You have probably heard or read the sixth line: "Boldness has genius, power and magic in it." This has been quoted in many books, including one of my own written twenty-plus years ago. In this compilation of wisdom from sixty of the most creative minds who have ever spoken to us through their written thoughts, I decided to include the total context of this universally accepted ideal of boldness.

While I was working on this book, as it progressed I read the material every day to my editor over the telephone. Every day she would say something like, "Wayne, you are amazing! I don't know how you daily come up with such great material. You're not just creating or writing it. You are first doing all the reading and research, and then creatively describing your take on what these philosophers and poets wrote. You inspire me!" I would smile inwardly at the compliment and comment that the answer was not a big secret. The answer to consistent creativity is to "Begin it, and then the work will be completed," which is the last line of "Lose This Day Loitering."

If I choose to loiter in this day I will lose it, and tomorrow will be the same, and I will end up lamenting the lost days. When Goethe asks, "Are you earnest?" I respond, "I am," and I "seize this very minute." I act on this powerful advice written by a man who filled his eighty-two years with greatness in many fields of endeavor.

Do not think about finishing a project, or about how overwhelming the task may seem. Do nothing more than begin, by seizing this minute. Whether it is writing a letter or making a telephone call, why don't you put this book down right now and

seize this very minute. Do nothing but begin it. Place a book-
mark here, and when you have *begun* your project, return to your
reading. What you will discover is Goethe's meaning of "Boldness
has genius, power and magic in it."

Thomas Edison's famous remark, "Genius is one percent inspiration and ninety-nine percent perspiration," is about learning to
seize the moment. That one percent is the recognition of your
thoughts and feelings. To actualize the genius that you are, you
must move to begin the implementation of your inspiration. I tell
my editor that my "secret" for getting this book and all the work
involved completed on time is simply that each and every day, at
a prescribed time, regardless of how many interruptions I have or
reasons for doing something else, I begin the next essay. I don't
vow to complete it, only to begin. And lo and behold, that boldness does indeed have genius, power, and magic in it, because
once I have begun the reading, research, and actual writing of the
opening sentence, I find that the work just manages to get completed. This has been true for me, without exception.

I suggest that you tape copies of Goethe's "Lose This Day Loitering" in the places you frequent when you are trying to avoid
seizing the moment. It will remind you of the creative aspects of
your life that you do not pursue with that bold step of beginning.
The reluctance to engage is what keeps you stuck and does not
allow your mind to heat up. The tendency to put it off, to pro-
crastinate, causes you to lose this day. The valuable technique of
beginning helps me complete the writing I love so much, and it
also helps me to seize the moments and begin activating other
facets of my life that provide me with equal pleasure and feelings
of being complete and in balance.

Rather than talking about a future time when my wife and I
can get away and just enjoy each other, which could never leave
the talking stage, I remember that boldness has power and that
engaging indeed heats up the mind and body. So I will say,
"Enough of us talking, let's make a reservation right now. I'm
putting it on our calendar and we are going to make it happen."
And it always does when we act against losing-the-day loitering.
Similarly, we have created many family activities because we both
stopped loitering and made it happen. Now!

The encouragement to act boldly comes from a man who was extraordinarily bold and accomplished himself. Carefully read Goethe's encouraging words and apply them in your life to make something move from the world of your thoughts to the material world of your immediate reality. Begin it, and watch the magic take over.

To practice boldness in the way that Goethe mentions in this passage from *Faust*, try out these suggestions:

- Jot down five things you have been thinking about for some time but, for whatever reason, have not been able to actualize in your life. Just the writing of these items on a piece of paper is the beginning point.

- Now, regardless of how much resistance you feel, do nothing but *begin* action on the first item. Do this for the next four days for each of the other items. Do not make a commitment to finish the project, simply commit to start it. You will see what Goethe meant when he said engaging heats you up.

- Stop the excuses you have come to rely on to explain why you don't get the really important things accomplished in your life. The main reason you haven't completed what you say you would like to is that you have refused to begin by seizing the moment. All the excuses are just that, excuses. In your heart you know this is true.

- Surround yourself with doers. Be around people who demonstrate their boldness. And conversely, remove yourself physically from those who encourage you to wallow in your excuses and explanations. Keep your immediate field of energy free from contamination.

IMAGINATION

What if you slept?
And what if,
In your sleep
You dreamed?
And what if,
In your dream,
You went to heaven
And there plucked
A strange and
Beautiful flower?
And what if,
When you awoke,
You had the flower
In your hand?

SAMUEL TAYLOR COLERIDGE
(1772–1834)

English poet and essayist Samuel Taylor Coleridge was the most perceptive English critic of his time and an intellectual spokesman for the English Romantic movement.

I have so much regard for this poem by one of the world's most renowned poets, literary critics, theologians, and philosophers, that I used it as the display quote for a book that I wrote about creating miracles, titled *Real Magic*. Coleridge's working life was consumed with expressing a fundamental creative principle that is applicable to human beings and the universe as a whole. The first step in creation, this unifying principle, is imagination.

This poignantly simple poem invites you to delve into your imagination and to reconsider your agreement with reality. What we know as real has its limits, but imagination is boundless in the dream state. Our agreement with reality invalidates the idea of being able to bring an object from the dream world into the waking world. But Samuel Taylor Coleridge suggests you reconsider. *What if* you were able to do such a thing? Ah, what then?

Consider what you are capable of in your dream state. Sleeping for eight hours each day means you will be in this dream state for thirty years if you live to the age of ninety. That is one-third of your life that you enter a state of awareness in which your agreement with reality is breached and you manifest everything that you need for the dream simply by the power of your thoughts. You have no concept of time, in fact you can go forward or backward in time at will. You talk to and can see the dead, fly if you so choose, walk through trees and buildings, change your shape instantaneously, become an animal if you so desire, breathe under water, and be in more than one place at the same time.

The most amazing part about all this dream activity is that for the length of the dream you are one hundred percent convinced that all of it is real. Your unlimited imagination is so convincingly powerful that for one-third of your life, you lose your agreement with reality.

When you wake, you say to yourself, this part is real and all that activity in my dream state is unreal. Samuel Taylor Coleridge spent his life examining the power of imagination to alter the perceptions of the two-thirds of your life called waking consciousness. In other words, "What if when you awoke, you had the flower in your hand?" You would have to bi-locate, which means to be in more than one place at a time.

Let's examine bi-locating, this quality of an extremely high level of awareness that gives one the ability to be in more than one place at a time. How could such a feat ever be accomplished? Go back to your dream state. Every character in your dream is you assuming those roles with your mind. When you are having a conversation with people in your dream, you are yourself, then at the same instant you are whomever you are talking to as well. You actually do not have conversations with someone else in your dream, you are those characters and yourself all at the same time. You are bi-locating. Similarly, the flower in your dream is not a flower in the same sense that you experience it while awake. In fact, you are the flower in your dream, and because your imagination shuts down to almost zero when you awaken, you lose the ability to create without limitation as soon as you leave your dream.

It is not absurd to think that it is possible to bring a flower from the imaginary dream state into this level that we agree is waking awareness. Everything you are capable of accomplishing, experiencing, and knowing in the one-third of life spent in pure imagination, you can accomplish, experience, and know in the remaining two-thirds. The key is to banish doubts and allow yourself the privilege of flying directly into that ecstatic state while awake.

This poetic expression of the dream and the flower, which I've read and recited thousands of times, always reminds me to work at being a waking dreamer by allowing myself the same kinds of privileges, freedoms, and, yes, powers, that I take for granted in my dream state. I remind myself of what another favorite poet of mine, William Blake, said about this fascinating world of imagination. "Imagination is the real and eternal world of which this vegetable universe is but a faint shadow . . . the eternal body of man is the imagination: that is God himself, the Divine body . . ."

To me it seems silly to think of being awake and being in the dream state as two distinct experiences of reality. I know that my dreams are not predictors of what is going to happen in my waking life, nor are they symbols that provide clues to the real me. For me, this dream state is like an open invitation into the mystical world of imagination. It is my opportunity to explore limitlessness, to know it firsthand, and to become totally convinced beyond all doubt of the realm of imagination. Then while awake I can go into my imagination and use it to travel miles beyond ordinary waking awareness. Then this waking world becomes but a canvas to my imagination.

When you rewrite your agreement with reality, you can use your experience of that one-third of your life while ensconced securely in your imagination to accomplish all that you desire without needing to go to sleep. Imagine yourself able to manifest into your material world whatever you are capable of conceiving in your mind, and let go of any doubts that you may have allowed to creep in.

As a young boy in a crowded Detroit public school class, I can recall getting into big trouble for my honesty in handling this dream/awake dichotomy. I was far away in a daydream, deeply blissful about the mental excursion I was on, when a teacher startled me by asking, "Would you care to rejoin us here, Mr. Dyer?" My immediate response was "Not really!"—for which I was once again sent to the principal's office as punishment for living out my imagination while awake in a classroom.

Do you believe it's possible to hold a flower in your hand that you plucked from a garden in your dreams? I know it to be possible, and so does Samuel Taylor Coleridge, the poet of the imagination.

To apply the power of your creative imagination in your life today, begin by:

• Always keeping in mind that you become what you think about, be very careful about any thoughts you harbor that involve doubt.

• Keep track of your dreams in the sense of remembering those "unreal" experiences that you were absolutely convinced of while they were occurring. Then work at eliminating your conditioned beliefs about their impossibility. You want to eradicate the word "impossible" from your consciousness. Truly, if you can conceive it, you can create it.

• Literally rewrite your agreement with reality so that it reads, "Anything I am capable of for one-third of my life I can add to the other two-thirds if I so choose."

• Live more in your imagination. Give yourself the freedom to wander into unfamiliar territory in your mind and to explore new possibilities in your fantasies, excluding nothing. These imaginative meanderings will ultimately become the catalysts for living an unlimited life.

Your imagination, just like your body, grows through exercise. Wake up and hold that flower in your hand.

NIGHTINGALE! THOU SURELY ART

I heard a Stock-dove sing or say
His homely tale, this very day;
His voice was buried among trees,
Yet to be come-at by the breeze:
He did not cease; but cooed—and cooed;
And somewhat pensively he wooed;
He sang of love, with quiet blending,
Slow to begin, and never ending;
Of serious faith, and inward glee;
That was the song,—the song for me!

WILLIAM WORDSWORTH
(1770–1850)

William Wordsworth was an English poet who poetically expressed his love of nature and a respect for humanity without regard to class distinctions.

*I*n my preparations for writing this collection of essays on applying the wisdom of the ages, I have read thousands of contributions from great thinkers and poets, from the present to thousands of years before Christ. One theme that persists, particularly in the poetry of the ages, is a fascination with nature. These soulful writers seem to immerse themselves in nature and create poems that stem from their state of bewilderment and ecstasy.

Of the thousands of these poems I have studied, I have selected this one to represent the topic of nature. It is from one of the world's most gifted and prolific poets, William Wordsworth, who wrote while Europe was exploding in revolution in the late eighteenth century. "Nightingale! Thou Surely Art" exemplifies

Wordsworth's ability to dramatize how imagination creates spiritual values out of the memory of sights and sounds in nature. His lesson to all of us is that the wilderness is therapy. Imagine the poet simply listening to the sounds of a bird, and listening with such intensity that he could write down words of this very basic yet universal human experience (who has failed to hear a bird singing?) and convey, "He sang of love, with quiet blending, slow to begin, and never ending; of serious faith, and inward glee; that was the song,—the song for me!" Allow Wordsworth's poetic observation to inspire you to go out into the wilderness, even if only your own backyard, or a public park if that is all you can manage, and listen, pretending to be one of the many poets who preceded you here. Memorize the sounds and sights of nature. By immersing yourself in the present moment, and shutting out all the distractions that fill your busy mind, you can allow one "Stock-dove [to] sing or say his homely tale, this very day," and it will be just for you. Indeed, the wilderness and all its natural sights and sounds is more than therapy; it is a connection, a link to your soul and the eternal creative energy of God.

This is the energy that nature uses each spring to write a new chapter in the Book of Genesis. Emerson observed on the western side of the Atlantic what Wordsworth noted on the eastern side, at essentially the same time: "Everything in nature contains all the powers of nature—everything is made of one hidden stuff." This includes all that is natural, including you. Yes, you too are a part of this world of nature. Your desire to be in solitude, to be free, to be your natural self, to follow your own intuition, to sing without being criticized, to flow as the rivers do, are natural instincts that are often ignored.

Ask yourself what are the most pleasant memories of your lifetime. They very likely are your personal ecstatic encounters with nature. The sound of the water or the wind, lapping or roaring against the shoreline. The feel of bitter cold on your face, or the sun penetrating your body at a beach. The sights and sounds of autumn leaves as you walk in the woods. A camping trip when you slept outside and listened to the mysterious sounds of the darkness. How did you lose your eyes and ears? How did you forget the ecstasy of nature? Go back to the place that Wordsworth describes: trees and breeze, cooed and wooed. These are more than a poet's rhyming schemes. These are tickets to a lost beatitude.

Several decades ago I was a professor at St. John's University in New York City. The afternoon hours just before my classes commenced were the most hectic time of the day. My outer office would be teeming with graduate students needing something from me, their adviser. My secretary would be buzzing my phone with unceasing interruptions, a dean could be demanding my attention for some administrative matter, and I would be filled with anxiety over all this push-pull pressure, knowing that I had a class to teach in a couple of hours.

Amid all this chaos, I would frequently excuse myself and announce to my secretary that I'd return in a moment, because I had an emergency. I would then retreat to a public park a block from my office. There I would find my favorite bench, surrounded by trees and the sights and sounds of nature, and I would just sit and listen for fifteen minutes. This tranquil setting was my therapy, my escape to sanity. No one in my department ever knew where I went, or why, during my frequent emergency escapes, but when I returned most of the problems had been resolved, and those who needed my attention were handled by a de-stressed professor. I look back now and realize I was applying the wisdom of Wordsworth's poetry to my situation, letting nature speak to me in her symbols and signs.

It is not an accident that so many of our most revered poets and writers have found nature to be the source of their artistry. It is in nature that one loses all judgments and false pretenses because nature does not judge. As the famed naturalist John Muir once said, "The grand show is eternal. It is always sunrise somewhere; the dew is never all dried at once; a shower is forever falling; vapor is ever rising . . ." When you treat yourself to nature you become one with the eternal show. Your soul has the opportunity to harmonize with you and your world.

Wordsworth's lyrical little poem is more than an observation of a bird in nature. It is a plea to all of us to let go of our obsessions with the pettiness that drives us crazy, and to seek out and live in the harmony that is in the sights and sounds of nature. Indeed, they all sing for you.

To explore what William Wordsworth offers you, try the following:

- Give yourself a designated time each week, or each day if you can, to walk barefoot on the grass, or to immerse yourself in nature and just listen. No assignments, no duties, just listen and observe the perfection of the natural world. Remember, the wilderness is therapy.

- Write your reactions to nature in the form of your own poetry or essay. Forget about rhyming schemes and rules of grammar. A friend of mine describes his experience as going from "pissed to blissed" by giving himself some time in a natural setting. Allow yourself to be a poet and record your divine intuition as you commune with nature, just as Wordsworth did a few centuries back.

- Plan extended time in nature on your next vacation. Consider a trek in the mountains, white water rafting, skiing, or camping. These are delights that will bring you the bliss you seek and the memories of a lifetime.

- Sleep outdoors one night, even if it is only in a tent in your backyard. Do it with your family, particularly your children, and notice the excitement they all feel by being in nature. This feeling of excitement is precisely what you can recapture in all areas of your life when you allow your own nature to play a more dominant and enthusiastic role in your life.

❧ ROMANTIC LOVE ❧

from *Sonnets from the Portuguese*

HOW DO I LOVE THEE?

How do I love thee? Let me count the ways.
I love thee to the depth and breadth and height
My soul can reach, when feeling out of sight
For the ends of Being and ideal Grace.
I love thee to the level of every day's
Most quiet need, by sun and candlelight.
I love thee freely, as men strive for Right;
I love thee purely, as they turn from Praise.
I love thee with the passion put to use
In my old griefs, and with my childhood's faith.
I love thee with a love I seemed to lose
With my lost saints—I love thee with the breath,
Smiles, tears, of all my life!—and, if God choose,
I shall but love thee better after death.

ELIZABETH BARRETT BROWNING
(1806–1861)

Elizabeth Barrett Browning was an English poet and the wife of poet Robert Browning. Her themes embraced her broad humanitarian interests; her unorthodox religious feelings; her affection for her adopted country, Italy; and her love for her husband.

This sonnet by Elizabeth Barrett Browning is perhaps the best-known poem of pure romantic love ever written. It would be a rare person who, upon hearing "How do I love thee," would not automatically follow it up with "Let me count the ways." It is a fabulous idea to indeed count the ways that you love another, particularly one whom you love in a romantic sense.

The story of Elizabeth Barrett and Robert Browning (a major poet also included in this book) is one of the great love stories of all time. These two sensitive poets were united in love, through their poetry, before they even met each other. Elizabeth had published in 1844 her second volume of love poetry, which was well received in London literary circles. In January 1845 she received a letter from the highly regarded poet Robert Browning, which read, "I love your verses with all my heart, dear Miss Barrett. I do, as I say, love these books with all my heart—and I love you too." They met later that summer and married the following year. Elizabeth had experienced a great deal of sickness as a young woman and was living with her father, who knew nothing of her courtship by mail with Robert Browning. In fact, they were married secretly and moved to Italy for her health without the consent of her father. He died in 1856, never having forgiven his daughter for her actions.

Elizabeth and Robert Browning lived in romantic bliss in Italy, where she gave birth to their only child in 1849. She wrote many passionate poems in opposition to slavery in the United States. In 1861, when she was fifty-five years old, her illness reappeared and she died in her husband's arms, as he told her of his undying love for her.

The story of Elizabeth Barrett Browning is embodied in this well-known sonnet from her collection of *Sonnets from the Portuguese.* Her closing line literally speaks to her great love for her husband, who loved her even before he ever saw her face, simply because of the grace of her soul, which she expressed with her poems of love: "And, if God choose, I shall but love thee better after death."

In this sonnet, a woman pours out her deep love for the man she loves and says to us all that being in love is not the result of a thunderbolt crashing down on you, rendering you speechless and wilting you by the magnitude of the love energy. It is not a purely physical attraction that makes one feel so in love. No, it is a multitude of little things that constitute that feeling of romantic love. As the sonnet says, "I love thee to the level of every day's most quiet need . . ." If you feel that scrumptious feeling, "count the ways" as a regular part of your relationship.

My wife, Marcelene, is a beautiful woman, and every time I look at her I think of how lucky I am to be in love with (and to have that love returned by) such an angelic-looking being. And yet, it is not her appearance that is the source of my love, just as Elizabeth Barrett Browning fails to mention her husband's good looks as even one of the ways she counts in her sonnet. The ways seem small when considered individually, but collectively they are the source of romantic love.

I watch my wife as she sleeps, and her hands are folded as if in prayer. She lies there the entire night not moving, looking exactly like an angel. That is one of the ways.

I see her with the children and note her smile of contentment in their joys and accomplishments, though it is subtle and often unreported by me. That is one of the ways.

I see in the early morning when I awake before everyone to go on my morning run, as I turn on the kitchen light, that she has done it again. She put out a glass and a stirrer for me to prepare my morning shake. Nothing huge, but I notice. And that is one of the ways.

I notice her when she comes back from her own exercising, sweating, glistening, and stunning as she enters the shower. Nothing magic. But I notice. And that is one of the ways.

I observe the soul inside the body, the voice that silently says, "I am here to serve. I care about everyone I meet. I give to others and seldom ask for any recognition. I have a tender heart for those less fortunate than I. I have immense respect for God. I am deeply saddened by violence. I am connected to you, and I will always be there for you, and it is endless. Death will not end it." I notice that soul that is silent but speaks to me alone. And that is one of the ways.

I could go on counting the ways that I love her for a thousand pages more, but I think the message is clear by now. It is in a multitude of everyday observations that our deepest love is revealed. It is a feeling that goes to the very core of our being, and yet it is most often unexpressed.

In this particular sonnet, the poet says she loves totally, yet she expresses it this way, "I love thee with the breath, smiles, tears, of all my life!" I too know this feeling. My breath is my very life itself, and I love you, Marcelene, with the same energy that allows me to continue to breathe. Your breath and my own are one, and that is how I love you. The smiles of our lives are the good times, the joys of a romantic dinner, touching your hand in a darkened movie theater, making love on a deserted beach after our own private picnic, the birthing of each child. The smiles are many, and you are loved through them all.

The tears of our lives also are a major part of the totality we call love. The disappointments, the arguments, the early times when we were anguished over being separated before figuring it all out. All the tears of all our lives are ways to count as I answer the question, "How do I love thee?"

Yes, it is the ability to love freely and purely, and in all of the so-called little ways, that makes the passion come alive and last. This particular sonnet speaks to all of us, some one hundred and fifty years after it was written, and it will speak to those who feel the fire of free and pure love in their hearts and souls for thousands of years to come. The message to all of us seems clear. Take the time to count the ways, and then take the even more important time to convey them to your beloved, and you will feel what Elizabeth Barrett Browning felt toward her beloved, and how I feel today as well. "I love thee to the depth and breadth and height my soul can reach." It doesn't get any better than that!

To put into your life the essential message of this world-class sonnet, begin to:

- Make a point of telling your beloved about the little things that you notice which you find so appealing and attractive. By saying them aloud, you give a voice to the love you share and create an atmosphere of appreciation.

- Become aware of who the person inside the body is rather than placing an inordinate amount of attention on the appearance of that body. Show affection for the kindness they exhibit, the love they feel for others, the reverence they show for the spirit in all life.

- Write your own poem or love note to your beloved. Forget about the quality of the writing and place your emphasis on conveying your feelings however they are represented in you. A personal poem that comes from your heart will be treasured forever by your beloved. In fact it will be framed and displayed prominently because it means so much.

NONCONFORMITY

from *Walden*

If a man does not keep pace with his companions, perhaps it is because he hears a different drummer. Let him step to the music which he hears, however measured and far away.

HENRY DAVID THOREAU
(1817–1862)

Henry David Thoreau was Harvard educated, but chose the unpopular career of writer and poet to satisfy his soul's urge. A force in the New England Transcendentalists, along with Emerson, he loved nature, freedom, and individuality.

The one comment that I am most pleased to hear, from those who have read my books or listened to my tapes over the years, goes like this, "Your words finally reassured me that I am not insane. All my life people have been telling me there is something wrong with me for the way I think. Your words made me realize that I am not crazy." I think that it was in reading Thoreau that I had the very same kind of epiphany.

I have often imagined myself in the shoes of Thoreau, living simply and deliberately in the woods, being self-sufficient and writing down what I felt most deeply in my soul. But more than writing it down, the idea of living these ideas, regardless of how others perceived me or reacted, seemed somehow noble.

Within each of us there is a voice that whispers, "Take the risks, pursue your dreams, live life to the fullest, as long as you're not hurting anyone else, why not?" Then, outside us there are voices that scream, "Don't be a fool, you're going to fail, be like everyone else, if you do what you want you're being selfish and hurting others."

These loud, incessant dictates of our companions urge us to keep up with them and threaten to ostracize us when we fail to do so.

I have observed that society in general always seems to honor its living conformists and its dead troublemakers. All those who have ever made a difference in any profession have listened to the music they hear and proceeded independent of the opinions of others. For doing so, they are labeled troublemakers, incorrigibles, even misfits. Yet they become highly respected after death. This applies to Henry David Thoreau, who was vilified for his position in his essay *On The Necessity of Civil Disobedience*, and jailed for refusing to obey what he considered absurd rulings. Yet today he is required reading in virtually all high schools and universities.

The beat that you hear within yourself is your connection to your soul's purpose. It will continue to plague you when you ignore it or suppress it in an attempt to conform with society. Those who implore you to march to the beat they hear are often well-intentioned and coming from a position of love for you. They will tell you, "I only have your very best interest in mind," and "I am the voice of experience; you'll be sorry if you don't follow my advice." You listen and you try so hard to be just like everybody wants you to be. Yet that nagging drumbeat that no one else seems to hear faintly thumps in the farthest reaches of your awareness. If you continue to ignore it, you will live a life of frustration. You may even learn to "suffer in comfort," which is the very best you'll be able to achieve.

Thoreau is speaking directly to you from the mid-nineteenth century about *your* own self-sufficiency and happiness. Whatever it is that you feel compelled to be or do is the voice of your soul pleading with you to have the courage to listen and act on the melody only you hear, as long as it does not interfere with any-one else's right to pursue his dreams. And so it is with those around you, who are also hearing a drumbeat that is foreign to you. They too must be allowed to step to the music they hear, even though it may sound strident and off-key to you.

If everyone marched to the same music and no one ever strayed from that conformity, we would all still be living in caves and preparing the same old recipe: "Take one whole buffalo, skin it, burn it, and devour it." Progress is the result of individuals first listening to what their hearts tell them, and then acting on those messages despite the protestations of the tribe.

In my own family we have eight beautiful children. Wouldn't it be nice if they all attended my lectures and decided to pursue my interests, and then took up my causes after I leave this world? But my wife and I both know better. Some of the children couldn't care less about my passion, and others cannot seem to get enough of it. Some want only to ride horses, and others want only to sing and perform. One child loves economics and accounting (ugh!) and another, advertising and skiing. They all hear their own drumbeat. And in some cases it is definitely far away from what I hear. I must honor their instincts and their choices, and merely guide them out of harm's way until they can be their own guides. I have always marched to my own beat. Most frequently it was inconsistent not only with my own immediate family, but with my culture as well.

I have written books that defied conventional psychological practice. I have said in my books what my common sense told me, even when it varied one hundred and eighty degrees from current popular professional wisdom. I could never find it in my heart to preach to my listeners to do it my way, when I've always pretty much ignored what was being preached to me.

Imagine yourself walking through the woods with Thoreau back in the 1840s, before the Civil War. His observations were based not on some philosophy he had read or heard, but on his own direct experience of feeling the outrage of conformity, and seeing the horrors of how Native Americans were being treated by the white man. He knew that the popular practice of removing Indians from their lands was our very own Holocaust. So he left to live in nature and experience self-sufficiency away from the pressures of the larger group. He did not keep step with his companions, and at the time he was criticized for it.

Yet time has revealed him to be one of those troublemakers we revere. Walk with Thoreau in your own mind. Listen to the voice *you* hear, and the drumbeat only you can feel, and honor it, while honoring it in those you love as well. It is the ultimate act of unconditional love. While it may not get you any awards while you are alive, you can take comfort in knowing that you

fulfilled your own divine purpose and encouraged others to do
the same.

To put Thoreau's advice into practice:

- Refuse to evaluate yourself as sane or insane on the basis of
  how you fit in with the expectations of those around you. If
  you feel it, and it harms no one, then it is authentic, and very
  sane.

- Remind yourself that you will have to incur the misunder-
  standing and perhaps even the wrath of those in your immediate tribes for having the temerity to march to your own
  drumbeat. Don't take it personally even for one moment. It is
  merely a strategy to get you to conform, and when you fail to
  react, the wrath will quickly disappear.

- Allow those in your immediate sphere—family and friends—
  to have the joy of blissfully marching to their own beat without having to explain or defend their choices. You will be
  substituting peace and love for anger and resentment, and all
  will enjoy the original music they hear.

REVERENCE FOR NATURE

There is no quiet place in [your] cities, no place to hear the leaves of spring or the rustle of insects wings. . . . The Indians prefer the soft sound of the wind darting over the face of the pond, the smell of the wind itself cleansed by a midday rain, or scented with piñon pine. The air is precious to the red man, for all things share the same breath—the animals, the trees, the man. Like a man who has been dying for many days, a man in your city is numb to the stench.

CHIEF SEATTLE
(1790–1866)

A member of the Suquamish-Duwamish tribes who befriended white settlers in the Puget Sound area, Chief Seattle participated in the Port Elliott Treaty of 1855, ceding Indian land and establishing reservations.

The following section is devoted to the wisdom of the Native Americans, whose words reflect their reverence for all that is sacred in our natural world. I will cite some of the Native Americans whose contemplative words of wisdom and peace have been left for us to read and share. It is to their memory and to our very survival as a people that this section is dedicated. Theirs is a legacy of deep love and respect for our environment.

Chief Seattle

Chief Seattle is best known as the man who wrote a now-famous letter to the President of the United States, asking him to consider the American Indians' point of view. Every part of the earth is sacred to his people, he wrote, and we are all part of the precious earth, as well as being brothers in spirit. In the passage quoted above, Chief Seattle asks us to increase our awareness of the soft sounds and the sweet smells of life. In so doing, we will treat our environment with greater respect not only for its natural beauty, but because we become aware that we are a part of this interconnected web of life. We all share the same breath, the animals, the trees, and one another.

Oren Lyons

In the following passage, Oren Lyons, known as the Onondaga Faithkeeper, tells us how his people think seven generations ahead when making decisions:

> In our way of life, in our government, with every decision we make, we always keep in mind the Seventh Generation to come. It's our job to see that the people coming ahead, the generations still unborn, have a world no worse than ours—and hopefully better. When we walk upon Mother Earth we always plant our feet carefully because we know the faces of our future generations are looking up at us from beneath the ground. We never forget them.

Would that we consider those unborn generations as we trample our forests and pollute our skies in the name of progress and our present day entitlement.

Wolf Song

Would that we also remind ourselves that everything is a circle and every living creature is a part of the sacred hoop of life, as Wolf Song of the Abenaki tribe puts it:

> To honor and respect means to think of the land and the water and plants and animals who live here as having a right equal to our own to be here. We are not the supreme and all-knowing beings, living at the top of the pinnacle of evolution, but in fact we are members of the sacred hoop of life, along with the trees and rocks, the coyotes and the

eagles and fish and toads, that each fulfills its purpose. They each perform their given task in the sacred hoop, and we have one, too.

In our cities we have lost much of our grace and naturalness in the name of civilization. We have created noisy, dirty, crowded places to gather and live in and in this process we have retarded our spirituality. For me there is nothing so rejuvenating as being out in nature and experiencing this sacred hoop directly.

Walking Buffalo

While our books and places of study do provide us with an invigorating environment, it seems to me that Walking Buffalo (Tatanga Mani; Stoney Indian) offers us an alternate milieu in which to profit from the terrain, scenery and immediate surroundings. He observes:

> Oh, yes, I went to the white man's schools. I learned to read from school books, newspapers, and the Bible. But in time I found that these were not enough. Civilized people depend too much on man-made printed pages. I turn to the Great Spirit's book which is the whole of creation. You can read a big part of that book if you study nature. You know, if you take all your books, lay them out under the sun, and let the snow and rain and insects work on them for a while, there will be nothing left. But the Great Spirit has provided you and me with an opportunity to study in nature's university the forests, the rivers, the mountains and the animals which include us.

We are being asked to consider the whole of creation and to embrace all living creatures and the whole of nature as something that is just as much connected to us, as are our feet, hands, and heart. This kind of thinking requires us to look beyond our own immediate feelings of separation from the rest and our sense of being limited in time and space. The Native Americans believed that "Everywhere is the center of the world. Everything is sacred."

Luther Standing Bear

The Indian people who lived here before we brought "refinement" and "culture" in the form of our civilizing efforts send us a
message as we seek to enhance our spirituality and regain our
connection to God. For the American Indian, God was known as
Wakan Tanka, and all life contained this essence. The winds and
drifting clouds were Wakan Tanka in action, the common sticks
and stones were revered as manifestations of the all-pervading
mysterious power that fills the universe. Luther Standing Bear, an
Oglala Sioux chief, expressed it poetically:

> The Indian loved to worship.
> From birth to death he revered his
> Surroundings. He considered
> Himself born in the luxurious lap
> Of Mother Earth and no place to
> Him was humble. There was nothing
> Between him and the Big Holy.
> The contact was immediate and
> Personal and the blessings of
> Wakan Tanka flowed over the
> Indian like rain showered
> From the sky.

You can see how much more peaceful and joyful your life
would be were you raised to have such reverence for all your surroundings. I love the idea of immediate contact with the "Big
Holy." This is something that each and every one of us long to
reestablish in our lives, and Luther Standing Bear's observation is
perhaps a method. Look around and be in a state of reverence,
while encouraging others to do the same.

Walking Buffalo

I return to the wisdom of Walking Buffalo. It would be absurd
to suggest that you leave your urban lifestyle to live in the
wilderness. Modern life has much to offer and our cities are definitely here to stay, the good with the bad. Yet our city life atti-

tudes may have disconnected us from the natural laws of spiritual harmony.

Walking Buffalo died in 1967 at the age of ninety-six. He had seen much of both worlds, and left these words for us.

Hills are always more beautiful than stone buildings, you know. Living in a city is an artificial existence. Lots of people hardly ever feel real soil under their feet, see plants grow except in flower pots, or get far enough beyond the street light to catch the enchantment of a night sky studded with stars. When people live far from scenes of the Great Spirit's making, it's easy for them to forget his laws.

He asks us not to move out, but to remember. To remember the sacredness of all life, and to be aware at all times of how these natural laws are always at work in this sacred hoop. Wherever you live, whatever your immediate environment looks like, these natural laws are at work. The air, water, trees, minerals, clouds, animals, birds, and insects all support life. Pay attention to our ancient ancestors who lived on these lands for thousands upon thousands of years with enormous reverence for the natural laws. This is what today we call ecological awareness. Native Americans thought seven generations ahead so that the preciousness of life would endure. The poetry of these Native Americans asks us to rekindle that flame. Consider it and begin to allow some of this ancient wisdom into your daily life.

I close this offering to us from some American Indians with this Ojibway prayer, which we all might well read and apply anew each day.

Grandfather,
Look at our brokenness.
We know that in all creation
Only the human family
Has strayed from the sacred way.
We know that we are the ones
Who are divided

And we are the ones
Who must come back together
To walk in the sacred way
Grandfather,
Sacred One,
Teach us love, compassion, honor
That we may heal the earth
And heal each other.

To put the essential message of all these Native American contributors to work in your life, start today to:

- Revere your surroundings by being in a constant state of gratitude for so much of what is taken for granted. Bless the animals, sunshine, rain, air, trees, and ground in silent rituals of thanksgiving each day.

- Promote ecological awareness in your life by contributing to organizations that work on behalf of the environment. Make a conscious effort to reduce pollution, eliminate litter, and practice recycling. Your individual actions can re-create respect and reverence for earth and the universe, our sacred web of life.

- Spend more time in the solitude of nature listening to the natural sounds and walking barefoot on the earth to reconnect yourself to all that supports and sustains life.

- Live by example. Rather than bemoaning the fact that people litter, pick up that aluminum can and dispose of it properly even though someone else was careless. Let young people see you act in these ways.

- Repeat the Ojibway prayer. Help heal the earth and each other with this reminder to live with love, compassion, and honor in your life each day.

FABLE

The mountain and the squirrel
Had a quarrel;
And the former called the latter "Little Prig."
Bun replied,
"You are doubtless very big;
But all sorts of things and weather
Must be taken in together
To make up a year
And a sphere.

And I think it's no disgrace
To occupy my place.
If I'm not so large as you,
You are not so small as I,
And not half so spry.
I'll not deny you make
A very pretty squirrel track;
Talents differ: all is well and wisely put;
If I cannot carry forests on my back,
Neither can you crack a nut."

RALPH WALDO EMERSON
(1803–1882)

American poet, essayist, and philosopher, Emerson was a steady optimist who believed that nature is a manifestation of spirit.

*M*y regard for Ralph Waldo Emerson is so high that he is the only person I have chosen to contribute twice to this collection; once through his poetry and a second time in one of his ground-breaking essays. Emerson was the founder of the Transcendentalist tradition in America. His philosophy emphasized the all-pervading spirit of the universe, wherein God existed everywhere. In "Fable," Emerson creates a poetic quarrel between a squirrel and a mountain that presents this view.

To understand the greatness of Ralph Waldo Emerson it is important to remember that during his period of history, spiritual guidance was the exclusive domain of the established religions. Emerson was challenging the dogma and rhetoric of traditional religion. Seeing divinity everywhere, Emerson spoke to a new consciousness in which God is not greater or lesser based on the appearance of the material form.

The squirrel, a furry little rodent, possesses the invisible God force, as does the mountain that can carry a forest on its back, yet cannot crack a nut. In this poem, Emerson is saying that each of us, regardless of our shape, size, or mobility, is a divine creation with unique opportunities to fulfill our destiny, independent of how others may do so. This includes all life forms in all shapes in all ways.

I recall a similar story told by a great teacher of mine, Nisargadatta Maharaj, who lived in India and was highly regarded as a mystical spiritual saint by many. A devotee wondered how Nisargadatta could say, "In my world, nothing ever goes wrong." Nisargadatta answered with this story of a monkey having a conversation with a tree.

"You mean to tell me," the monkey said to the tree, "that you actually stay in one place for an entire lifetime and don't move from that spot? I don't understand!"

"You mean to tell me," the tree said to the monkey, "that you actually go from place to place using your energy to move about all day? I don't understand!"

Nisargadatta's story was meant to help his devotee recognize that her identification with her body got in the way of her understanding of his spiritual perspective. Engaging in judgment about the other created a scenario that was like the monkey trying to understand the tree, or vice versa. As in the Emerson poem, the higher reality is that both life forms contain the same universal organizing intelligence, yet cannot begin to understand each other. This fable of Emerson's and the story of Nisargadatta are particularly relevant to my life.

I recently wrote a book, along with my wife, Marcelene, called *A Promise Is a Promise*. It is the true story of a mother who has cared for her comatose daughter for over twenty-eight years, feeding her every two hours around the clock, turning her, giving her insulin every four hours, raising the money to pay all expenses, and sleeping in a chair every night next to her daughter's side. Twenty-eight years ago, Edwarda, then sixteen years old, pleaded, "You won't leave me will you, Mommy?" as she was slipping into a diabetic coma. Kaye, her mother, responded, "I will never leave you darling, I promise. And a promise is a promise."

In the ensuing twenty-eight years Edwarda O'Bara has moved from a stage one coma wherein she was catatonic and had to have her eyes taped shut, to a stage nine, where she appears to recognize voices, smiles, and cries when saddened. She voluntarily closes her eyes and sometimes appears to react to stimuli in the room. But the most amazing part of this story concerns the effect that Edwarda has on those who have visited her. Some claim to have experienced miraculous healings, and everyone feels the unconditional love Edwarda radiates from her immobile body.

I myself, along with my wife, have felt a deep sense of compassion and love because of our association with Kaye and Edwarda. I feel blessed to have had the opportunity to use my gifts for writing and speaking to tell this incredible story of love and compassion and to contribute the proceeds toward reducing their massive debts. I have been able to disempower my ego's self-importance and serve at a more giving spiritual level because of Kaye and Edwarda.

Even though Edwarda does not move about, remains essentially immobile, and has been labeled handicapped by the rest of the world, even though she never speaks and needs continuous care, I know that she is doing her work. And who knows, maybe she is reaching more people through me and my writing and speaking than she ever could were she awake. Maybe she is able to help create miracles in others because she has left her body and its limitations. Who is to say?

Yet this much I know. Edwarda O'Bara's life is as valuable as anyone else's on this planet. Life is not necessarily about moving around and talking. The life force that exists within her comatose body is the same life force that is in every body and in every

mountain, every squirrel, and every nut that the squirrel cracks.
Edwarda's life has a mission, and she accomplishes it each day in
her destined way. She teaches us to be compassionate and she
teaches us about unconditional love. She has provided me with an
opportunity to see firsthand that all life has infinite value. I don't
pretend to understand why this young girl has lived in this state,
unattached to life support, for over a quarter of a century. There
are some things I'll never understand, and I like it that way.

What I have learned through my association with the O'Baras
and in writing *A Promise Is a Promise* is that I am like the monkey
talking to the tree or the squirrel conversing with the mountain.
They both move about and chatter to the silent and stationary,
whose immobility and mute silence are a different form of the
same life force.

Emerson's "Fable" offers us a poetic insight into this life force that
is everywhere. Being able to acknowledge that life force, without
judging oneself superior in any way because of differing physical
traits, is a great lesson to learn on the road to your spiritual growth.

To put this important lesson to work in your life:

• Refuse to make judgments about the importance or value of
  others based on what you have come to assess as normal. See
  the unfolding of God in everyone and all life. Know that no
  one is superior in the invisible realm of the spirit, and that our
  outer shells all come in a variety of shapes, sizes, and conditions.

• See the genius in everyone you encounter. Just as the mountain cannot crack a nut though it can carry a forest on its
  back, so too does every living creature have its own perfection
  built into it. Make every effort to look for that perfection
  rather than being misled by appearances of the host container.

• Begin to practice the simple wisdom: "There are many things
  I do not understand, and I like it that way."

• Let go of judgments that compare others to what has come to
  be labeled normal. Just because most people can see, that
  doesn't render the blind insignificant. And just because most
  folks walk about and talk, that does not imply that those who
  lie in silence are less precious in any way.

❁ SELF-RELIANCE ❁

from "Self-Reliance"

These are the voices which we hear in solitude, but they grow faint and inaudible as we enter into the world. Society everywhere is in conspiracy against the manhood of every one of its members. Society is a joint-stock company, in which the members agree, for the better securing of his bread to each shareholder, to surrender the liberty and culture of the eater. The virtue in most request is conformity. Self-reliance is its aversion. *It loves not realities and creators, but names and customs.* [Emphasis added.]

Whoso would be a man, must be a nonconformist. He who would gather immortal palms must not be hindered by the name of goodness, *but must explore if it be goodness.* Nothing is at last sacred but the integrity of your own mind. [Emphasis added.]

RALPH WALDO EMERSON
(1803–1882)

American poet, essayist, and philosopher known for challenging traditional thought, Emerson developed a philosophy that upholds intuition as the way to comprehend reality.

The ideas of this one essay, "Self-Reliance," have influenced all my writing, and I consider Emerson one of my greatest teachers even though he passed on well over a century ago. Ralph Waldo Emerson was known as much for his essays as for his poetry. In perhaps his best-known and most frequently quoted essay, "Self-Reliance," this provocative American author, known as the father of the Transcendentalist movement, examined in depth the basic tenets of what it means to be your own person. I can still remember the impact that the essays "Self-Reliance" and "On the Necessity of Civil Disobedience"—by Emerson's contemporary Henry David Thoreau—had on me when I was a seventeen-year-old high school student.

In this brief excerpt, Emerson speaks to the necessity of being a nonconformist to be fully alive, and of resisting enculturation. Society demands conformity at the expense of individual liberty, he asserts—it demands that you fit in or be an outcast. Emerson insists on the integrity of the individual mind, maintaining that it is essentially sacred. Now, remember that Emerson was also a minister, who is informing us that the mind is what is sacred: not the rules, laws, and societal mores, but your mind. Further on in "Self-Reliance" Emerson declares, "No law can be sacred to me but that of my nature." This profoundly courageous statement is from a fearless man who knew that divinity and sacredness are not in the institutions of the church but in the minds of individuals. Our conduct makes us divine creatures, not our memberships. How we use our minds as free-thinking people is what makes us sacred, not how well we cite the laws to protect our malice or vanity.

When you stop to consider most of the evils that have been perpetrated on humanity, they have virtually all been accomplished under the protective custody of society's laws. Socrates was murdered because the law said it was proper to so dispose of intellectual dissidents. St. Joan of Arc was burned at the stake because it was the law. Herod ordered all the male babies in an entire country to be systematically murdered because it was his rule. When my own mother was born, one-half of the population—that is, one hundred percent of the women—could not vote in America because the rules said so. At the time I was born, millions of people were being herded into death camps and all their possessions confiscated because of inhumane laws. It was the law that required black people to sit in the rear of buses, drink at separate drinking fountains, and live lives of separate and inferior opportunity. So please don't cite the laws and rules of society to justify your actions.

People who truly understand what is meant by self-reliance know they must live their lives by ethics rather than rules. It is possible to find some obscure law or rule or societal tradition to justify virtually anything. Those who do not give priority to the integrity of their own mind will indeed cite laws to explain why they do what they do. Aspiring to be a more sacred being means shedding your reliance on conformity.

Emerson went on in this provocative essay to say, "I am ashamed to think how easily we capitulate to badges and names, to large societies and dead institutions." He spoke openly of the long-held but immoral institution of slavery, which was protected by law. "I ought to go upright and vital, and speak the rude truth in all ways. If malice and vanity wear the coat of philanthropy, shall that pass?" Recall, if you will, that Emerson was speaking and writing like this while slavery was legal and protected by society.

What does this essay on self-reliance say to us today? It encourages us to cultivate ethics rather than rules or laws as the governing inner light for ourselves. If we know it is right, it will be in harmony with spiritual principles, many of which have been written about in this book.

For example, mercy. The law shows no mercy when it lawfully executes prisoners. When lawmakers, jurors, or the press say that the perpetrator showed no mercy, so why should the law, you must seek your sense of what is right to formulate your opinion. If mercy is an essential aspect of your spiritual practice, then citing someone else's lack of it is hardly a justification to ignore your own inner truth. This is self-reliance, not thinking like the herd or citing its rules as your rationale for your own inner truth. Emerson does not ask you to deliberately disobey any law, rather to use your own sense of ethics in running your life. He makes it clear that "Whoso would be a man [or woman], must be a nonconformist."

I suggest that the best way to employ this profound truth from Emerson is to learn how to be quietly effective in your life. That is, have no need to make public pronouncements about how you refuse to conform, and instead take solace in the comfort of your own inner strength, and proceed as a silent individual who knows how to rely on yourself.

I practiced Emerson's philosophy starting with my discovery of his essay when I was seventeen. In 1959 I was nineteen, in the navy, stationed aboard an aircraft carrier, the USS *Ranger*. President Eisenhower was scheduled to fly over our ship, and all the sailors were required to get into full dress uniform and spell out HI IKE! on the flight deck as the President flew to a political meeting in San Francisco. When I learned that I was expected to participate I was outraged at this insult, yet I seemed to be a small minority. Apparently the majority of the crew did not mind conforming in "group formation" to create this greeting made of human letters. Rather than launching a protest, I recalled the words of Emerson, "Whoso would be a man, must be a nonconformist," but I had to do it silently. I let the conformists go about their task while I disappeared into the bowels of the ship until this insult to my self-reliance as an individual with dignity was completed. No outbursts, no useless fighting, simply being quietly effective.

The rules are not reasons to live a certain way. It is the integrity of your own mind that you must first consult if you are ever to experience this quality of self-reliance. This lesson applies to all areas of your life, from making decisions for yourself about how you spend your free time, to how you will dress, to what you will eat, to how you will raise your children. Don't let the voices within you grow faint and inaudible in favor of that societal conspiracy. Be yourself and run your life by what you know to be right and in harmony with your spiritual essence. That is, by the integrity of your own mind.

Here are some ideas to help you put this message of self-reliance from Ralph Waldo Emerson, to work for you:

- Read the entire "Self-Reliance" essay and list the points Emerson makes in this classic piece of writing.

- When you are about to cite a rule or law to justify why you are acting a certain way, stop and shift to your personal integrity. Do what you do because it is right and it fits in with your spiritual truths. If you know forgiveness to be divine, then don't cite a law to justify your unwillingness to forgive.

- Practice asking yourself if you are dressing or behaving in ways that please you, or to fit in. "Am I wearing this or doing that because I like it, or because it is so important for me to fit in?" Then make the self-reliant choice and see how much better you feel.

- Declare your independence from your society in terms of your own self-identification. Twenty-five hundred years ago Socrates declared, "I am not an Athenian I am a citizen of the world." You too are a creation of God, and not restricted by any societal labels.

- Refuse to do anything simply because everyone else is doing it. If it fits with your definition of ethical and right, then by all means proceed, irrespective of what those around you are saying or doing.

In summary, be yourself. Respect yourself, and create a harmonious relationship between the integrity of your own mind and your daily conduct.

A PSALM OF LIFE

Tell me not, in mournful numbers,
Life is but an empty dream!—
For the soul is dead that slumbers,
And things are not what they seem.

Life is real! Life is earnest!
And the grave is not its goal;
Dust thou art, to dust returnest,
Was not spoken of the soul.

Not enjoyment, and not sorrow,
Is our destined end or way;
But to act, that each tomorrow
Find us farther than today.

Art is long, and Time is fleeting,
And our hearts, though stout and brave,
Still, like muffled drums, are beating
Funeral marches to the grave.

In the world's broad field of battle,
In the bivouac of life,
Be not like dumb, driven cattle!
Be a hero in the strife!

Trust no Future, howe'er pleasant!
Let the dead Past bury its dead
Act,—act in the living Present!
Heart within, and God o'erhead!

Lives of great men all remind us
We can make our lives sublime,
And, departing, leave behind us
Footprints on the sands of time.

Footprints, that perhaps another,
Sailing o'er life's solemn main,
A forlorn and shipwrecked brother,
Seeing, shall take heart again.

Let us then be up and doing,
With a heart for any fate;
Still achieving, still pursuing,
Learn to labor and to wait.

HENRY WADSWORTH LONGFELLOW
(1807–1882)

American poet, translator, and college professor, Henry Wadsworth Longfellow is considered both a popular and a serious poet.

Longfellow is one of the few poets included in this book who enjoyed enormous popularity during his lifetime. "A Psalm of Life," first published in 1839 from a collection of poetry called *Voices of the Night*, became enormously popular in America and in Europe, as did his later even more famous works, "The Wreck of the Hesperus" and his classic "The Song of Hiawatha." This poem, written by the man who holds the title as the most popular American poet of the nineteenth century, is a tribute to one word, and that word is "enthusiasm." The original Greek meaning of this word is "a god within." Longfellow's "Psalm of Life" encourages you and me to take a thoughtful look at the brief span of time given to us, which is our life, and to adopt an enthusiastic and grateful attitude for all that we are and all that we experience.

In 1861 Longfellow was plunged into melancholy when his second wife died after accidentally setting fire to her dress. After losing two wives to untimely deaths, Longfellow longed for spiritual relief, and much of the poetry of his last twenty years reflected his quest for making connection with the divine. "A Psalm of Life" stands as a memorial to the spirit of this great and popular poet.

In this poem, Longfellow tells us that the soul is our true essence, "and things are not what they seem." Our bodies and our material surroundings are but a myth, and a way of thinking that leads us to a dull and unfulfilled life. He reminds us that the grave is not our goal; when we speak of aging we should refer only to the body, for the soul, the source of our "God within," is not composed of dust. He asks us to forget about our sorrows and our pleasures and instead turn our attention to our own growth and vow to be farther tomorrow than we are today. Our body is on a funeral march to the grave, but the God within will never know such a thing as a burial.

I love his choice of words to get us out of the doldrums of a life in which we often act like dumb, driven cattle, doing whatever our herd mentality directs us to do. Rather, he says, be a hero, which I interpret to mean, be enthusiastic until it positively thrills you. Demonstrate your enthusiasm for life and radiate it outward in everything you do until it infects all those around you. This is heroism. You don't have to run into a burning building to save a child to be a hero, you just have to be in touch with that God within.

Enthusiasm is not something granted to some and absent in others. All of us have a God within. Some of us choose to be in touch with it and display it, while others mask it and allow it to remain dormant. We let our inner God be dust even though the poet reminds us, "Dust thou art, to dust returnest, was not spoken of the soul." Enthusiasm is a quality that nourishes success. When people ask me the secret of giving a great talk, I tell them it is being authentically enthusiastic. Be this and you will be loved and forgiven for any flaws.

As the great Greek dramatist Aeschylus once proclaimed, "When a man's willing and eager, God joins in . . ." Enthusiasm spreads joy because there is nothing depressing about it. It has faith on its side since all fear subsides when enthusiasm is present. It is accepting because all doubt has been banished and there is no uncertainty. Enthusiasm is a choice that you can make right now.

A contemporary of Longfellow's, Ralph Waldo Emerson, also recognized the value of enthusiasm. He wrote: "Every great and commanding movement in the annals of the world is a triumph of enthusiasm . . ." Make your own life a great and commanding movement, by practicing what this "Psalm of Life" offers you. "Let us then be up and doing, with a heart for any fate."

Notice those people who have this "heart for any fate" and continue to achieve and pursue regardless of their circumstances. They love to laugh. They get excited over even the smallest of things. They don't seem to know how to be bored. Give them a gift and they will hug you in appreciation and put it to use instantly. Give them a free ticket to a concert and they bubble with delirium over the unexpected opportunity. Go shopping with them and their eyes are open appreciating everything in sight, and never complaining. Don't you just love being around them? This is enthusiasm. It is the God inside all of us that wants us to know what Longfellow means when he says, "Life is real! Life is earnest!"

And truly, as he puts it, "the soul is dead that slumbers." Let your soul come alive, and experience life through your physical being. You can begin by reading this popular poem every day and permitting Longfellow's greatness to inspire your enthusiasm. Then try some of these practical suggestions:

• Any time you are beginning an activity, like walking along the beach, or attending a soccer game, pretend to yourself that it is both the *first* and the *last* time you are having this experience. This gives you a fresh eye and a sense of enthusiasm for whatever you are doing. I have eight children, and I couldn't tell you how many talent shows; concerts; auditions; recitals; soccer, basketball, and baseball tryouts, games, and playoffs I have attended. I practice this suggestion each time I attend. I'll pretend that this is the very first time I've ever done this, and the experience comes more alive. Or I'll pretend that this is the very last time I'll ever get to have this experience, and again my enthusiasm soars.

- Change your mind about how you have defined yourself until now. Rather than "I've always been a nondemonstrative person," shift to "I am going to let my enthusiasm for life show." It is always a choice to have your soul slumbering or enjoying its embodiment through you.

- Lessen your inclination to be a nonparticipant in life. Standing on the sidelines while others partake of the action is all fine and good, but when you allow your enthusiasm for life to triumph, you will experience what Longfellow meant when he reminded you to be up and doing!

- Another of Longfellow's great poems tells of Paul Revere's ride and begins with the famous lines, "Listen my children and you shall hear . . ." Read it also in its entirety and feel the excitement of that epic moment and how Longfellow brought his enthusiasm to the telling of that story. Even while mourning the loss of his wife, this man was able to continue being "up and doing, with a heart for any fate."

IMMORTALITY

THE SINGLE HOUND

This quiet dust was gentlemen and ladies,
And lads and girls;
Was laughter and ability and sighing,
And frocks and curls.
This passive place a summer's nimble mansion,
Where bloom and bees
Fulfill'd their oriental circuit,
Then ceased, like these.

EMILY DICKINSON
(1830–1886)

Emily Dickinson is an American poet who spent her life in Amherst, Massachusetts. She wrote close to two thousand poems during a reclusive life dominated by a stern Calvinist father. Like Walt Whitman, Robert Frost, and Ralph Waldo Emerson, she wrote about an inner spirit in nature and mankind.

I have always been intrigued by this poem, and quote it frequently in my lectures. I feel as if I am personally delivering a message from one of my favorite nineteenth-century poets. When you look around at your body and your world through this poem you have to admit that everything you see, everything you experience with your senses, will someday be "quiet dust." Yet the part of you that is noticing all this is never the "quiet dust."

When you die, the instant after you leave your body, it will weigh precisely the same as when you were alive. Imagine that! Your body is the same weight alive or dead. My conclusion is that if the body weighs the same when life leaves as it did when life occupied it, then life is weightless. You cannot weigh, measure, compartmentalize, identify, or otherwise put boundaries on life. Emily Dickinson poetically describes this part of ourselves, the part that defies the dust bowl of the material world.

Scientists explain this material world as a planet with a finite supply of minerals. By this, they mean that the total supply of minerals is already here on the planet; there is no outside source of minerals. If you could determine how much iron is here, for example, you would have a total count that you could identify as earth's supply of iron. It is a finite amount, and when we use it all up, we can not go to another universe to replenish our iron supply.

Within your own body you possess a specific fraction of our total finite supply of iron. When you have a blood test, you can know whether you are high or low on iron. Now, for the million-dollar question. Where was the iron that now flows through your body before you showed up here on this planet? And where will it go when you make your departure? This is a part of the mystery that Emily Dickinson addresses in her poetic observation.

Hold up a handful of quiet dust and ask yourself what it was yesterday and yesteryear. Was it an elephant's trunk? A Jurassic creature? Michelangelo's eyeball? Every material particle is in a constant state of change. The more graphic scientists remind us that we are all tomorrow's food. All things in our physical universe will eventually become this quiet dust.

In a sense, in this poem, Emily Dickinson is poetically saying the same thing that Aristotle did when he wrote, "Let us live as if we were immortal." They are both informing us that everything and everyone has a circuit to fulfill, and that when it is complete, it ceases in its current form and shifts to another. The material of our bodies is recycled, while our true essence remains. In another of her short poems, Emily Dickinson writes:

> Because I could not stop for death,
> He kindly stopped for me.
> The carriage held but just ourselves.
> And immortality.

This awareness is a great source of liberation; it is your ticket to eternity. It allows you to stop fearing death. In many ways, the death of your body can be a great teacher, rather than something to fear.

I recall being asked by a teacher in my life to sit in deep meditation. During this quiet exercise I was instructed to imagine myself leaving my body and observing it from overhead, then I was to move farther away and ultimately to actually leave the city, country, hemisphere, and finally the entire planet. As I observed the earth from an imaginary position out in space, I was then given the assignment of picturing our planet without me on it. This was a great exercise for subduing my ego. At first it just seemed too weird to contemplate, because my ego kept saying, "What's the point? What good is an entire planet without me on it!" Then I began to identify more with the part of myself who was doing the watching than with the aspect of myself who was being watched.

It is the quiet dust that we watch, and that dust is what our ancestors were actually made up of chemically. But the watcher needs no chemicals, no dust. When you become the "noticer" full-time, you will completely lose your fear of dying. Your essence was never born and can never die. Eternity is not something that you pass into, you are already in it. In other words, now is eternity.

Your mind has not been trained to believe in your immortality, therefore it does not know you are immortal. It has been trained to identify with only what it sees. There is a command center in your brain where all your decision making, emotions, and human experiences seem to originate. Yet within that command center is an invisible, formless commander that is incapable of dying. Only through the awakening of that divine nature will you come to the awareness that you are immortal. That commander in your command center gives the orders, yet you've never seen him or her with your eyes. To know your internal commander, you must shut your eyes and directly experience your eternal divine nature.

The experience of the immortal self does not come from education, conditioning, or science. This idea rises from the depths of your being and you quite simply *know* it to be true. Your invisible nature is real, yet we know also that it can never be surveyed and mapped. We know this because we can look beyond the dust of our bodies and in quiet divine meditation experience immortality for ourselves.

Emily Dickinson in her beautifully simple poetry asks us to stop and realize that the bodies we inhabit, the cars we drive, the clothes we wear, and all things made up of chemicals and dust, are destined to fulfill their prescribed circuits and then cease. "Death" is what we call that cessation process. But that which is beyond chemicals is free to ride forever in the carriage with you; yes, you and immortality as the only passengers.

You can have a more direct experience of what Emily Dickinson wrote about if you practice the following suggestions:

- Use your own death as a teacher, a companion that is always with you. Imagine that you are talking to your dying body from a perspective of acceptance and love, rather than fear. Remember, death is experienced only once. But if you fear it, you will die in every minute of your life. Use your death as a reminder to live more fully each day.

- Do the meditation exercise of viewing the earth without you on it, which I described earlier in this essay. This will help you to shift your allegiance and your identity away from what you notice to the immortal noticer that is always with you.

- Remind yourself that all the time that passed before you showed up here did not cause you to be filled with fear and anxiety, nor will the time after you leave this body be any more troubling.

- Remember the last words of Robert Louis Stevenson, "If this is death, it is easier than life . . ." and also these final words of Thomas Edison, "It is very beautiful over there." Indeed it is just dust returning to dust, while the eternal remains. This awareness is your ticket to eternity.

PERFECTION

The year's at the spring
And day's at the morn;
Morning's at seven;
The hillside's dew-pearled;
The lark's on the wing;
The snail's on the thorn;
God's in His heaven—
All's right with the world.

ROBERT BROWNING
(1812–1889)

The English poet whose romance and marriage to Elizabeth Barrett was told in the play The Barretts of Wimpole Street, *Robert Browning enjoyed enormous success with the publication of* The Ring and the Book *after forty years of writing sensitive poetry.*

Robert Browning and his equally famous wife, Elizabeth Barrett Browning, were Victorian poets who were faulted for the spiritual and metaphysical optimism they expressed in their poetry and dramatic writing. A century and more after his death, Robert Browning's eight-line masterpiece reflects that metaphysical optimism for which he was so chastised in his lifetime. Browning speaks of a majestic awe and perfection in the universe as if he is saying to us, "Take a look around you. Everything is just as it should be."

If you appreciate Browning, then you agree with him that springtime and morning are miracles to behold. They represent the birth of new life, which remains a mystery. A heart starts beating inside a mother's womb a few weeks after conception, and all our greatest scientific and pessimistic observers are totally mystified. Where was that life before? Where will it go after here? What begins it? What stops it? Why? These questions baffle the critics and are the wellspring of great poetry.

The very essence of living one's life feeling "awe" rather than "awful" is to see the simple spiritual truth in Browning's poetic observation. The dew still covers the hillside even though the poet is buried beneath it, and the lark flies above all graves. God is in His heaven, and all's right with the world. Anything you notice that is inconsistent with Robert Browning's poetic observation is not the fault of God.

Rather than seeing ourselves as connected to this world, we often feel we are in it to push it around and make it conform to us. Rather than accepting it, we twist it to feed our ego, creating havoc, imbalance, and what we then call imperfection. Then the ultimate irony, we blame God for the very conditions we create out of the perfection that is our gift from God. The poet says, be at peace, don't judge the world, observe it. Don't try to straighten it out, accept the perfection of its crookedness and live in harmony with it. Don't manufacture problems. Be in awe of the perfection of it all.

In another passage Robert Browning observes, "All the wonder and wealth of the mine in the heart of one gem: In the care of one pearl all the shade and the shine of the sea. . . . Truth, that's brighter than gem, trust, that's purer than pearl." He is asking us to look at our world with new eyes. Eyes that are filled with wonder at the miracle that is in every cubic inch of space. Eyes that are moist with appreciation for the truth and trust that transcend their material counterparts called gems and pearls. A vision that is void of judgment and focused on the dazzling landscape can change any day that is filled with depression, anxiety, or stress.

To imply that the world is perfect is to draw the ire of many social commentators who prefer to notice a multitude of imperfections. They focus on all that is wrong with the world, and encourage us to do the same and thus to become part of the large number of people who despair over the imperfection of the world. To those who say, "All's right with the world," as Robert Browning does, there will be a truckload of skeptics to tell you how absurd your thinking is, just as there were in the

Victorian days when critics pointed to slavery, economic disasters, and warfare as their response. Yet Browning chose to look beyond the manmade world, and this is what I encourage you to do as well.

Look to the perfection that is the universe of which you are part and parcel. See how the earth continues to orbit and hurl through space independent of your and everyone else's opinion about it. See how every single day, "morning's at seven," and go back through all of the "isms" that have tried, failed, and tried again, and still, "morning's at seven; the hillside's dew-pearled." This is really only a simple turnabout from noticing what's "wrong" to noticing the perfection of our world.

For instance, consider the necessity of lightning-inspired forest fires over the centuries for the proper maintenance of the ecological balance. We have a tendency to say God shouldn't burn down our forests, or blow so hard as to create hurricanes, or rumble about so as to incur earthquakes. We think these things should not occur, yet they too are a part of the perfection of it all, and when we see them from a larger perspective, we begin to acknowledge the perfection in the chaos.

The way to a peaceful life is to notice the perfection in God's world and in ourselves, and nurture that perspective. Robert Browning's wife, Elizabeth Barrett Browning, wrote two lines in "My Kate" that nicely sum up all of this: "The weak and the gentle, the ribald and rude, she took as she found them, and did them all good." When you look out with wide eyes of wonder and appreciate all that you see as a gift from God, including your own life working in harmony with nature, you will know what the poet meant when he wrote, "God's in His heaven—All's right with the world."

To adopt this metaphysical optimism begin to:

- Give yourself a gift of five minutes of contemplation in awe of everything you see around you. Go outside and turn your attention to the many miracles around you. This five-minute-a-day regimen of appreciation and gratitude will help you to focus your life in awe.

- Allow the word "perfection" to be a part of your vocabulary. From the Prince of Peace, "Be ye perfect, even as your Father which is in Heaven is perfect." You don't always have to perceive yourself and the world from the perspective of judging it and trying to improve it. Enjoying the perfection is one way to apply the wisdom of the ages.

- Remind yourself that you are just as much of a miracle as that dew, lark, and snail. You, in fact, are what God is doing. Trust in and value your own divinity as well as your connection to nature. Seeing God's work everyplace will be your reward.

SOULCENTER

from *Moby Dick*

For as this appalling ocean surrounds the verdant land, so in the soul of man there lies one insular Tahiti, full of peace and joy, but encompassed by all of the horrors of the half-lived life.

HERMAN MELVILLE
(1819–1891)

American novelist, short-story writer, and poet, Herman Melville is best known for Moby Dick, *his tale of a literal and a heroic journey.*

When I read this quote, I have a vivid mental picture of visiting the sweet little chapel in Assisi, Italy, where St. Francis lived and performed his well-documented miracles in the thirteenth century. The chapel, like most of Upper and Lower Assisi, has been largely preserved so that visitors can experience this holy place exactly as St. Francis did. It is easy to feel as if you have stepped back into the Middle Ages. Millions of people have pilgrimaged from around the world to pray in this ancient but well-preserved little church.

The original chapel sits in the center of a much larger, more ornate building that was built hundreds of years after the death of St. Francis. This surrounding edifice has majestic columns, enormous cathedral ceilings, and an array of church tributes to St. Francis, who was a simple, gentle, and extremely passionate man. Walking in the outer chambers I felt as if I were in a museum dedicated to a highly spiritual man.

When my wife and I entered the original chapel in the center, we both felt the joy and peace that this place represents. It comes back to me whenever I read, ". . . in the soul of man there lies one insular Tahiti," We tingled with bliss, cried tears of joy, and felt the energy of unconditional love that St. Francis represents. After meditating for thirty minutes or so, we left with the feeling of communicating with something divine. Since that time we have often remarked how it was a turning point in our lives together. Our marriage shifted to a spiritual partnership in which our role is to assist each other in our spiritual growth.

Herman Melville's words take me back to that peak experience in Assisi. The original chapel in the center represents the soul, a place of divine truth and bliss. The surrounding edifice is like our physical body. It is always a step removed from the beauty and truth that reside in the center. A half-lived life, as Melville describes it, is one in which we do not get to that inner place of peace and joy, that "insular Tahiti."

The half-lived life is lived exclusively in the trappings and the structures that are the outer world. These are the horrors that Melville tells us encompass the soul, as if one were unable to find the center where bliss resides. You sense that there is a deeper, richer experience of life available, yet you somehow continue to flail around in the external ocean, glimpsing that verdant Tahiti, that peaceful chapel from a distance.

Perhaps the most devastating scenario imaginable is to face death knowing that because of some imagined fear, you have always chosen a half-lived life in which you avoided doing the things your heart beckoned you to do. I urge you to change the scenario now. Start living your life with the courage to step ashore and experience your insular Tahiti.

I encourage you to read and reread the poignant words of Herman Melville, written in the nineteenth century for you to apply today. That space in the center that he calls your soul has no boundaries, no form, no dimensions to measure. Yet it is the very core of your being. When you are able to experience that space, you will know the peace and joy that comes from a life fully lived and fully appreciated. That inner space that Melville calls your soul is silent and indivisible.

You can get there by meditating and then listening to your heart rather than your head. Your heart speaks a silent language of purpose, while your head often gives you intellectual reasons that you can't follow your bliss. Accomplished musicians say, "It's the silence between the notes that makes the music." Without that formless, dimensionless silence there can be no music.

You can access your verdant Tahiti, your peaceful chapel, by working your way through that appalling ocean and those architectural structures, past the shell of your body composed of bone and sinew, and arriving at that indivisible silent place within. Then just listen and glow and know that a half-lived life is not for you. Write your truths, speak your innermost feelings, let go of what you've been told you must do or not do. You will feel fulfilled in your work, your family, your entire life.

What is it that your heart begs you to do? What verdant island inside the ocean of your body beckons you to come and visit? It could be a travel bug to explore the Galapagos or the Himalayas. Perhaps it is a feeling that is heartfelt which implores you to open an art gallery, or work with the Eskimos. Maybe it is a gnawing itch to write your own poems or your own symphony.

What is your secret in the center? Robert Frost wrote, "We dance round in a ring and suppose,/But the secret sits in the middle and knows." He must have known what Melville was speaking about in *Moby Dick*. Whatever you feel within you, but have avoided for whatever reason you've manufactured in your mind, give yourself permission to explore it with new eyes and ears. As you practice accessing this silent center, be careful how you use your intellect. If you proceed to tell yourself that it is one thing to explore your inner chapel, but quite another to live there, then carefully note how you are setting yourself up to continue wallowing in the outer chambers. You *will* act on what you think about. And if you think, "It's impossible, impractical, and beyond my reach," then this is precisely what you will act upon, and it is back to the appalling ocean you go.

Melville wrote in the nineteenth century, but he was writing to you and me. He left this planet before we showed up, yet his words ring true. The same life force that flowed through this great novelist also flows through us today. He felt the horror of a half-lived life was a result of ignoring the inner, silent spark of life that gives peace and joy to all of us.

Here are my suggestions for implementing this wisdom today:

- Practice a daily meditation in which you go to that silent space within. This inner place will give you a sense of peace that is impossible to know when you are enmeshed in the turmoil of that appalling ocean.

- Listen to your heart, not your head. Your feelings are a sensitive barometer for what you love to do. Imagine yourself visiting your expression of the verdant Tahiti. Experience in your soul and then in your mind all the details of doing what you love and loving what you do.

- Take the risks involved in listening to your soul, but be very careful to avoid projecting thoughts of fear, failure, and catastrophe onto your decisions. Remind yourself each day that Herman Melville was writing to you, and that when the Angel of Death comes calling—and the call is inevitable—you won't say, "I am horrified, wait, I've only lived halfway." Instead you will know the joy of listening to your soul and you will say, "I am at peace. I have no fear. I have been to Tahiti."

REGRETS

from "Maud Muller"

Alas for maiden, alas for judge,
For rich repiner and household drudge!
God pity them both! And pity us all,
Who vainly the dreams of youth recall:
For of all sad words of tongue or pen
The saddest are these: "It might have been!"
Ah, well! for us all some sweet hope lies
Deeply buried from human eyes;
And in the hereafter angels may
Roll the stone from its grave away!

JOHN GREENLEAF WHITTIER
(1807–1892)

A Quaker devoted to social causes and reform, John Greenleaf Whittier was a popular New England poet. After the Civil War his poetry emphasized religion, nature, and New England life.

The above-quoted passage is the final stanza in a fifteen-stanza poem titled "Maud Muller," written by John Greenleaf Whittier, a prolific and sensitive nineteenth-century American poet. I urge you to read and reread the entire poem, which tells a story that has a profound message for everyone who has the courage to accept this sage advice.

The poem opens with Maud Muller, a beautiful young maiden, raking hay in a meadow looking up and seeing a handsome judge on a horse, riding toward her. Her heart beats intensely as she speaks to the judge while giving him a drink of water from her tin cup. Her mind races at the thought of what it would be like to be with the kind, sensitive man who spoke to her "of the grass, and flowers, and trees. Of the singing birds and the humming bees." She forgot the tattered clothes she wore and her unkempt appearance and allowed herself to fantasize about her dreams: "A wish, that she hardly dared to own, for something better than she had known."

As the judge rode away, her heartfelt thought was, "Ah, me! That I the judge's bride might be!" But it was not to be. Instead she married a man who brought her sorrow and pain. As Whittier writes it, "A manly form at her side she saw, and joy was duty, and love was law." Then she took up the burden of her life again, saying only, "It might have been!"

The poet describes the young, handsome judge who rode off that day with a deep longing in his heart, but one that he was unwilling to fulfill. Afraid to jeopardize his position in life, he was unable to act on his feelings for the young maiden and her way of life. "Would she were mine, and I today, like her, a harvester of hay; no doubtful balance of rights and wrongs, nor weary lawyers with endless tongue." And so he left his heartfelt longings and pursued a life that had been arranged for him by the decisions of others. "But he thought of his sisters, proud and cold, and his mother, vain of her rank and gold; so closing his heart, the Judge rode on, and Maud was left in the field alone."

Whittier then tells of how the judge married someone of his own rank and position and how he daydreamed of his soul connection back in the field: "Oft when the wine in his glass was red, he longed for the wayside well instead."

> And the proud man sighed, with a
>   secret pain,
> "Ah, that I were free again!
> Free as when I rode that day,
> Where the barefoot maiden raked
>   her hay."

As the story of Maud and the Judge comes to its poetic conclusion, the final verse builds to an emotionally charged conclusion. The two lines that Whittier is most remembered for are words that I kept in large letters on my bulletin board for my students to read when I was a school counselor many years ago. They are words that today I remind my children to internalize when they fear making a mistake, or when they avoid taking a risk by remaining silent. These are words to live by, written by a brilliant poet more than a century ago. "For of all sad words of tongue or pen the saddest are these: 'It might have been!'" Indeed, *it might have been* is the lament of the unfulfilled dreamers who ponder the past with regret over what they failed to say or do because they feared the consequences.

In my own life I have made many mistakes but I can honestly say that I have no regrets today regarding anything I've done. Absolutely none. Yes, there are things I said that I wouldn't say today. Yes, there were people I hurt along the way, and today I have learned from those behaviors. Yes, I've made some bad investments, written some horrible words, consumed some toxic substances, lost some competitive contests, and even been lost in my own self-importance far too frequently in my past. But, as I said, I have no regrets about anything I've done. I've worked at not repeating those blunders and I know I cannot undo the past. Yet I am not free of regrets. My own regrets are in what *I didn't do.*

At a twenty-year high school reunion I met a woman whom I absolutely adored when I was a seventeen-year-old boy. I finally had the courage to tell her how I felt two decades later! She responded, "I always liked you and would have given anything if you would have called and asked for a date." I was floored by my regret. At seventeen I trembled with fear at thoughts of being rejected or appearing foolish. I imagined she was way too "cool" and gorgeous to go out with me, and consequently I allowed the opportunity to pass.

If you feel something in your heart and know it resonates within you as something you should try, yet you hold back out of fear, you set yourself up for regret. Make no mistake about it, regret is an appalling waste of energy. You cannot build on it, you cannot grow from it; all you can do is wallow in frustration.

Whatever you feel deeply about but fail to act on will cause you regret. The words you didn't say for fear of being ridiculed, the action you failed to take for fear of failing, the trip you didn't take for fear of being alone are the stairs that lead, one step at a

time, to the attic of despair in your later years. As Whittier puts it
so succinctly, "God pity them both! And pity us all, who vainly
the dreams of youth recall."

You undoubtedly will encounter some disapproval. Some
results you produce will not always be to your liking. You will
experience ridicule. But you will not know regret if you speak up
or take action. What you will know, no matter what, is a sense of
your own spiritual destiny. As Jesus put it, "No man having put
his hand to the plan and looking back is fit for the Kingdom of
Heaven."

To practice this no-regrets advice from Whittier's classic poem
of Maud Muller and the Judge, consider the following:

- Visualize yourself as an older person looking back on yourself
  today. How do you want to feel then? Full of regret, or satisfied that you did what your heart advised?

- Instead of asking yourself what everyone else's opinion is
  going to be and how your action will be perceived by others,
  ask yourself, "How do I want my life to be lived?" Then proceed to take a small risk in the direction of that new action.

- Contemplate how you are going to feel, in advance. First,
  imagine taking the potentially regret-producing path of inaction. Then imagine what the very best outcome would be
  were you to take this risk. By picturing both scenarios in
  advance, you can avoid the regret of what might have been.

FEAR AND RISK-TAKING

I ENVY NOT IN ANY MOODS

I envy not in any moods
The captive void of noble rage,
The linnet born within the cage,
That never knew the summer woods:

I envy not the beast that takes
His license in the field of time,
Unfetter'd by the sense of crime,
To whom a conscience never wakes;

Nor, what may count itself as blest,
The heart that never plighted troth
But stagnates in the weeds of sloth,
Nor any want-begotten rest.

I hold it true, what'er befall;
I feel it, when I sorrow most;
'Tis better to have loved and lost
Than never to have loved at all.

ALFRED, LORD TENNYSON
(1809–1892)

An English poet who was appointed poet laureate in 1850, Alfred, Lord Tennyson is considered highly representative of the Victorian age in England.

Alfred Tennyson was the chief representative of what is known as the age of Victorian poetry. Yet no poet that I have ever read about could be called less Victorian. He was hopelessly addicted to tobacco and port, he was a wanderer, and he remained largely unsettled throughout his life. The poet Thomas Carlyle described him in a letter to Ralph Waldo Emerson as "A man sultry and sad in an element of gloom . . . one of the finest looking men in the world . . . His voice is mightily loose. Fit for loud laughter and piercing wail." From all that I have read of Alfred Tennyson, he was a deeply passionate man who loved to take risks and was willing to take the consequences when his investments or his pursuits did not turn out as planned.

In this selection, the poet sends us a message that is all too often ignored by those who live in fear of failing. He tells us to go on in life as if failure were not a consideration, and ignore our fears as we proceed. He does not envy the songbird who remains safely ensconced in a cage; freedom is what he values, despite the inherent risks. He does not envy those who, fearing the risks of partnership in marriage, choose the safety of noncommitment. The last four lines of this poem are among the most memorable and oft-quoted in all of literature. Yet they are also perhaps the most unheeded.

> I hold it true, whate'er befall;
> I feel it, when I sorrow most;
> 'Tis better to have loved and lost
> Than never to have loved at all.

I second this notion and remind you that Tennyson is not just writing about love relationships. He could just as easily have written:

> 'Tis better to have acted and fallen
> Than never to have acted at all.

I suggest you consider a radical idea: *There is no such thing as failure!* Failing is a judgment that we humans place on a given action. Rather than judgment, substitute this attitude: *You cannot fail, you can only produce results!* Then the most important question to ask yourself is, "What do you do with the results you produce?"

Suppose, for example, that you want to learn to hit a baseball or to bake a cake. You step up to the plate and you dribble the ball off your bat after several misses. In the case of your baking, your cake comes out of the oven and collapses in a pile of crumbs before your eyes. In truth, you have not failed, you have acted and you have produced a result. Now what do you do with the results you produce? Do you label yourself a failure, announce that you are uncoordinated and untalented in the kitchen and mope about your genetic deficiencies, or do you step back up to the plate or head back into the kitchen and learn from the results you have produced? This is what Tennyson is asking you to understand and apply in your life, in all areas of pursuit.

In relationships you have not failed if you have been through breakups or divorce court. You have produced a result. It is better to jump in and experience life than to stand on the sidelines fearing that something might go wrong.

Consider for a moment what your very nature is like. As an infant, before you ever had any opportunity to be subjected to the conditioning that leads you away from risks for fear of failing, your nature was programmed to learn how to walk. For a while you just lay down, then your nature said, "Sit," and you did. Then your nature commanded, "Crawl," and you obeyed. Eventually your nature said, "Stand up on two feet, balance yourself, and move from an upright position." And you listened.

The first time you made the effort, you fell down and returned to crawling. But your nature wouldn't let you stay satisfied with crawling and you ignored your fears and the results you had produced and stood up again. This time to a wobble and then another fall. Eventually your nature won out and you walked upright. Imagine if you had succeeded in overcoming your natural programming. You would still be crawling on all fours and not know the advantages of an upright life!

And so it is with everything in your life. It is far better to have acted and produced results that you will grow from than to ignore your nature and live in fear.

The word "fear" can be thought of as an acronym that translates to *False Evidence Appearing Real*. In other words, we look at what we imagine to be a strong reason for inaction and then we allow it to become our reality, even before we make an attempt. Our fear is supported by an illusion that it is possible to fail, and that failure means we are worthless. Another acronym for "fear" is *Forget Everything And Run*. This is the flight mentality in the face of the prospect of failing. This is not what Tennyson is promoting!

Alfred Tennyson was elevated to the peerage eight years before his death, and he became the national poet of England in his later years. But the younger Alfred Tennyson was a man who pursued his interests with vigor, was willing to make mistakes, and was most anxious to love. Even knowing that losing was a probability, he preferred that to never having loved. He did indeed experience rejection and sorrow, but as he says so poignantly, "I envy not in any moods."

Know in your heart that you have never failed at anything and you never will. The artificial judgments of failure only keep you from erring or making a mistake. Yet those mistakes and errors are the very stuff of growth. I've always enjoyed Thomas Edison's response to a reporter who asked him how it felt to have failed twenty-five thousand times in his efforts to invent a battery. "Failed," replied Edison, "I haven't failed. Today I know twenty-five thousand ways not to make a battery!"

Put the lesson of Tennyson's classic poem to work in your life with the following suggestions:

- Refuse to ever use the term "failure" again about yourself or anyone else. Remind yourself that when things didn't go as planned you didn't fail, you only produced a result.

- Then ask yourself this powerfully life-enhancing question, "What am I going to do with the results I've produced?" And proceed to act in such a way as to be grateful rather than resentful for those less than glorious results.

- When others use the term "failure" about you, gently correct them by saying, "I have not failed, today I know another way not to bake a cake."

- Deliberately pursue activities in which you have previously shown little or no aptitude. The way out of fear or failure is to face it and laugh at the results rather than be embarrassed or intimidated by earlier outcomes.

PHYSICAL PERFECTION

To me, every cubic inch of space is a miracle . . .
Welcome is every organ and attitude of me . . .
Not an inch, nor a particle of an inch is vile . . .

WALT WHITMAN
(1819–1892)

American essayist, journalist, and poet, Walt Whitman made his
major themes the sacredness of life in all its forms, even death, and
the equality of all people.

The physical body, composed of molecules and atoms, is constantly changing. Inside the body in a "placeless place" is the eternal observer, which is the unchanging divine nature. Walt Whitman honored his body and its continuous state of change from this sacred perspective. He once observed, "If anything is sacred the human body is sacred . . ." What is your reaction to that statement? How do *you* feel about the body that you occupy? Your answer has a great deal to do with the quality of your life—both your material life and your spiritual life.

Your attitude toward your body literally impacts the atoms and molecules that comprise your body. Deepak Chopra, M. D., often says to his audiences, "Happy thoughts make happy molecules," pointing out that the chemical composition of tears of joy varies dramatically from the chemical composition of tears of sadness. So be at peace with your body and treasure its various organs, rivers of fluids, and solid structures of bone, and have an attitude of awe as it moves, thinks, dreams, calculates, loves, and constantly changes. This state of wonder is what Walt Whitman is asking you to embrace when you contemplate the miracle that is your ever-changing body.

There is nothing about your body that is vile or imperfect. It is not too short, tall, stocky, dark, fair, or anything else. The color of your hair, the amount that is left, the places that it grows are all in divine order. Your breasts are just the size they are supposed to be, your eyes the right color, and your lips the proper fullness. While your happy thoughts can create healthy molecules, and your mind has a great deal to do with your level of health, essentially your body is a naturally functioning system. You actually showed up in this body. Its shape, size, and what have erroneously been called handicaps are all in perfect order.

A few weeks after conception, a heart started beating inside your mother's womb, and your body began to form, independent of your opinion about it. This process of body building is a mystery to everyone on the planet. Who can explain it? Out of nothing your body began to journey, fingers and toes forming from a tiny drop of human protoplasm. How? From where? Who is to question the wisdom of the future pull inside that seed? Now you reside in this body that is changing just as drastically outside the womb as it did inside. And you get to observe it all. You, the invisible I, the ghost inside the machine, the occupier of this perfect creation.

This body of yours is like a curriculum in school, only this is your curriculum to God. This is your house of God, and it is in this body, while it is here on this planet, that God can be realized. To find anything about this house of God to be vile or disgusting is to sully the temple that is the one place in the universe where you know you can realize God. No one can stop the process that is the ever-changing body. No one can alter the fundamental structure of the body. You live in something that has an invisible future pull, taking it wherever its nature will take it. Do not detest any part of it unless you wish to deny the wisdom that created you.

Treat your body like a guest who visits and then must leave. While it is here don't neglect it, don't poison it. Honor it, welcome it, and allow it to take its course which is ultimately to leave as it came, back to where it came from. Make it fun to watch your body go through its designated phases. Be in awe of every inch of it.

When you stub your toe or cut a finger or pull a muscle, and are constantly brought back to this little pain that makes even the simplest of functions most noticeable, stop and remind yourself how grateful you are to have toes, fingers, and muscles. Remind yourself how they work perfectly with no awareness at all from you most of the time. Why ever have an unwelcome thought about your body, or ever look at this ever-changing divine creation with contempt? You are privileged to have the body you have. Honor it as if it is the garage in which you park your soul. Refuse to have contemptuous thoughts about your soul's garage, your body. Don't complain about its size, color, or worn-out places.

As long as you are grateful and in a state of awe, you will be unlikely to neglect it. You will be much more likely to keep it repaired, sparkling and clean, healthy and vibrant, when the you inside looks with amazement and wonder, views with awe, every inch of this universe knowing there are no mistakes. If your hair chooses to grow in your ears, on your shoulders, and in your nose, rather than on top of your head, then so be it! If your skin loosens around your bones, then applaud the loosening process. Refuse to cling to the flesh as though it were going to last forever. Each body is gripped by death, and yet the paradox remains; within that same body dwells the immortal self. See your body as a place from which to observe the world. Choose to do so from the miraculous, sacred perspective that Walt Whitman cited so frequently in his magnificent poetry.

Here are some suggestions for applying the wisdom of Walt Whitman's observations to your daily life:

- Give thanks every day for this temple that houses your soul. Give verbal appreciation for your liver, your eyesight, your pancreas, every organ, every inch of your body. Simply say, "Thank you God for this always changing and always perfect place for me to observe from."

- Become more aware of how you choose to treat this miracle of a body. Talk to it as you give it exercise, good food, and generous amounts of fresh water. "I bless you, wondrous body of mine. By being more aware of what a perfect creation you are, I will avoid mistreating you."

- Observe the changes that take place in your body with joy rather than displeasure. Refuse to call any part of your body flawed. God does not deal in flawed material.

- A body that is cared for has a greater opportunity to advance the spiritual life. It is out of the spiritual invisible dimension that the material world is created. Purity of thought will help you to maintain a pure, healthy body. Remember, thoughts heal the body, not the other way around. This is why a welcoming attitude of awe and gratitude toward the body is such an important factor in the enhancement of your spiritual life!

AGELESSNESS

from *Alice's Adventures in Wonderland*

FATHER WILLIAM
After Southey

"You are old, Father William," the young man said,
"And your hair has become very white;
And yet you incessantly stand on your head—
Do you think, at your age, it is right?"

"In my youth," Father William replied to his son,
"I feared it might injure the brain;
But, now that I'm perfectly sure I have none,
Why, I do it again and again."

"You are old," said the youth, "as I mentioned before,
And have grown most uncommonly fat;
Yet you turned a back-somersault in at the door—
Pray, what is the reason of that?"

"In my youth," said the sage, as he shook his gray locks,
"I kept all my limbs very supple
By the use of this ointment—one shilling the box—
Allow me to sell you a couple?"

"You are old," said the youth, "and your jaws are too weak
For anything tougher than suet;
Yet you finished the goose, with the bones and the beak—
Pray, how did you manage to do it?"

"In my youth," said his father, "I took to the law,
And argued each case with my wife;

And the muscular strength which it gave to my jaw,
Has lasted the rest of my life."

"You are old," said the youth, "one would hardly suppose
That your eye was as steady as ever;
Yet you balanced an eel on the end of your nose—
What made you so awfully clever?"

"I have answered three questions and that is enough,"
Said his father, "don't give yourself airs!
Do you think I can listen all day to such stuff?
Be off, or I'll kick you downstairs!"

LEWIS CARROLL
(1832–1898)

*English author, mathematician, and photographer, Lewis Carroll is
most widely known for* Alice's Adventures in Wonderland *and*
Through the Looking-Glass.

Charles L. Dodgson was a shy English mathematician, photographer, and novelist who was deaf in one ear, spoke with a stammer, never married, yet was fascinated with and loved being around children. He was able to speak naturally and easily around children and enjoyed making up stories as he was telling them. He frequently took his young friends on picnics, where his imagination created stories of Alice and her underground adventures. He recalled some twenty-five years after the publication of *Alice's Adventures in Wonderland* "how, in a desperate attempt to strike out some new line of fairy lure, I had sent my heroine down a rabbit hole, to begin with, without the least idea what was to happen afterwards."

This hobby of telling endlessly provocative stories about a heroine named Alice would eventually become *Alice's Adventures in Wonderland,* and Charles Dodgson would become known as Lewis Carroll, one of the best-known authors of children's books to this day. This excerpt is from that famous story first told in 1862 to a group of children who accompanied Charles as they rowed up the Thames River from Oxford to picnic on the river-bank. Today his stories are read by children and adults the world over.

"Father William" is a humorous ballad depicting a conversa-tion between a son and his father, who is perceived as an old, dried-up nonentity by the child. Father William's responses send a twin message to all of us as we face the reality of a body that is aging, but also houses an ageless soul. These two messages are: (1) You are only old if you believe it; and (2) You can be expert at whatever you choose. Father William replies to each of the child's questions with a reference to his own youth, which we all know is universally ignored by children, and with a silly and ironic action response as well. He stands on his head because old age has erased the youthful idea of having a brain that needs to be pro-tected, he proclaims. He turns back-somersaults though fat, and he chews bones though his jaws are weak. The beauty of Lewis Carroll's writing is in the irony and the whimsy. He is telling us all that growing old is a given, and being ridiculed and misunder-stood by our younger generations is to be expected, yet it ought to have no relevance to how we continue to function in our own lives.

Father William's response to the young man is my signal to absolutely refuse to allow an old infirm person to enter my body. He reminds me that I can maintain an attitude of sprightly alive-ness, and this inner decision will allow me to perform at whatever level I dictate, irrespective of age. I love this advice and I apply it every single day.

For over two decades now, in fact almost a quarter of a cen-tury, I have told my body that it will go out and run every single day, regardless of whatever ailments it may be experiencing. I have instructed my body to swim in the ocean regularly and to play tennis at least five times each week. I tell it to walk up the stairs whenever possible rather than ride in elevators. I frequently inform it that it will walk rather than drive to its appointed rounds of chores. I tell it to do those sit-ups and abdominal crunches, and to play basketball, soccer, and whatever other activ-ities my youngsters engage in, right alongside them. Not only that, but I remind these same youngsters and their friends, with equal whimsy and lighthearted sarcasm, that I can do it all day without getting tired like they do. To their teasing, I say, like Father William, "Do you think I can listen all day to such stuff? Be off, or I'll kick you downstairs."

You do not have to take on an aging attitude with the natural progression of your body's journey through its life stages. You can easily give in and call yourself an old person, and with that self-label become an *in*valid as well as inv*al*id. Or you can take the example of Father William and look your body right smack in the eye and say to it, "You are not going to stop me from living fully."

The second message I glean from Father William's nonsensical responses to his young son's inquiries is that it is unnecessary to limit ourselves to one area of expertise. You *can* be outstanding both as an intellectual and as an athlete, even though many consider these polar opposites. I have long heard that there are great writers and there are great speakers, but it is not possible to be great at both. These observers have told me that writers are introverted and communicate with words and paper, while speakers are extroverts who communicate with people and therefore are not generally talented in writing.

I see this as just as nonsensical as Father William saw his son's inquiries, and I choose to do both just as I know that I can choose to enjoy listening to classical music and watching a football game, or even playing in one. You can love poetry as well as romantic novels. You can be just as much at home on a virtual reality ride at Disney World as you are in a discussion group on existentialism. There are no compartments that you have to stuff yourself into in order to know yourself. You do not need to find out what your innate interest is and then pursue one or two areas that are commensurate with your God-given talents. You can enjoy a high level of expertise in virtually any area of pursuit that you decide on. You are an eclectic rather than a one-dimensional being. And as you hear the questions put to you by those wise-cracking youths who see you as dried up and limited in abilities, keep in mind Father William, the feisty character that Charles L. Dodgson, a. k. a. Lewis Carroll, created from his wildly imaginative mind, who responds by standing on his head, balancing an eel on the end of his nose, and doing somersaults while good-naturedly sending his young critic away, telling him, "don't give yourself airs, . . . be off, or I'll kick you downstairs."

I suggest that you literally kick downstairs any and all attitudes that you may be cultivating, or that you have already adopted, which identify yourself as an aging or a limited body. To get this process started I suggest you:

- Talk to your body and force it to become more active, despite its objections. If you have accustomed your body to living as a couch potato, it will resist walking and running and being dragged through exercise routines. Note those protests, and then do it anyway.

- Resist impulses to label yourself with descriptions that limit you in any way. Statements such as, "I'm not good at . . . ," or "I've never been interested in . . . ," only serve to strengthen your self-image of limitation. You can be good at and enjoy anything if you decide to.

- Put yourself through a self-improvement project that is designed to maximize your state of mind, body, and spirit. Write your own personal curriculum and apply it each day.

- Take classes in something new or unfamiliar, such as archery, bridge, yoga, meditation, tai chi, tennis, dancing, or anything that you have never experienced before.

KINDNESS

DO NOT WEEP, MAIDEN, FOR WAR IS KIND

Do not weep, maiden, for war is kind.
Because your lover threw wild hands toward the sky
And the affrighted steed ran on alone,
Do not weep.
War is kind.

Hoarse, booming drums of the regiment,
Little souls who thirst for fight—
These men were born to drill and die.
The unexplained glory flies above them;
Great is the battle-god, great—and his kingdom
A field where a thousand corpses lie.

Do not weep, babe, for war is kind.
Because your father tumbled in the yellow trenches,
Raged at his breast, gulped and died,
Do not weep.
War is kind.

Swift-blazing flag of the regiment,
Eagle with crest of red and gold,
These men were born to drill and die.
Point for them the virtue of slaughter,
Make plain to them the excellence of killing,
And a field where a thousand corpses lie.

Mother whose heart hung humble as a button
On the bright splendid shroud of your son,
Do not weep.
War is kind.

STEPHEN CRANE
(1871–1900)

*American novelist, short-story writer, poet, and war correspondent,
probably best known for* The Red Badge of Courage, *Stephen
Crane, who died at age twenty-nine, managed to produce work
that assured him a permanent place in American literature.*

Stephen Crane, the youngest of fourteen children, lived a short
but highly explosive life. He wrote about what simultaneously
seemed to both attract and repel him. The violence of the streets
and the victims it creates was the subject matter of his first novel,
Maggie: A Girl of the Streets, a sympathetic story of an innocent girl
from the slums and her descent into prostitution and eventual
suicide. In 1893 this topic was so taboo in literature that the book
was privately printed and Crane had to use a pseudonym. This
was followed in 1895 by his classic story of the horror of war, *The
Red Badge of Courage*.

He wrote of his aversion to violence, his sympathy for victims
and the downtrodden, yet he was equally attracted to report and
to experience firsthand these outrages, and once lived with a former brothel-house proprietor. Stephen Crane's career as a writer
and a journalist covering wars wherever they cropped up on the
planet was brief. He died at age twenty-nine of malarial fever and
tuberculosis contracted while he was in Cuba covering the Span-
ish-American War.

For me, this poem of deep irony is not only a disparaging
attack on war and all of horror, but a classic statement against violence of any kind. Also included is the violence that we observe
daily of man's inhumanity to man, and the rage and fury within
our own hearts. These are equally as destructive and are also the
subject of the poet's lament against war. His ironic poem *War Is*

Kind is a commentary on what he termed those little souls who thirst for fight, who find virtue in something so horrifying as slaughter, and excellence in a field of a thousand corpses. For me, this is a lesson to look within myself for any remnant of a little soul who might find glory in the trumpeting of man's inhumanity to man. It is a reminder to allow my big soul to triumph over its lesser compatriot, and to suppress curiosity about or fascination with violence of any kind.

There are people who carry guns and leave maidens weeping all over the world, be it on battlefields, or in our homes, schools, streets, and playgrounds. All seem to be men who were born to drill and die, yet we do not believe that anyone has such a destiny at birth. This carnage is the result of our own curiosity about and fascination with warfare and killing, with violence and rage so that we attract into our collective lives the very thing we fear the most. We live, in a more subtle fashion, the same kind of life as the poet Stephen Crane, attracting to ourselves that which repels us. If we don't harness that little soul we too will become victims of the search for the unexplained glory of the battle-god and his kingdom where a thousand corpses lie.

Our fascination with violence and its ultimate implementation, killing, is reflected in our preoccupation with action films wherein human life is reduced in value so much so that the taking of these lives is considered entertaining. Killing for the sake of keeping the customers happy takes its toll on our collective consciousness whether we recognize it or not. We defend the need and the right to carry handguns and they therefore become a high-profit item in the world of commerce. A gun for every man, woman, and child is now the goal of this industry and we are getting closer each day. Do not weep, war is kind.

Yet there is much to weep about, and there is no shortage of tears. Maidens howl in anguish every hour of every day as loved ones fall victim to our almost insatiable attraction to war and unnecessary violence. We live in the most violent society on earth, where hundreds of thousands are killed and maimed yearly with barely a flicker of attention from our "leaders" who are busy chastising others on human rights violations. Recently state officials from China were not granted full diplomatic recognition in an official visit because their country was being bitterly criticized for its stand on human rights. This seemed to me to be as ironic as Stephen Crane's poem, "Do Not Weep, Maiden, for War Is Kind."

To make a huge dent in this kind of fascination with war, killing, and violence, we must first look within our own hearts and allow the big soul to triumph over those inclinations. We must find the place within ourselves where we know that in some non-earth based way, we are all connected by an invisible organizing intelligence and we need to live in this awareness. We must refuse to participate in any form of activity that purports to be entertainment which trivializes violence and killing. We must teach our young sons that they were not born to drill and die, not born to throw their hands toward the sky in some kind of ego ritual to dying in battle as a badge of courage. We must raise them to have disdain for violence, and to check the impulses of fury brought on by an overidentification with ego's need to be triumphant in battle. We must teach them and ourselves the value of cooperation over competition, and the great wisdom in the Native American homily, "No tree has branches so foolish as to fight among themselves."

We must elect those who see the horror in having a world filled with weapons and live ammunition. They have to pursue at all costs, with true courage, the end of all weapons that are designed to kill, from megadeath nuclear bombs to low-caliber handguns. If they are meant to inflict death, we must find another way. And finally, we must look within our own hearts to quell our little soul's attraction to violence and instead find our fascination with kindness and love.

"All we need to do is be a little kinder toward each other." This was Aldous Huxley's answer when he was asked on his deathbed for his advice to mankind after a lifetime of study and exploration of the human spirit. Simple words with a simple solution. War is most assuredly not kind. Being kind is the solution not only in the world as a collective whole, but in our individual lives, where it all begins.

To put this awareness of Stephen Crane's poem to work in your own life, begin to:

- Eliminate your personal participation in movie going, television watching, or reading that promotes violence or reduces the value of human life by making killing and maltreatment any form of entertainment.

- Teach young people to value kindness over killing. Talk to them about why you don't want them using play guns and weapons. Explain that they can change the world by choosing kindness over killing as a way to play.

- Catch yourself when you feel violent impulses, and have a quiet self-talk that allows you to reprogram yourself along the lines of kindness rather than rage. By recognizing rage when it crops up, you will allow the big soul to begin to tame the baser tendencies of the little soul.

- Support organizations that have as their mission the eradication of violence on our planet. There are many organizations from the United Nations to local groups that want to elect more kindness-oriented people to commissions and government offices. Choose at least one to give your support to.

 LAUGHTER

A CHILD'S LAUGHTER

All the bells of heaven may ring,
All the birds of heaven may sing,
All the wells on earth may spring,
All the winds on earth may bring
All sweet sounds together;
Sweeter far than all things heard,
Hand of harper, tone of bird,
Sound of woods at sundawn stirred,
Welling water's winsome word,
Wind in warm wan weather,

One thing yet there is, that none
Hearing ere its chime be done
Knows not well the sweetest one
Heard of man beneath the sun,
Hoped in heaven hereafter;
Soft and strong and loud and light—
Very sound of very light
Heard from morning's rosiest height—
When the soul of all delight
Fills a child's clear laughter.

Golden bells of welcome rolled
Never forth such notes, nor told
Hours so blithe in tones so bold,
As the radiant mouth of gold
Here that rings forth heaven.
If the golden-crested wren
Were a nightingale—why, then,

Something seen and heard of men
Might be half as sweet as when
Laughs a child of seven.

ALGERNON CHARLES SWINBURNE
(1837–1909)

English poet and man of letters, Algernon Charles Swinburne is
known for his rebellion against Victorian social conventions and
religion, and for the pagan spirit and musical effects of his poetry.

*A*ttempt to imagine the sounds that Swinburne presents in the opening of this sensitive poem on a child's laughter. Try to hear and see the bells and birds of heaven, the wells of earth springing; the winds, harps, rustling trees, and tones of singing birds. They are for the most part naturally melodic sounds that bring to mind the peace and serenity of nature. God's sounds, if you will, which can delight us when we calmly listen.

Algernon Charles Swinburne, the prolific mid-Victorian poet who wrote this poem, is described as a master of word-music and word-color, terms that I find fascinating. He used his unparalleled artistry to liken the most beautiful natural sounds in our world to the sound of a child's laughter, and concluded they might be half as sweet! I love to read this poem over and over. I concur whole-heartedly with the poet. There is no sound sweeter than the sound of laughter, particularly the laughter of a child.

When our youngest daughter, Saje, was an infant, she had the most infectious glorious laugh I had ever heard. If something impressed her as funny, even at ten or eleven months old, she would break into raucous laughter from somewhere deep down inside her belly. When this outbreak of hilarity occurred, everyone in the family gathered around and tried to get her to repeat her beautiful laugh. We all loved sharing the joy that our baby was experiencing.

Just today, my young son, Sands, got a soccer ball stuck way up high in a palm tree after an earnest high kick at a soccer field where several hundred people were gathered. After many futile attempts to get the ball by throwing objects at it, I suggested to my friend Steve that I get on his shoulders with a rake in my hand and as he lifted me I could poke the ball free. The sight of two grown men grappling with a rake, holding on to a tree, and balancing on a friend's shoulders sent my children into spasms of laughter.

We did retrieve the ball, although we were laughing so hard that we could barely compose ourselves. But when the task was completed, scores of people approached us telling us how much they enjoyed the sideshow. The fun of solving the problem and being silly and laughing will never be forgotten by our children.

The way to cultivate the habit of laughter and a healthy sense of humor is to get reacquainted with the child that resides in each one of us, regardless of chronological age. Very often we have the tendency to equate growing up with becoming serious, as if being mature means stifling our childish laughter. The speakers I enjoy hearing inject a sizable amount of humor into their presentations, and I particularly like the ones who laugh at themselves, rather than making fun of others.

The teachers for whom I have the most reverence, without exception, had a wonderful sense of humor, and they were unafraid to bring it into the classroom, be the subject chemistry, mathematics, or literature. The people I most enjoy being around in my life are those who can laugh—frequently and raucously—and provoke the same reaction in me. All my children fit this description. When I see their faces light up with laughter I am thrilled all over. In fact, just sitting here writing these words and picturing my children laughing sends waves of good feelings throughout my body. Just *thinking* about laughing can be therapeutic!

There is something about laughter and a sense of humor that is extremely healing. I love the observation made by Voltaire, who used humor and satire so brilliantly in his writing. "In laughter," he said, "there is always a kind of joyousness that is incompatible with contempt or indignation . . ." Voltaire was reminding us of the value of the sound of laughter, saying that it is virtually impossible to be sad and to laugh at the same time. When you get into bed at night and review your day and discover that you haven't laughed very much that day, I recommend that you get out of bed and do something that constitutes pure fun. Just doing that will probably make you begin laughing! As you do, notice how much better you feel both physically and emotionally.

When Norman Cousins was told that he suffered from a disease that was virtually incurable, a deterioration of the spinal cord that would claim his life, he decided to have as many hilarious films brought to his hospital room as the family could find. He spent every day watching reruns of comedy shows such as those of the Three Stooges, Abbott and Costello, and Jack Benny. His therapy was laughter. His true story, *Anatomy of an Illness*, was a best-seller that described how he was cured of his terminal illness through the medicine of laughter. When we laugh, we literally change the chemistry of the body. We introduce peptides and endorphins into our bloodstream that can have an enormous healing impact on the body. Isn't it fascinating that tears of laughter have a different chemical makeup than tears of sadness?

Swinburne wrote of the sweetness of a child's laughter long before we had scientific medical evidence of the mind-body connection, or the medicinal value of laughter, as both tranquilizer and stimulant with no harmful side effects. Our instincts tell us that we need to laugh, to make life fun, to rid ourselves of stodgy thoughts and hardening of the attitudes. It is not just the sounds of those things around us—birds, trees in the wind, waterfalls, and rain— that are natural, as Swinburne points out in this melodious poem. There is "Something seen and heard of men" that is also natural.

The sounds of fun are the sounds that not only heal the body, as Norman Cousins told us, but also heal the spirit. An ancient Oriental proverb reminds us, "Time spent laughing is time spent with the gods." We have a natural instinct to include laughter in our lives. We all want to enliven our lives, to feel more connected to one another, to heal what ails, and to impact the world in a positive way. One of the simplest and most basic ways to achieve these lofty ideals is to spend more time just plain having fun and deliberately laughing out loud. As Swinburne puts it, "Heard from morning's rosiest height—when the soul of all delight fills a child's clear laughter."

I never really considered Saje's glorious outbursts of laughter when she was a baby as coming from the "soul of all delight," until I read this poem many times. Now I know that the natural inclination to laugh and let it out without inhibition indeed comes from a divine space inside each of us.

To put the wisdom of this poem into your life, try these suggestions:

- Spend some time observing children interacting with one another. Notice how frequently they laugh as they play. Then remind yourself of the child in you who also has those same inclinations. Be childlike and less controlled in your life and allow that inner child to express itself in fun ways.

- If you have labeled yourself as a "serious person" or someone who doesn't have a sense of humor, change the label right now. You do not have to stay stuck in any mode simply because you've become used to it.

- Make a conscious effort to laugh more often, and don't let a day go by when you fail to laugh. This is particularly important on "bad days," as Norman Cousins revealed. He changed his bad days to good days through the use of laughter.

- Invite as many fun things that will provoke laughter as you can into your life: going to amusement parks, concerts, comedy clubs, and funny and silly movies; playing fun games like Twister or Old Maid. All these kinds of activities will help you to rekindle the healing effect of laughter in your life. "Be a child, be a child." Keep repeating this valuable lesson.

- Let yourself be a little crazy, it lightens up your life. And when people ask what you're on, tell them, "I'm on endorphins!"

❀ VISUALIZATION ❀

There is a law in psychology that if you form a picture in
your mind of what you would like to be, and you keep and
hold that picture there long enough, you will soon become
exactly as you have been thinking.

WILLIAM JAMES
(1842–1910)

*American philosopher, psychologist, and teacher, William James
was a gifted writer in the fields of theology, psychology, ethics, and
metaphysics.*

William James was part of an incredibly accomplished family.
His father, Henry James, Sr., was a highly respected philosophical
theologian who developed his own philosophy based on the
teachings of Emanuel Swedenborg. William's brother, Henry, one
year younger, became a world-class novelist who wrote *Daisy
Miller, The Portrait of a Lady*, and *The Ambassadors*.

Many consider William James the father of modern psychology. In this one brief statement he offers a powerful tool for all of
us to use each and every day of our lives. It is glorious in its simplicity, and when fully understood it is also one of the great
secrets of becoming exactly the kind of person you would like to
be. Yet, because of its simplicity, it is often ignored by those who
attribute their unhappiness to factors such as bad luck, or the
gods, or circumstances, or the economy, or genetics, or family history, or a potentially endless litany of excuses explaining their
failures and flaws.

William James was a much sought after lecturer in religion,
philosophy, and psychology, which he personally transformed
from a nonscientific philosophy to a laboratory science. He abandoned the philosophy of determinism, proclaiming, "My first act
of free will shall be to believe in free will." He refers to the state-

ment at the beginning of this piece as "a law in psychology." This
process of forming a picture in our minds is often referred to as
visualization and is based on the biblical idea "As you think, so
shall ye be." This goes well beyond the idea of positive thinking. If
you want to see your life work at an entirely new level, I encourage you to discover how this law works for you.

We think in pictures, just as we dream in pictures. Not words,
sentences or phrases, but mental images. The words are symbols
enabling us to communicate or describe those pictures. It is this
picturing process that William James is saying that you control
with your free will. If you can learn to hold those pictures long
enough, without allowing anyone to weaken them, you will actually convert those pictures into your reality. You will become a co-
creator of your very existence and all that shows up in your life.

I have written an entire book, called *Manifest Your Destiny,* on
the principles involved in this process, and I choose not to repeat
those nine principles here. What I will do is offer you what I
think of as the "Four Rs" for putting this idea to work beginning
today. Here are the "Four Rs" in one sentence. *What you Really,
Really, Really, Really, want, you will get.*

The first "R" stands for what you *Really-wish.* Here is where
you form a picture of what you would like in your life, such as a
promotion, a new car, weight loss, nonaddiction, or whatever.
Once the picture is formed, you wish for it by seeing yourself in
the job, or driving the new car, or at your desired weight, or non-
addicted. Everything you manifest begins with a wish based on
an inner visualization.

The second "R" stands for what you *Really-desire.* The difference between merely having a picture in your mind that you
wish for and a desire is in your willingness to ask for it. "Ask and
you shall receive" is not an empty promise. Whatever it is that you
have wished for in your imagery, ask out loud, but privately, to
receive. "God, I am asking for your cooperation in bringing this
picture to me in a material way."

The third "R" stands for what you *Really-intend.* Now you
take the picture that you have wished for and asked for and you
frame it into a statement of intention or will. It goes like this, "I
intend to bring this picture into my world with the cooperation

of . . ." whatever you prefer to name as the creative intelligence. There is no room here for doubt with such statements as "If everything works out okay," or "If I am lucky." A statement of intention is based on the law that William James formulates for you at the beginning of this chapter.

The fourth "R" stands for what you feel *Really-passionate* about, or what I call the hardening of the will. You are unwilling to allow anyone to discourage your passionate purpose or put a damper on your picture. You resist the negative opinions of others, and you remain silent as much as possible on what you intend to produce into your life. This passion is what William James meant by "And you keep and hold that picture there long enough . . ." Those who are *Really, Really, Really, Really* accomplished at attracting into their lives all that they desire, are by no means lucky, nor do their circumstances create their desires. They have all "Four Rs" working for them at all times, and particularly the fourth "R," *Really-passionate.*

Virtually everything in my life, including all my books and tapes, are the result of applying this "law in psychology." It all begins with a wish. This book began with a *wish* I could write a book that interpreted the great wisdom of the people I've so admired all my life and what they offer all of us today even though they've all left our planet. I actually saw a picture of the various poems and contributions at the top of sixty pages, and my essays to you, the reader. I then expressed this *desire* to my wife and my agent along with my editor, at the same time that I asked for the ability and the cooperation of the universe in bringing it about.

This was followed by an *intention* to create such a book that I relayed to the various people and departments involved in the publishing process. Some liked it, some were a bit skeptical, telling me all the reasons that poetry analyses were not popular, and some discouraged me. I had my picture of the book, and I loved the idea of bringing these great masters to my readers' lives.

Finally, my *passion* took over and it was impossible for me to ignore my picture. As William James said, "You will soon become exactly as you have been thinking." And here it is, right in your hands. The key to this is putting all "Four Rs" to work and really using them.

"What is it that you weren't willing to do to make it happen?" is my response to the question I frequently hear wondering why something didn't materialize as pictured. When the passion is there, and you refuse to allow any interference from any external sources, nothing will stop you. According to William James, it is a law!

To activate this law in your life, I suggest you implement the "Four Rs." Here are my suggestions:

- Be willing to wish for anything you want. You are entitled to share in the abundance of the universe. Refuse to limit yourself or see yourself as unworthy. You are a divine creation of God, and are as much entitled to prosperity, love, and health as anyone who has ever lived on this planet.

- Express your wishes in the form of a request to your name or phrase for the creative intelligence that many call, God. Be willing to ask for help and don't be embarrassed to put your request in writing as well as voicing it. "Ask and you shall receive" is not an empty promise.

- Practice phrasing your requests in terms that eliminate doubt. Use words such as "I will," "I shall," "I intend," rather than camouflaging your desires in the wishy-washy terminology of language that seeks but doesn't expect to receive.

- As much as possible keep your pictures to yourself, along with your intentions to materialize them. When you encounter resistance, instead of using it to become discouraged, transform the negative feedback into the energy of your passion to bring your picture into clear, touchable focus.

Family and Home

ROOFS
(For Amelia Josephine Burr)

The road is wide and the stars are out and the breath of the
    night is sweet,
And this is the time when wanderlust should seize upon
    my feet.
But I'm glad to turn from the open road and the starlight
    on my face,
And leave the splendor of out-of-doors for a human
    dwelling place.

I never have seen a vagabond who really liked to roam
All up and down the streets of the world and not to have a
    home:
The tramp who slept in your barn last night and left at
    break of day
Will wander only until he finds another place to stay.

A gypsy-man will sleep in his cart with canvas overhead;
Or else he'll go into his tent when it is time for bed.
He'll sit on the grass and take his ease so long as the sun is
    high,
But when it is dark he wants a roof to keep away the sky.

If you call a gypsy a vagabond, I think you do him wrong,
For he never goes a-traveling but he takes his home along.
And the only reason a road is good, as every wanderer
    knows,
Is just because of the homes, the homes, the homes to
    which it goes.

They say that life is a highway and its milestones are the
    years,
And now and then there's a toll-gate where you buy your
    way with tears.
It's a rough road and a steep road and it stretches broad and
    far,
But it leads at last to a golden Town where golden Houses
    are.

JOYCE KILMER
(1886–1918)

American poet, remembered chiefly for his poem "Trees," Joyce
Kilmer died in battle in France during World War I.

While Sergeant Joyce Kilmer is known primarily for his twelve-
line poem that begins, "I think that I shall never see a poem lovely
as a tree," I have chosen to highlight this poetic tribute to home,
which by way of inference is a call to value and appreciate all that
a home encompasses, particularly family and loved ones. Under-
neath those roofs that Joyce Kilmer eulogized in this poem is what
we all need to be most mindful of as the greatest source of love
available to us in our lifetimes. Those roofs cover over our places
of comfort. For most of us home has a very deep significance. It
represents the anchor to our temporary earthly visit. It symbolizes
a sense of safety, and those who live there with us help guide us
through the uncertainties of a world filled with strangers. While
home life is far from idyllic for many of us, nevertheless there still
seems to be a universal sense of security in having a home to
return to regardless of how far we decide to travel.

I have visited all over this planet, and I have seen homes of
every description. People living in grass shacks in Polynesia, and
igloos in the frozen tundra. Some occupying tiny apartment
dwellings with many others in Hong Kong, and others choosing
to live in tents along the edge of the desert. Even those who are
labeled homeless usually have some location, even if it is a large
box or a spot of their own beneath a freeway overpass. The uni-

versal inclination seems to be to find some shelter that provides a source of comfort and a sense of safety and call it home.

Joyce Kilmer writes of these two unifying human inclinations both to wander and to have a place to wander back to. Truly, he is saying, it is great to be on the road, but there is no place like home. This poem appeals to me because of my own vagabond nature but my inclination to love being home. Somehow it conveys a way to combine those two seemingly opposite predilections that are present not only in me, but in most of the people that I meet and receive mail from.

All of us want to see the world, to travel, to get up and go. A common fantasy involves roaming free, as an unemployed vagabond, and letting go of all those anchors that hold us back. But at the same time, as the poet says, "the only reason a road is good, as every wanderer knows, is just because of the homes, the homes, the homes to which it goes." Everywhere you travel, you see people congregating in their shelters, and sure enough, it makes us homesick.

"Roofs" reminds us to adopt an inner attitude of appreciation for that place of shelter and comfort that we call home, to look around and count our blessings in being safe not only from the elements, but from the fear of not having a home. Moreover, these structures that we call home are more than the locations and the building materials. Under these roofs are those who care the most about us, those who have been willing to support and feed us, those who are always there regardless of how troublesome things might get.

I have known some people who appear to be kinder to strangers than they are to the people under their roof who care the most about them.

Many of our most basic problems and miseries came from our inability to deal effectively with those who reside with us under our roof. Nevertheless, for the most part there is a bond that exists between family members who share the same home, that is rarely ever severed. I think of my own brothers whom I have not lived with for many decades, whom I see only a few times during the course of a year, and yet the times of being together under one roof have bonded us in a circle of love that can never be broken. It is this feeling of connectedness to others that a home symbolizes. It cannot be measured by any accounting methods. It is a feeling of being in a state of unity with others who share that space. Joyce Kilmer asks you to treasure that feeling, and appreciate whatever it is that you call home, and whomever you have had the opportunity to live with inside the confines of those walls, and under those roofs.

By all means succumb to your travel lust, take that wide road and see all you can, but also, while on that road, know that all along those wide roads, on either side and at the end, are places that someone calls home. Therefore, when coming back and traveling down that most familiar road, stop before opening the door and feel a deep sense of appreciation not only for having a home of your own to return to, but for those before you who built a home for you to grow up in, and provided you with all your experiences, good and bad, easy and difficult. Be a wanderer today and then return to your home. It took a lot of love, and care, and food, and work, and energy to keep you out of harm's way and to make you self-sufficient. It is all that loving and caring that a home represents.

The poet who wrote these sentimental lines was a sergeant in the U.S. army during World War I. This sensitive young man who volunteered to wander far from his earthly home in New Brunswick, New Jersey, was killed in action in France in 1918 at the young age of thirty-one. His last lines of this poem seem prophetic. "It's a rough road and a steep road and it stretches broad and far, but it leads at last to a golden Town where golden Houses are."

I cannot imagine a rougher or steeper final road than the trenches of World War I, but somehow Sergeant Joyce Kilmer knew about an even grander home, where the soul resides. It is evident in the last lines of this poem, as well as in "Trees": "Poems are made by fools like me, but only God can make a tree."

Here are a few suggestions for putting the message of this poem into your life:

- Take a few moments each day to be in a state of appreciation for the immediate surroundings that you call home, regardless of how grand or humble they might be. Give thanks to those who provide this home, to those who share it with you, and to God for the blessing of a shelter.

- Do whatever you can to assist those in our world who do not have a home. While some may make the choice to be vagabonds and have a new place to call home each day, others are homeless through no deliberate choice. Be of service, financially, spiritually, or physically, to those who would love to have a more permanent place called home.

- Teach those who share your home with you to honor and revere it, not only for its physical attributes, but for the space of shelter and love that it represents.

SOLITUDE

Laugh, and the world laughs with you;
Weep, and you weep alone.
For the sad old earth must borrow its mirth,
But has trouble enough of its own.
Sing, and the hills will answer;
Sigh, it is lost on the air.
The echoes bound to a joyful sound,
But shrink from voicing care.

Rejoice, and men will seek you;
Grieve, and they turn and go.
They want full measure of all your pleasure,
But they do not need your woe.
Be glad, and your friends are many;
Be sad, and you lose them all.
There are none to decline your nectared wine,
But alone you must drink life's gall.

Feast, and your halls are crowded;
Fast, and the world goes by.
Succeed and give, and it helps you live,
But no man can help you die.
There is room in the halls of pleasure
For a long and lordly train,
But one by one we must all file on
Through the narrow aisles of pain.

ELLA WHEELER WILCOX
(1850–1919)

A theatrical personality attracted to Spiritualism, Theosophy, and mysticism, Wisconsin-born Ella Wheeler Wilcox was much loved by the readers of her volumes of poetry and her syndicated column of prose and poetry.

The title of this poem is "Solitude." I think a far more fitting title would be "Attitude"! What Ella Wilcox is saying to us via this oft-quoted poem is that whatever attitude you decide to adopt is precisely what you will attract into your life. Think sad and you attract emptiness. Think mirth and the world will laugh right along with you. This beautifully simple poem is also a very elementary presentation of energy field theory, written before fields of energy were contemplated.

Essentially, energy field theory says that there is an invisible vibratory field of energy surrounding all living objects, including human beings. This field is created by how we think and process our experiences wherever we are in the world. At certain levels of consciousness, the energy field vibrates fast. At other levels of consciousness, the energy vibrates slowly. Essentially, there is a continuum along which varying levels of consciousness are responsible for creating the field of energy.

We encounter different energy fields when we are within one another's physical proximity. Where there is strong, continuous energy for extended periods of time, even when people are gone, the field of energy can remain intense. For instance, we often feel sad or happy without realizing that we have entered a field of energy that is invisibly present. While touring the home of Anne Frank in Amsterdam, I almost had to force myself to breathe. The air seemed so heavy throughout this house which is now a museum where millions of people have come to share the story of Anne Frank.

The joyous energy field also remains in places where it predominates. In the presence of highly advanced spiritual people, one can feel love and be transformed in consciousness just by being in their field of energy. Ella Wheeler Wilcox, unknowingly captured the essence of field energy theory with those two famous opening lines; "Laugh, and the world laughs with you; weep, and you weep alone."

Many years ago while walking on the beach I had an experience that illustrates the message in this popular poem. A woman who was moving to Florida from Chicago approached me, having recognized me from a television appearance the night before. She said, "Do you live here in south Florida?" and I responded that I did and was taking a beach walk after returning from an all-night flight. Then she asked me a commonly heard question, "What are the people like here?" I responded with a question of my own: "What are the people like in Chicago?" She smiled broadly and told me how warm and friendly people were in the Midwest, and I told her immediately, "That's pretty much what you're going to find here."

On my return walk along the same beach, a woman whose husband was being transferred to Miami from New York stopped me to say that she had seen me on television the night before and had enjoyed the show. We struck up a conversation and then she asked me the same question I had heard only an hour before on the very same beach. Naturally, I asked her the same question in return. "What are the people like in New York?" She launched into a tirade on how insensitive, cliquey, and unfriendly it was in the big city, and I responded, "That's pretty much what you're going to find here." We attract into our lives pretty much what we ourselves project with our own attitudes. In general, those who feel that the world is a cesspool notice the vermin, while those who believe in the goodness of humanity see others of like mind.

Many people lament the poor quality of service in contemporary America. "You just can't got good service" is a gripe you hear daily. In fact, *Time* did a cover story on the decline of service in every field, from retail stores and restaurants to watch repair. Recently on a television show where everyone on the panel unanimously agreed on the poor quality of service, I disagreed. I explained that I felt expectation attracted what it expected. When I enter any retail store or restaurant, I *expect* to be treated cheerfully and politely, and that is pretty much what I get. If I can't find a salesperson to wait on me, I refuse to contaminate my energy field with thoughts of displeasure and disgust. Instead I begin sending out the energy that I want to find. If I encounter a surly waiter I immediately bring him into my field of energy with "Looks like it's been a tough day. I understand, and you've just been rewarded with a customer who appreciates you and how tough your job is!

Take your time." Lo and behold, the poet is right: "Be glad, and your friends are many; be sad, and you lose them all."

Your field of energy radiates at whatever vibratory frequency you generate. You are impacting and being impacted by the energy fields of many people each day. "Refuse to give energy to things you don't want or don't believe in" is a very powerful piece of advice. Any time you opt for weeping rather than laughing, sighing rather than singing, grieving rather than rejoicing, sadness rather than gladness, fasting rather than feasting, or pain rather than pleasure, you are making a choice to slow down your vibrations and to pollute your immediate mental energy field.

Every morning, as you take in your first view of day, you have the choice to say, "Good morning, God," or "Good God, morning." Whichever you choose is precisely the energy that you will invite into your life. Indeed, "There is room in the halls of pleasure for a long and lordly train." Remember Ella Wheeler Wilcox's poem while you increase the vibration of your energy field with these adjustments to your attitude:

- When experiencing any of the negatives in the poem, such as sadness, sighing and weeping, ask yourself, "Who really wants to be around me when I'm this way?" Then begin deliberately shifting out of that state.

- As you make the choice to shift states, even if you have to fake it, take notice of how you begin to attract what you want rather than what you don't want into your immediate field. The magnet you are becoming, can be either negatively or positively charged, and whichever you opt for will determine what comes rushing into your life space.

- When entering into a field where you feel there is too much negative energy, consciously make an effort to deflect the negativity by being a polar opposite. Smile in situations when all about you are frowning, and radiate cheer instead of criticism.

- Lighten up. The lighter you take yourself, and the more you detach from self-importance, the more fun you will attract into your life. We have total control over how much laughing, singing, and rejoicing we are experiencing, regardless of how much we have convinced ourselves to the contrary.

MYSTERY

POINTS TO PONDER

I have observed the power of the watermelon seed. It has
the power of drawing from the ground and through itself
200,000 times its weight. When you can tell me how it
takes this material and out of it colors an outside surface
beyond the imitation of art, and then forms inside of it a
white rind and within that again a red heart, thickly inlaid
with black seeds, each one of which in turn is capable of
drawing through itself 200,000 times its weight—when
you can explain to me the mystery of a watermelon, you
can ask me to explain the mystery of God.

WILLIAM JENNINGS BRYAN
(1860–1925)

*American political leader and orator William Jennings Bryan was
one of the most popular lecturers on the Chautauqua circuit and is
perhaps best known as a prosecutor in the celebrated Scopes trial.*

Whenever I read this observation made by William Jennings
Bryan on the power of a watermelon seed, I never fail to lapse
into a state of deep awe and appreciation for the endless miracles
that are in everything and everyone I behold. Though he is not
considered a poet, philosopher, or spiritual emissary, I included
Bryan in this collection because of this one piece he wrote on
the mysteriousness of life and what it says to each of us.

William Jennings Bryan was known as the most electrifying
orator of his time. He lost three bids for the presidency of the
United States by rather narrow margins, and he served as Secretary of State under President Wilson. Yet perhaps his most lasting
impression was as the assistant prosecutor in the famed Scopes

monkey trial in 1925, where he provided masterful oratory on a literal interpretation of the Bible and defended the doctrine of divine creation.

But this essay is not about where you stand on Darwinism versus creationism. It is about the glorious mystery of life and what it teaches each of us about living at a higher level each day. The power that is in one watermelon seed is of course invisible, yet its presence still cannot be denied. It is an awesome power indeed as illustrated by Bryan's observation that it is "capable of drawing up through itself 200,000 times its weight" and producing a perfect creation "beyond the imitation of art."

To our minds, such creativity is simply inexplicable. We know we cannot do such a thing ourselves. We sense the perfection that exists in every seed for producing life, without making a single mistake. The watermelon seed never makes the mistake of involuntarily producing a pumpkin or an apple! This force that no one can see, touch, smell, hear, or taste is perfect. Let me call this invisible perfect force a future pull, for want of a better name. This same purposeful future pull that is in the seed also is responsible for the beginning of every single human being who has ever lived anywhere at any time in this universe, including you! And I believe there has never been a mistake here as well. Everyone shows up exactly as that mysterious future pull dictates, on time, in order, looking just as it has been so ordained, and destined to leave on schedule.

Unlike the watermelon seed, however, you and I are subject to an enormous paradox. We are doomed by the future pull, in the cellular structure of our beginning seed, just like the watermelon, and at the very same time we are creatures who make choices and possess a free will. Thus the mystery for us magnifies beyond that of the watermelon. We get to contemplate the paradox of being doomed to make choices. We humans are aware of the mysterious future pull, and ponder to what extent we are drawn to a conclusion about which we have nothing to say.

F. Scott Fitzgerald, a contemporary of William Jennings Bryan, described this paradox. "The test of first rate intelligence is the ability to hold two opposed ideas in mind at the same time and still retain the ability to function. One should, for example, be able to see that things are hopeless and yet be determined to make them better." It seems to me that the lesson in both Bryan's and Fitzgerald's comments is to simultaneously choose life while serenely knowing that the mysterious future pull is doing exactly what it is supposed to be doing as our bodies age and die. Thus we are in charge and we are not in charge, both at the same time, and it is all right for these two opposites to coexist.

With this mindset in place, you are liberated from worry about what is happening to your form and all the forms you see around you. It is in the hands of the same future pull that is in the watermelon seed, and you are free to witness these mystical happenings with love and acceptance and freedom from fear.

It is a grand experience to do nothing more than just be in a state of metaphysical acceptance. In this state you look at everything, including your own body, with joyous detachment. This is the subject matter of all the poets and philosophers in this volume who express this immortal human truth: *There is life that we experience with our senses, and there is the invisible experiencer inside who is beyond our senses.* They all advise us to become aware of the mysterious future pull and then make a choice about viewing it with appreciation or judging it and being perplexed.

As you ponder William Jennings Bryan's words and the enigma of the watermelon seed realize that the same future pull is also within you. You too are a part of the drama that creates forms millions of times greater than the originating seed. Your awareness is your apparent advantage over the watermelon. You, unlike the watermelon, know that your form will follow its prescribed path, and then turn to dust. You have the greatest of all gifts, a conscious mind to contemplate all this and to be either joyful or jaded in your assessment of it.

I suggest that you take on the demeanor of one who accepts your form and its future pull, and choose to identify with that which is the actual acceptor inside; not the command center itself, but the commander inside, who is impervious to boundaries and beginnings as well as ends. Your gift is your power of awareness. You need not explain the mystery of God, since even one tiny seed containing an invisible future pull stymies all of us. Far more sensible to be aware of this presence, to feel it within

yourself, and to allow yourself the great joy of feeling connected
to it all.

Rather than being in a state of confusion over whether you
do or don't have a voice over what is called your destiny, far better to surrender and be willing to hold two opposing ideas in
your mind simultaneously. You live in a body with boundaries,
and in a boundary-less inner world at the same time.

Implement this kind of an appreciation for the mystery of life
with the following suggestions:

- Whenever you feel yourself slipping into judgment or worry,
  use your mind to shift gears. An affirmation that says, "This
  very moment is a miracle, as is everything around me," will let
  you use your thoughts in appreciation rather than anxiety.

- Remind yourself daily that everything is in order. The seed of
  a watermelon, the seed that began you, and the seed that
  began the universe all contain a future pull independent of
  your opinion about it. This is an intelligent system that you are
  a part of, and trusting in that intelligence is far more fulfilling
  than questioning it or even trying to figure it all out.

- Try to be less rational and intellectual about your life and how
  you organize it. Let go of your mental inclination to compute
  and just allow yourself to be and to be pulled by that future
  pull that is the source of your life. And by the way, enjoy the
  luscious watermelon, rather than attempting to understand it.

WORK

When you work you are a flute through whose heart
the whispering of the hours turns to music. To love
life through labor is to be intimate with life's inmost secret.
All work is empty save when there is love, for work is
love made visible.

KAHLIL GIBRAN
(1883–1931)

*Lebanese mystic, poet, dramatist and artist, Kahlil Gibran lived in
the United States after 1910.*

*I*f I were pressed to put down in percentages what part of me is
visible and what part is invisible, I would divide myself up this
way. One percent visible, ninety-nine percent invisible. This is my
conclusion based on the ancient biblical reminder, "As you think,
so shall ye be."

Our thoughts, that invisible part of our humanity, determine
everything about our physical, visible self which is the major
chunk of our earthly existence. Here also, in the invisible domain,
rests the part of us that is real, the aspect which we may think of as
the soul, or the eternal self that resists change; the death-defying
aspect of oneself. Take a few moments right now to think of *yourself* in this way. Contemplate yourself as one percent material and
ninety-nine percent spirit.

Now, with this image in place, remind yourself that all of our
actual working represents only a small portion of that one percent. Perhaps less than one-fourth of one percent of our total
humanity is invested in the actual physical activity called work.
But our thoughts about work represent the larger portion of our
humanity. Our thoughts, the soul, derived from the ninety-nine
percent are always with us. To spend our life energy over our

chosen work, immersing our soul in displeasure, anger and frustration here in the material realm of existence, is to have our priorities completely reversed. If we are ninety-nine percent invisible, then this is the place where love ought to rule supreme.

Your thoughts about the work you are doing are ninety-nine percent of who you truly are. When you hate your work, ninety-nine percent of your human essence is directed to one percent of your total humanity. These thoughts originate in the realm of yourself where feelings of inner peace reside. Kahlil Gibran calls this "life's inmost secret." If you do not love what you do and do what you love, you have chosen mayhem over music.

There is absolutely no excuse for continuing in a state where you are not doing what you love and loving what you do. You have two simple choices: (1) Change what you are doing and embrace something that you love, or (2) change how you feel about what you are currently doing to reflect the love that you want to dominate your life. To continue without making either of these choices is to sacrifice the major part of your life for the purpose of satisfying less than one percent of your humanity.

When you are born into this world your work is born with you. You have been made for some particular work, and the desire for that work was put into your heart at the moment you showed up here. If you are unable to feel connected to that purpose because you have opted to do something that you don't love, regardless of how all that got started or what keeps you there today, you can benefit greatly by listening to the poetic advice of that great Lebanese poet Kahlil Gibran. Whatever risks are involved, your humanity, your soul itself is at stake.

I know how easy it is to reject this advice. We all can find many practical and solid reasons for being unable to do what we love, but the message of the poet will never be silenced. "All work is empty save where there is love." If you want to feel empty, and sacrifice the music of your soul in nonlove every day in the name of practicality, then you have made a choice to abandon your specific purpose in this life.

But if you want to feel at work as if you are "a flute through whose heart the whispering of the hours turns to music," I invite you to shift around your inner perceptions about why you are working in the first place. Your first answer is most likely to do with making money. You think you must do what you've been trained to do, or what you've always done to keep the money flowing. I ask you to challenge this conclusion by recognizing it as a dictate of your cultural conditioning.

I suggest that you shift to doing first and foremost what you love, what your soul prompts you to do, and see if the money doesn't follow. In the ancient Hindu holy scripture, the *Bhagavad Gita,* God (Krishna) tells his student (Arjuna), "While the unwise work for the fruits of their actions, the wise offer all results of their action to me." The message is that in work, do what you enjoy, what you love, and let the universe take care of the details. Know in your heart that doing what you love, and loving what you do, is far superior to loving what you may produce or the compensation you receive for your labor.

Read Gibran's advice and contemplate the joy and playfulness in what he offers. You are a flute and your work is love made visible. The more you blur the line between work and play, the more you follow the poet's advice.

I personally make no distinction between my work and my play. I hardly know which is which. I pursue my own vision through whatever I do and I leave others to determine whether I am working or playing. As I write, I feel joy for I am doing what I love. Whether it is work or play, I simply cannot decide. The same is true when I speak, play tennis, or romp with my children. I always seem to be doing both, work and play.

Indeed, work is love made visible. I can offer no more powerful advice than Gibran provides. Do what you love, love what you do. It is a choice you can make beginning now. To do so, try these suggestions:

• Make a conscious decision to stop finding fault with your daily work activity. Practice being grateful for the opportunity to work. Send love to each person you encounter and make being joyful a deliberate act on your part, regardless of how it is received by others.

• Take the risk to make a major change, regardless of your age or seniority. Decide what you most enjoy doing in your life, regardless of whether it is dancing, gardening, writing, or working crossword puzzles. Then devise a plan to make this activity your work/play regimen for a week or two. Before long you will have overcome your cultural conditioning that says that work is what you have to do, and that it is a laborious and dull activity in order to pay the bills. Shift to the lesson that Kahlil Gibran wrote for you. "Work is love made visible."

• When you do decide to do what you love and love what you do, let go of your temptation to anticipate disaster. Stay focused on your purpose and the joy of living there, and refuse to allow other thoughts to interfere with your vision. Remember, the love you feel for what you do is a thought.

• When you are inspired in your work, everything seems to fall into place. You don't focus on lack of money, being tired, or hungry. Your inspiration alone seems to make everything you need show up right on schedule, as if God were right there with you, guiding you along. The word "inspire" originates from in-spirit. Indeed, when you are inspired you are in bliss as you are working with and for spirit.

• Work can be thought of as the daily chores of your life. Practice loving thoughtfulness in every so-called chore of your day. Notice spirit, life, soul—the ninety-nine percent of you that is invisible as you sweep, make a bed, shop, pick up a pencil, and so on. Your loving attention directed toward every physical movement you make is a beautiful and practical way of loving your life through your labor.

INSPIRATION

IF

If you can keep your head when all about you
Are losing theirs and blaming it on you;
If you can trust yourself when all men doubt you,
But make allowance for their doubting too:
If you can wait and not be tired by waiting,
Or, being lied about, don't deal in lies,
Or being hated don't give way to hating,
And yet don't look too good, nor talk too wise;

If you can dream—and not make dreams your master;
If you can think—and not make thoughts your aim,
If you can meet Triumph and Disaster
And treat those two impostors just the same:
If you can bear to hear the truth you've spoken
Twisted by knaves to make a trap for fools,
Or watch the things you gave your life to, broken,
And stoop and build 'em up with worn-out tools;

If you can make one heap of all your winnings
And risk it on one turn of pitch-and-toss,
And lose, and start again at your beginnings,
And never breathe a word about your loss:
If you can force your heart and nerve and sinew
To serve your turn long after they are gone,
And so hold on when there is nothing in you
Except the Will which says to them: "Hold on!"

If you can talk with crowds and keep your virtue,
Or walk with Kings—nor lose the common touch,
If neither foes nor loving friends can hurt you,
If all men count with you, but none too much:

If you can fill the unforgiving minute
With sixty seconds' worth of distance run,
Yours is the Earth and everything that's in it,
And—which is more—you'll be a Man, my son!

RUDYARD KIPLING
(1865–1936)

Born in India of English parents, Rudyard Kipling was a success-
ful novelist, poet, and short-story writer. During the five years he
lived in Vermont while publishing The Jungle Book *and* Cap-
tains Courageous, *his popularity in America was second only to*
that of Mark Twain.

This oft-quoted poem by Rudyard Kipling has long been a
great favorite of mine. When I read it, I picture myself with any
one of my eight children on my lap while I impart the wisdom
of the ages to his or her open and eager mind. In this fantasy my
child listens intently while I describe the secrets of the universe,
as though I am the enlightened master who has discovered them
through a lifetime of struggle, and now with fatherly wisdom pass
them on to the next generation, who will use this knowledge to
transform their world. End of fantasy!

Rudyard Kipling's poem "If" does indeed inspire such a vision
whenever I hear it, but it is purely a fantasy of mine. I have discovered truth in many of the tidbits of advice Kipling offered to
his son in this poem, but frankly I still work on applying this kind
of advice in my own life every day. This famous poem by Rudyard Kipling, who won the Nobel Prize for Literature in 1907,
has so much to offer every one of us. The lofty ideas in his four-
stanza poem inspire me to be a better man each time I read it and
share it with my children, students, and audiences. I have included
"If" in this collection because of my desire to share it with you
also. That is, I want you to feel inspired not only to be able to
help others to improve their own quality of life, but also to feel
inspired to become a better person yourself.

There are so many messages in these thirty-two lines of
poetry. Let me tell you what inspires me in this poetic advice.

I am inspired by the idea of being self-directed enough to maintain my own sense of balance and integrity when I do not allow myself to become part of the madness around me, irrespective of what others might think. "Be yourself" is the advice, not only here but in many of the selections in this book, and when I am able to do so, without judging those around me, I feel heartened. I want my children and any others who may decide to make me their teacher to cultivate their personal integrity and balance in the face of any and all circumstances.

I am inspired when I am able to use the hypocrisy I encounter to remind me of how much I dislike hypocrisy. At earlier times in my life I frequently used others' hypocrisy as a starting point for mine. If people lied to me I could, at one time, choose to give them the same treatment, even though I disliked it myself. It feels much pleasanter to dislike being lied to so much that I work at not being that way myself.

I am inspired when I am a good loser in life. I have not always been this way, and I'm not always that way now, but I am much better at it today. I love the action and competition as much as ever, and I can now retreat in peace when the contest is over, and know in my heart that the real me is unattached to outcomes. The act of participating means that you will win some and lose some, and the results are impostors, posing as the real you. I would like my children to know that they are not their victories, nor are they their defeats.

I feel terrific when I can read a lousy review of one of my books and honestly feel pretty much the same as when I read a glowing review. Trust me, it hasn't always been that way. I used to ask my agent, "Where am I on the best-seller list?" Now I know the difference between myself and my books, and I don't ever inquire, but if I did, I now know to ask, "Where is my book on the best-seller list?" Knowing the difference indeed makes all the difference. I now know that I am not what I do, I am now identified with that eternal invisible soul that watches the doings and knows that the wins and losses are mere shadows of the real me. I would love for my children and students to know this freedom.

I am inspired when I can make my decisions in life based on how I feel rather than how things will turn out. Those are the times when I can turn down a lucrative offer to host a television show in favor of speaking at a benefit and not only not worry about it, but not feel the need to mention it to anyone, and the times when I can be generous, anonymously.

I am inspired when I am able to suspend judgments based on appearances, achievements, and acquisitions, and truly only see the unfolding of God in people. The temptation to compartmentalize people by these extremes is at times overwhelming, and I talk to my children about never losing their common touch. My family has been richly blessed with the ability to purchase. I am so proud when I see them share those blessings and resist the temptation to see themselves as more valuable than others based on this purchasing power.

I am inspired when I see myself living from my heart and needing less and less to prove myself worthy. I am inspired when I can read poetry all day and then write about that rather than taking on a more financially rewarding activity. I am inspired when I notice that I no longer am compulsively attached to convincing others that I am right, even if I know the truth of what I am saying to be exactly right for me.

I want my children and my students to know the joy and fulfillment of following their own destinies and pursuing their own heroic missions, even if those around them, including me, would prefer another course.

All these qualities that Kipling so brilliantly portrays in his poem "If" signify to me what he truly means in his conclusion. If you can do all of these you too will feel inspired and "Yours is the Earth and everything that's in it, and—which is more—you'll be a Man, my son!" This was his way of saying to his son that maturity is being your own person without judgment of others. When you are grown-up in these ways you will have everything you could ever want.

To put the words of this classic poem to work in your life today I have a simple suggestion for you:

- Copy this poem and read it to yourself and those you would like to help acquire emotional and spiritual maturity. All the lessons are built right into the poem. That is, keep your head, trust yourself, be honest, be a dreamer, be detached, be a risk-taker, be independent, be humble, be compassionate, be forgiving. It is all right there in this classic poem. The question you might have now begins with the one-word title, "If" . . .

# SOUL LOVE

WHEN YOU ARE OLD
After Pierre de Ronsard

When you are old and gray and full of sleep,
And nodding by the fire, take down this book,
And slowly read and dream of the soft look
Your eyes had once, and of their shadows deep;

How many loved your moments of glad grace,
And loved your beauty with love false or true;
But one man loved the pilgrim soul in you,
And loved the sorrows of your changing face.

And bending down beside the glowing bars
Murmur, a little sadly, how love fled
And paced upon the mountains overhead
And hid his face amid a crowd of stars.

FOR ANNE GREGORY

"Never shall a young man,
Thrown into despair
By those great honey-colored
Ramparts at your ear,
Love you for yourself alone
And not your yellow hair."

"But I can get a hair-dye
And set such color there,
Brown, or black, or carrot,
That young men in despair

May love me for myself alone
And not my yellow hair."

"I heard an old religious man
But yesternight declare
That he had found a text to prove
That only God, my dear,
Could love you for yourself alone
And not your yellow hair."

WILLIAM BUTLER YEATS
(1865–1939)

*Irish poet and dramatist William Yeats is generally considered one
of the greatest poets of the twentieth century.*

William Butler Yeats was a fascinating visionary who sought wisdom and brotherhood through mysticism and loved to write of the soul's cry for release from the material world of circumstance. Indisputably one of the most significant modern poets, and renowned as a dramatist, Yeats was an Irish National politician when Ireland became a free state in 1922, and he received the Nobel Prize for Literature in 1923. He was consumed by his interest in the occult and magic, as well as the sinister forces that seemed to be drawing the world toward a cataclysmic battle of good versus evil. He died shortly before the outbreak of World War II.

In addition to writing of Ireland, Yeats wrote of a love that transcended preoccupation with physical beauty. He had fallen in love with Maud Gonne, an Irish beauty who was also brilliant and a rebel, and whose passion was lavished on Ireland. She rejected Yeats's overtures and refused his proposal of marriage. Interestingly, Maud's daughter also later rejected his proposal of marriage. He had many loves but was not married until the age of fifty-two.

The two selections here represent his poetic embrace of love that is inspired by more than a physical attraction. In 1907 Yeats had traveled through Italy with Anne Gregory, a beautiful woman with golden hair. He writes to her, "That only God, my dear, could love you for yourself alone and not your yellow hair." This same theme appears in "When You Are Old": "How many loved your moments of glad grace, and loved your beauty with love false or true; but one man loved the pilgrim soul in you, and loved the sorrows of your changing face." Here he says to you and me, the truest test of love has nothing to do with appearances, and though I admire your outward beauty, I urge you to love as God does, for yourself alone.

One of my most memorable moments as a doctoral student in the 1960s occurred during a seminar in an advanced course on counseling psychology, taught by the most prestigious professor at the university. I, along with eleven others, studied the research and conclusions on self-actualization, including the specific characteristics of highly functioning people. These exceptional people, some of them historical figures, were called self-actualizers. The purpose of this advanced seminar was to teach us how to identify these traits and to help others embrace them to live fuller and more deeply passionate lives.

The traits of these self-actualizers included appreciation for beauty, sense of purpose, resistance to enculturation, welcoming the unknown, high enthusiasm, inner-directedness, detachment from outcome, independence of the good opinion of others, and absence of a compelling need to exert control over others. Each week we discussed the strategies we could employ as therapists to encourage clients to become self-actualized. At the halfway point of the semester, our distinguished professor gave the midterm examination, which consisted of only the following question.

"A self-actualized person arrives at a dinner party at which everyone is dressed in formal attire. He is wearing blue jeans, a T-shirt, sneakers, and a baseball hat. What does he do? You have thirty minutes to write your answer." All twelve of us wrote furiously for the next half-hour, and then we were each asked to read our responses aloud. Some of the responses I remember were: He wouldn't pay attention to those appearances; he wouldn't leave or make excuses; he would just act as if nothing were amiss; he would just go on and enjoy the gathering and not worry about how others perceived him. I remember feeling particularly proud of my answer, which dealt with his feeling of purpose and a higher mission.

When all of us had finished reading our answers, our professor said, "I'm sorry, you have all failed the midterm exam. You only needed to write three words. And he proceeded to put the three words on the chalkboard. "He wouldn't notice."

The highest level of awareness is one in which the self-actualized person does not notice appearances and sees only the unfolding of God in each person encountered. It is this kind of love that William Butler Yeats writes of in these two selections.

What a challenge! To look past what we see with our eyes and to feel total affection for the soul, rather than the physical appearance. What a challenge in a society where we are bombarded with advertising propaganda designed to sell us products that are almost exclusively about improving physical appearances! In this mindset, wrinkles must be hidden or, better yet, removed by surgical procedures; silver hair must be disguised; and all signs of a natural aging process must be concealed.

Yeats asks us to look beyond those advertising messages, to love in a God-like way that has nothing to do with outward appearances, to literally not notice superficial characteristics. We all had this ability at one time in the past. There was a time when we didn't notice the color of the skin or the shape of a playmate's eyes. When the conditioning process of our culture took over, we began to identify more on the basis of the appearance of the container than on the soul inside the package.

Four of the most powerful lines of poetry I've ever read are in one of my favorite Yeats poems, "Sailing to Byzantium."

> An aged man is but a paltry thing,
> A tattered coat upon a stick, unless
> Soul clap its hands and sing, and
>   louder sing
> For every tatter in its mortal dress.

As physical beings we are all eventually heading toward being "a tattered coat upon a stick." If we love only for what we observe with our senses, that becomes a paltry thing indeed. But when the soul claps its hands and sings, the aging part becomes insignificant. Yeats asks you to first look beyond the superficial, and then, when this becomes your self-actualized way of being, to get to the point where you don't even notice. Let the soul of those you love receive your attention, and while you're at it, do yourself a favor and let your own soul clap its hands and receive your applause. Love yourself as God does, for yourself alone.

Here are some suggestions for adopting this kind of love into your life:

- Begin to see yourself as a soul with a body rather than a body with a soul. Look at those indicators of aging as merit badges and try to look past them into the part of yourself that has never aged and never will.

- Ignore the incessant propaganda that bombards your consciousness each day encouraging you to hang on to eternal youth and to judge yourself and others on the basis of appearances only. Be proud of yourself not for how you look, but for the content of your character. Repeat often the famous phrase from *La Cage aux Folles*, "I am what I am."

- When meeting others see first the unfolding of God in those people and resist the temptation to talk about the superficial traits that you've been trained to focus on. Simply comment on others on the basis of their inner beauty and refuse to partake of gossip that emphasizes appearances.

- When telling the persons that you love of your feelings emphasize what you truly love about them rather than how they happen to look. Talk to their eternal soul rather than the garage that houses it.

I came out alone on my way to my tryst. But who is this
   me in the dark?
I move aside to avoid his presence but I escape him not.
He makes the dust rise from the earth with his swagger;
He adds his loud voice to every word I utter.
He is my own little self, my lord, he knows no shame;
but I am ashamed to come to thy door in his company.

RABINDRANATH TAGORE
(1861–1941)

One of the leading personalities of modern India, mystic and painter Rabindranath Tagore received the Nobel Prize for Literature. His works are classics, renowned for their lyrical beauty and spiritual poignancy.

*T*here are two people living inside each of us. The first person I call ego. Ego wants to be right. Ego also believes that he is separate from everyone else and that he is competing with all those others. He feels that his very existence depends on being better than everyone else. Consequently he strives to have not only more things, but more expensive things. He feels best when he is able to defeat someone else, and thus he evaluates his worth as a person, on the basis of how he stacks up to all those others he so desperately wants to conquer. If he is number one this is his dream come true. But being in the top ten percent is still pretty good, and staying in the top half is absolutely essential.

Ego not only loves to win, he needs it desperately and he is always in a state of striving. He wallows in his achievements, counts his awards, rewards, and badges of honor frequently. Ego can have the nicest cars, fanciest clothes, finest foods, most spectacular drugs imaginable, kinkiest sex, and all manner of pleasures, and when they have all worn off and become passé, a brand-new list of demands appears. Ego is impossible to satisfy as long as there is someone out there whom he must defeat, or more stuff to buy and own so that he can be a winner. He strives, but he never arrives.

The second person residing inside each of us I call spirit. He is not interested in any of the same things that capture the fancy of ego. He could care less about acquiring anything, he is not the least bit interested in being better than anyone else, let alone in defeating others. In fact, he never even compares himself to anyone. He only seems to want one thing, and is single-minded when it comes to this desire. Spirit overlooks all the needs of his omnipresent twin, ego, and desires only to be at peace. Yes, spirit is the desire to be at peace.

When it comes to competition, he will compete, but he never feels any need to lord it over those who also compete. When it comes to possessions, spirit truly enjoys them, but never seems to be possessed by them, and is just as likely to give them away. While the mantras of ego include more and better, spirit's mantra is always the same: peace. He radiates this peace to others and promotes this kind of tranquillity at all times, even in the midst of chaos.

Here they are then, our two constant inner companions, ego and spirit. The question is not how to slay one in favor of the other, but how to subdue the part that keeps us in a perpetual state of turmoil and never allows any peace. How can we move from striving to arriving? I ask myself this question many times in the course of a day. Who am I allowing to run things here? In fact, I wrote an entire book on the subject; maybe to help myself understand the power I had given to my ego in my own life. I called it *Your Sacred Self*, and it is devoted to the theme of Tagore's famous dialogue with Krishna (God) at the beginning of this essay.

How can we tame the part of ourselves that feels separate from everyone else and needs to conquer, win, and acquire in order to feel good? I have borrowed thoughts from famous poets like Tagore and Rumi, who are essential contributors not only to this book, but to my daily life, and created the following prayer that I say each morning on my way to begin the day.

Dear God, my ego is demanding, pushy, obsessed with being right and is always in search of more. It never seems to be satisfied. My sacred self is inclined to being peaceful, noncompetitive, nonjudgmental, and it never makes demands. Please send messages from one to the other.

Tagore in his dialogue with God is doing much the same thing. He wonders, "Who is this me in the dark" that he cannot seem to escape; who is this who swaggers through life with his self-importance infecting every word, who is shameless. But also he recognizes that the entranceway to the highest realm is blocked by this shameless "little self." This poet was given the Nobel Prize for Literature in 1913 for one of his greatest collections of poetry, yet felt no kinship with such an honor. He lived his life writing about how to rid oneself of identification with such prizes.

Reading Tagore's sensitive poems, and this particular piece, offer each of us a valuable reminder of the benefits of subduing the ego and listening to the spirit who beckons us to peace. The "dust rising from the earth" is the turmoil that will clog your life pores if you ignore spirit and fail to see ego's responsibility for the dust. Tagore personified quiet dignity and a peaceful countenance in his life, which is reflected in his beautifully simple poetry.

Here are some suggestions for applying the wisdom of Tagore's poetry into your daily life:

- Listen to your heart before you react to anyone. See if you can tame your ego once today. Before speaking, ask yourself, "Is what I am about to say for the purpose of making someone else wrong and proving myself special? Will I create more turmoil or more serenity?" Then make the decision to be kind and loving. Notice how your ego reacts and allow it to take a less dominant role once or twice a day until it becomes a habit, a new way of being.

- Be aware of how frequently you use "I" in conversation and see if you can let your sentences begin with "you" a few times each day. Pass up the need to brag and boast in favor of applauding the accomplishments of others.

- Work at being less attached to the things you've accumulated and begin a practice of letting go. Giving more of yourself to others by giving some of your stuff away is a helpful way to tame the attachment to acquisitions and to retrain ego and allow the peace that spirit desires.

- Converse with your ego in much the same way I do in my daily prayer. Speak from your highest self. Here is an example of a letter to her ego that Shirley Ross Korber wrote to me after reading *Your Sacred Self.*

> Journaling is a daily routine for me and has been for thirteen years. This morning I wrote a letter in my journal to my ego. It is as follows:
>
> "Dear Ego, you are hereby given notice that we have a new leader. You are welcome to stay on as a silent partner. I (my sacred self) am taking over my life and my business. I have brought in the number one consultant in the universe, God. God and I will confer on the restructuring of my life and my business. You will no longer have a voice in any of my decisions. I have no bad feelings towards you, but it is not in my best interests or those of my business to allow you to influence my decisions."

PRIVACY

Strength of numbers is the
delight of the timid.
The Valiant in spirit glory in
fighting alone.

MOHANDAS KARAMCHAND GANDHI
(1869–1948)

Known as Mahatma, which means "great soul," Gandhi advocated nonviolence in his fight for independence and civil rights for the people of India.

*B*oth the secret for manifesting what you desire into your life and the mysteries of quantum physics are partially revealed in these words of Mohandas Gandhi. This is clearer when we consider that we can divide the universe of our personal experience into the seen and the unseen, or the material and the spiritual. The world of the seen is what we experience with our senses. It is this world that we are most interested in when it comes to having the things that we desire.

But where do *things* come *from*? How does this so-called reality manifest? Quantum physicists search for the answer to that question, and I contend that the first quantum physicist was not Bohr, or Einstein, but St. Paul, one of the authors of the New Testament. In the words of St. Paul, "That which is seen hath not come from that which doth appear." It seems to me that St. Paul stated precisely what contemporary quantum physicists have concluded: *Particles themselves are not responsible for their own creation.* Quantum mechanics involves studying matter (the material world) at the tiniest level while looking for the source of our physical world. The conclusion is that the world of the seen comes from the world of the unseen. So how does all this relate to Gandhi's viewpoint of the valiant in spirit fighting alone? Read on.

The two divisions of our one reality are ego and spirit. Ego is often described as standing for Earth Guide Only because one cannot create or manifest from the dimension of ego; and the unseen world is called spirit. Particles (the material itself) are not responsible for their own creation. To manifest your dreams you must be free of your ego. Ego is nothing more than an idea you carry around that insists you are separate and in competition with others, and also separate from God (or your source). As long as you believe yourself to be separate from everyone and from your source, you lose the power of your source. When you reconnect to your source, or make conscious contact with the unseen (spirit) you regain the power of your source. This means you regain the power to manifest, to heal, and to attract what you desire into your life. However, even reconnected to source, ego wants to be involved.

The moment that you begin to tell others about what you desire and how you are going to create the kind of life you know is your personal destiny, you invite ego. As you begin explaining your radical ideas you will be asked to defend yourself. Then you will feel the need to argue about how this fits or fails to fit into the perceptions of those you are talking to. And most debilitating of all, you will be expected to listen to the logic of those you choose to share your dreams with as they tell you to "get real" and look around at the circumstances of your life.

Once the ego becomes involved, you literally lose the ability to create what your heart tells you is your destiny. Thus, by sharing your innermost desire you seek out the strength of numbers, which Gandhi says is the "delight of the timid." Make no mistake about it, the timid do not manifest their own dreams, they join the ranks of the unfulfilled.

By fighting alone for what you know to be your destiny, regardless of what others say, you become the "valiant in spirit" who "glory in fighting alone." Spirit is the source of all that you see, all that you witness, all that you observe. You can reconnect by avoiding ego's influence. This means specifically keeping your dreams to yourself and sharing them only with God, or whatever you call that invisible source of everything in our material world. Reconnect to that source and regain all the powers of that source; invite the ego and you ensure separation from your source.

As a young man I had a vision of creating financial independence. I shared my "plan" with family and friends. Each time I related how I was going to first pay myself one-fifth of everything I earned, before anything was spent elsewhere, I heard all sorts of objections to my financial strategy. I remember being told, "You're out of touch with reality. You can't save twenty percent of your income, pay taxes, pay your bills, and take care of your family, it's impossible." I defended my plan, explaining how compounding the interest and not touching the principle would lead to living off the tax-free interest in less than fifteen years. But I would become discouraged listening to the "experts" who were majoring in poverty. I learned to keep my mouth shut and proceed silently. I found that the less I needed to tell others of my vision, the faster my vision began materializing.

By removing my dream from the ego state, and instead relying on the silent power, I attracted into my life a financial independence that reflected my inner vision. Gandhi's words remind me of that earlier time of my life, and they are a succinctly powerful reminder in today's world. Resist the need to have many people endorse your dreams and instead be a valiant spirit who glories in trusting your inner guidance. Another way of saying this is less sophisticated but equally as profound: "If you follow the pack, you are going to end up stepping in a lot of what they leave behind."

My suggestions for putting Gandhi's words into practice include the following:

- When you are about to seek the endorsement of anyone for your dreams, stop and remember that once the ego becomes involved, you lose both your spiritual and your scientific means for creating what you want.

- To satisfy your need to announce your plans, describe in a journal what you are going to manifest into your life. At the very least, your journal will not give you reasons to doubt your dreams.

- Keep uppermost in mind that the process of creation moves from the unseen to the seen, from the spirit to the material. Trust deeply in your ability to make conscious contact with that invisible world. Conscious contact is the difference between knowing *about* God and *knowing* God.

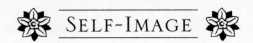
This is the true joy in life: The being used for a purpose recognized by yourself as a mighty one. The being a force of nature, instead of a feverish, selfish little clod of ailments and grievances complaining that the world will not devote itself to making you happy. I am of the opinion that my life belongs to the whole community, and as long as I live, it is my privilege to do for it whatever I can.

I want to be thoroughly used up when I die—for the harder I work, the more I live. I rejoice in life for its own sake. Life is no "brief candle" to me; it is a sort of splendid torch which I have got hold of for the moment, and I want to make it burn as brightly as possible before handing it on to future generations.

GEORGE BERNARD SHAW
(1856–1950)

Irish dramatist, critic, and social reformer George Bernard Shaw used his plays and essays as vehicles for his theories and causes, some of which were political and economic socialism, a new religion of creative evolution, antivivisection, vegetarianism, and spelling reform.

George Bernard Shaw worked into his nineties as a brilliant dramatist, literary critic, lecturer, music critic, theater critic, and essayist on every subject imaginable. He won and refused the Nobel Prize for Literature in 1925 for *Saint Joan*, and he is best remembered for his mesmerizing *Man and Superman*, and of course, *Pygmalion*, from which *My Fair Lady* was adapted. This one passage perfectly reflects how George Bernard Shaw, the most significant Irish playwright since the seventeenth century, lived his life.

I was ten years old when Shaw died, and I still remember reading about his passing. I seem to always have been attracted to his life philosophy. Here he promotes living as if we are being used for a purpose that we recognize as "a mighty one." This idea of seeing ourselves as naturally purposeful speaks directly to our self-image. Does anyone aspire to the image he describes as "a feverish, selfish little clod of ailments and grievances complaining that the world will not devote itself to making you happy"? Probably not, yet don't we all see people who fit this description?

People who enjoy life as if their being is a force of nature are doers who are fully alive, have little patience for complainers and whiners, and generally are active every day of their lives. They are not active just to stay busy, but are rejoicing in their life activities. They have no time or interest for petty grievances, nor are they preoccupied with this kind of activity themselves. Shaw asks us to let go of our self-absorption and get involved in the true joy of life, which is to feel that you are being used for a purpose.

In this passage the dynamic and witty philosopher conveys his enormous enthusiasm for life and encourages us to embrace a comparable attitude toward everyone and everything. Let go of grumbling, moaning, and passivity by changing how you choose to perceive life in general, says Shaw. He asks us to rejoice in life, not for the outcomes and rewards that come our way, but purely and simply for its own sake. This advice, from one of the greatest examples of a fully functioning person, is to shuck your passivity and your search for a reason to be happy. Instead, bring a joyful knowing that your life has a natural purpose to everyone you meet and everything you do. How does one accomplish this?

My personal way is to remove myself from the energy fields of those who violate the principles that Shaw is writing about. When I begin to hear grievances, complaining, and bitching, I deliberately and quietly move out of that space as quickly as possible. Generally I will do or say nothing that might be interpreted as rejection. I simply refuse to have that kind of energy in my immediate surroundings. I have also found that the less I verbalize, the less I have to complain about. Almost twenty years ago I decided to stop using these sentences: "I'm tired," "I don't feel well," or "I'm getting a cold." This was a conscious choice based on my reading of this particular phrase of Shaw's, which I partially included in some of my earliest writing. By not using these sentences, I was forced to rethink my inner attitudes about fatigue and illness. I found that just by eliminating the verbal grievances I generally did not have those ailments in my life.

When I encounter other people telling me how tired they are, or how they feel a cold coming on, I usually respond, "Don't think tired thoughts," or "Don't think 'cold' thoughts." I often receive a puzzled look, yet the message is conveyed and I also let them know that I am not going to be seduced into a discussion of their complaints and grievances.

If you are willing to apply this advice, this one selection of George Bernard Shaw's, taken to heart, can literally change the state of your mind. If each day you see yourself as a mighty one and forgo self-importance and complaints in favor of viewing life as a splendid torch that illuminates your life in a magnificent way, you will know what Shaw means by "the true joy of life." I love the idea of being thoroughly used up when we die. To me this means not having thoughts that keep us immobilized or in any way removed from our own heroic mission. It means absolutely refusing to think and act in any way that denies that we are a force of nature, and here for a purpose. Any inner thoughts that keep us from knowing and mobilizing this force will be first identified and then, step by step, rejected. It means that you are not going to die with your music still in you!

You may feel that this advice is fine for a genius like George Bernard Shaw, but does not apply to you, because in many ways you do see yourself as a selfish little clod. This attitude reflects a self-image that you have chosen to adopt, and the essential message here is that you also can choose to change that self-image. Remember, self-image derives from the self, and it is not the responsibility of anyone else. It is purely yours.

These words have guided my life since I first read them as a young man. Try these alternatives to being in any way described as a "feverish, selfish little clod," if you want to put them to work for you:

- Remove from your vocabulary statements about anything that you do not want to manifest into your life. Catch yourself

when announcing your ailments, fatigue, or fears, and stay
silent rather than radiating a self-fulfilling prophecy.

- Remove yourself physically as subtly as you can from those
  who persistently insist on burdening you with their grievances.

- Put energy into your life by taking on new interests or projects, and generally being consumed with rejoicing in life. Dis-
  continue dismal habits that you've adopted which reflect a
  poor self-image. Eliminate self-denigrating labels or comments
  and let others who do this to you know privately that you do
  not want to be identified this way any longer.

- Be a doer rather than a critic, complainer, or explainer. Let
  who you are speak for you, and get in the habit of no longer
  suffering fools gladly.

- Ignore criticism. My favorite quote from Albert Einstein, a
  contemporary of Shaw's, hangs on a poster in my office.
  "Great spirits have always encountered violent opposition
  from mediocre minds." You are a great spirit! Live that way.

SUFFERING

from *Sayings of Paramahansa Yogananda*

Man has falsely identified himself with the pseudo-soul or ego. When he transfers his sense of identity to his true being, the immortal Soul, he discovers that all pain is unreal. He no longer can even imagine the state of suffering.

PARAMAHANSA YOGANANDA
(1893–1952)

Born to a devout, well-to-do Bengali family, Paramahansa Yoga-nanda graduated from Calcutta University in 1915 and estab-lished the Self-Realization Fellowship in Los Angeles in 1920 to offer a science of spiritual exploration for self-harmony leading to a more compassionate and peaceful world. His Autobiography of a Yogi *introduced millions to India's age-old philosophy of yoga and its time-honored tradition of meditation.*

*P*aramahansa Yogananda's message of divine inspiration—that it is possible to imagine suffering is impossible—may seem impossible to you. I have included this statement from a man I deeply admire precisely to encourage you to look at this business of suffering in a way that will very likely lead you to see your life from an entirely new perspective. You are invited to let go of some firmly entrenched ideas and the false identity Yogananda refers to.

In the essence of your true being—what Yogananda calls the "immortal soul"—pain is unreal. We, though, live in a world that is real, with problems that are definitely real, and with elements of suffering that you know to be real. This advice to transfer our sense of identity and enter a space in which we can no longer even imagine suffering probably seems impossible.

An answer that works for me is to become as a spectator, wherein I lose attachment to the impermanent. A great teacher of mine, Nisargadatta Maharaj, put it this way, "You do not suffer, only the person you imagine yourself to be suffers. You cannot suffer." Once again, he refers to your true being as that which is quite distinct from your ego/body. Overcoming your inclination to believe so strongly in your suffering by becoming the spectator to your life is an awesome challenge.

Let's take the most common kind of suffering, which is called pain. Suppose you are in some kind of pain, such as a severe headache, and you don't want to hear some swami telling you that it isn't real or it is only in your imagination. But bear with me here just for a moment to see if you can let go of your attachment to that suffering. What if you could become a spectator to that ache in your head by actually transferring your sense of identity to what Yogananda calls your true being?

By putting your attention on that ache you could identify its precise location, describe its size, color, shape, and any and all characteristics of it that you perceive. If you concentrated long enough, you could actually move that pain from one point in your head to another. Once you have accomplished this movement, you have the new awareness that you can move it right out of your head as well. This means that the suffering was eliminated by your becoming the observer and detaching yourself completely from the painful experience. Some call this activity mind control, but I see it as a powerful means to stop identifying ourselves with what we have come to call suffering.

Most of the suffering we experience outside of outright physical pain occurs because of our identification with our own self-importance. As I was planning how I would approach this topic of ego and suffering I recalled a conversation I had with my close friend Deepak Chopra. As I debated whether to include what he had told me in that conversation, the telephone rang, and sure enough, it was Deepak calling. I told him that only ten seconds before I had jotted down his name on a piece of paper to remind myself about what he had said about ego and suffering, and I meant to call him to get it correctly.

He chided me, saying, "I got your message in the unified field and so I called you." What he had told me was how a Buddhist teacher had been asked what one single thing could he always remember and use when he felt himself in any state of suffering. The teacher said, "Just remember this and you will never suffer again. Nothing should be clung to as me or mine." Here are nine words that if repeated often enough, particularly when you feel sorrow and therefore suffering, could eliminate that false identity with the ego. The ego is all about self-importance.

Deepak and I talked for a few more moments and he said, "As long as you are writing about the ability to end suffering, I suggest that you give your readers a phrase from the Ojibway Native American tribes that I use on myself whenever I get too involved in my own self-importance by getting upset over some trivial matter." He said, "I simply repeat this phrase to myself and almost by magic the mental suffering disappears." So here it is, from the Ojibway via Deepak Chopra, through me, and to you. "Now and then I go about pitying myself and all the while my soul is being blown by great winds across the sky."

It is a wonderful image to call into play when you feel that you are suffering and you become immersed in your own self-importance. As a spectator, you can observe your suffering, and from that vantage point you can actually choose to love it and give yourself to it completely. You can treat it as a great gift that will help you to let go of that identity crisis with your pseudo-soul, and to put your inner attention and energy on that which is able to watch all that sorrow from a completely detached point of view.

This is an extremely liberating approach to ending all suffering. When you live as Yogananda did, you can actually say, "I can't even imagine the state of suffering." Somehow I can hear Yogananda saying that you should learn to rejoice in suffering, for everything is done by God for one's own betterment. The pain is a messenger to remember God and your soul being blown across the sky, invisible though it may be, and then pain is not pain anymore, and suffering is not suffering anymore, and you will have removed your vulnerability to sorrow and suffering by no longer identifying with your body/mind.

This is not some trick, it is a here-and-now means for looking at all your attachments, all your "me" and "mine," all your self-importance, and reidentifying yourself with that which is eternal. Truly this works, and you do discover, as Yogananda promises, that all pain is unreal.

To make this divine advice come to life for you, begin to:

- Make an honest assessment of what you feel is the source of your sorrow or suffering. Then begin a practice of repeating to yourself, "The cause of any suffering is in me alone, and I am going to stop blaming anyone or anything for it."

- Now make an effort to notice everything you can about your actual state of suffering. If it is just a mental state of sorrow, note where it lives, where it shows up, what its appearance is, and every characteristic you can identify.

- When you find yourself in a state of self-pity, try repeating the words of the Ojibway to yourself. You will soon see how trivial your self-suffering feelings are in comparison to your eternal soul that knows absolutely nothing of such feelings.

- Ask yourself, as I always do, "What is the lesson for me in this experience?" Once I know that I have something to learn from this sorrow, as I have from all the disappointments and sorrows of my life, I can turn that sorrow into a song almost instantly.

❧ LOVE'S ENERGY ❧

Someday, after we have mastered
the winds, the waves, the tide
and gravity, we shall harness for God
the energies of love.
Then, for the second time in the history
of the world, man will have discovered fire.

PIERRE TEILHARD DE CHARDIN
(1881–1955)

*French-born Jesuit priest, paleontologist, scientist, and philosopher
Pierre Teilhard de Chardin made his lifework the reinterpretation
of Christianity in the light of evolution. He perceived matter and
spirit as two distinct aspects of one single cosmic stuff without the
need for any intellectual conflict.*

$\mathcal{P}$ierre Teilhard de Chardin writes here of a theme that, once
understood by each of us, will have a monumental impact on
humanity. He speaks of love and energy as being interconnected,
suggesting that love contains within it an energy that can unite
human beings because it alone joins all of us by what is deepest
within ourselves. Think of the magnitude of what this brilliant
philosopher and man of God offers us with this observation. He
assumes that the time will come when we will learn how to tame
the winds, waves, tides, and gravity to make them subordinate to
our endless need to supply energy for ourselves as a people.

Notice that all of these energy sources are movements orches-
trated by an invisible power supply. No one has ever seen the
wind; all we can observe are the results of the wind. We watch the
trees rustle, see the rain swirl in the air, and feel the air on our
faces, but the wind itself remains an unseen thing. So too with
waves, tide, and gravity.

We watch as the waves move ceaselessly against the shore, in and out on schedule each day, and yet what it is that is doing the moving remains impervious to our investigation. We see objects falling from trees, but what propels them downward is also a mystery to our sensory apparatus. Now consider for a moment the latent power, virtually untapped, in love. All we ever get to see are the results of the energy. No one can agree on what or where it is, yet we all know and feel it when its results are made manifest.

Within each and every cell of our individual humanity are infinitesimal atoms and subatomic particles. When we line up a given number of electrons within one atom of one molecule we produce a force that is a mystery. I will not pretend to know the scientific formula, but let's say theoretically that an atom contains one billion electrons. When we artificially line them up one at a time, one right under the other, eventually we reach what physicists call a critical mass. Theoretically we get 375 million electrons lined up, with the remaining 625 million flitting about randomly. When we align the 375 millionth electron, a force within the structure of the atom propels all the remaining electrons to align as well. This point is called phase transition, the point at which the inner force within a cell, or a molecule, or an atom, or a subatomic particle is activated to create this new alignment. This energy within a cell is what Pierre Teilhard de Chardin called love. He put it this way: "Love is the affinity which links and draws together the elements of the world . . ."

Now think of yourself as one cell in the total body of humanity, which contains some six billion cells. When each of us aligns in a certain way, we too reach a critical mass. The field of energy created by that critical mass is love. Just as it does in the microcosm, it produces results in the macrocosm, or the material world as we see it. Teilhard speaks of humanity reaching this critical mass and igniting the invisible force of love as equivalent to the discovery of fire. This begins with individuals aligning in ways that spiritual teachers have indicated throughout the history of this world.

Pierre Teilhard de Chardin was both extremely well respected and virtually unknown during his lifetime. As a Jesuit priest he was prohibited from publishing certain ideas, and the major body of his teachings was not published until after his death. The essence of his philosophy is that there is a mental and social evolution drawing us toward a spiritual unity. We need only to "imagine our ability to love developing until it embraces the totality of men and of earth . . ." He called this latent energy of love the universal synthesizer. Love is an energizing elixir with a power to nurture and bring together humanity in much the same way that cavemen were drawn to the first bonfire. Imagine, if you will, a similar state of wonder and the impact on our survival of a discovery with the magnitude of fire.

We can apply the teaching of Teilhard by understanding that injuring a single human being is injuring the divine power within each of us. This universal synthesizer, love, is part of all of us just as each electron shares the force within the confines of one atom. Thus when we act with any mean-spiritedness in our thoughts or actions, we literally inhibit the phase transition that will lead us to discover fire for the second time in the history of the world. Every single act of hatred or injury toward another is an action that keeps us from harnessing the energy of love. It may sound gushy and way too sugary to accomplish, but I believe we can all tame our mean-spiritedness and bring about this universal phase transition that Pierre Teilhard de Chardin predicted was our destiny.

I am reminded of my all-time favorite biblical quotation, the famous statement on love in I Corinthians 13, which begins: "If I speak in the tongues of men and of angels, but have not love, I am only a resounding gong or a clanging cymbal." It continues beautifully saying we gain nothing without love. It speaks of the patience and kindness of love; the absence of envy, boasting, rudeness, self-seeking; and how love does not delight in evil, but rejoices with truth, and concludes with this formidable message. "And now these three remain; faith, hope, and love. But the greatest of these is love."

Yes, even greater than faith and hope is the ability and willingness to cultivate love. How do we cultivate love? We can let go of impulses to judge others. We can refuse to feel good about the mistakes or sufferings of anyone. We can *live* the lessons of kindness rather than only read about them in church. We can remove our desire for revenge and replace it with forgiveness. We can choose love wherever and whenever we are by simply making that choice. This energy is so powerful that it literally holds together every cell in our universe. It is the glue that unites us. Robert Browning described our world without love: "Take away love and our earth is a tomb." You know when the energy of love is absent, and you can do your part to revive the energy of life with love.

You can put Teilhard's famous words to work in your own life right now. Here are a few suggestions for harnessing the energies of love:

- See yourself as the one cell in this body called humanity that can activate the energy for that phase transition to universal love. You do make a difference, and every thought of love, followed by an action, moves us a step closer to discovering fire for the second time.

- Push out thoughts of judgment, revenge, anger, and hatred by becoming aware of them as they surface. Simply tell yourself, "I don't want to think this way, and I refuse to allow it anymore."

- When confronted by mean-spiritedness and hateful gossip, respond to it from your position of love: "I don't want to make any judgments. " Rather than criticizing the mean-spirited person, silently project love. Be the person in any gathering who defends the absent in a kindly manner.

- Frame I Corinthians 13 in your home as we have done. I read it every time I walk down the hallway to the children's bedrooms, and it reminds me that the greatest gift I can offer them, and the world, is the universal synthesizer. Love!

INDIVIDUALITY

here is little Effie's head
whose brains are made of gingerbread
when the judgment day comes
God will find six crumbs

stooping by the coffinlid
waiting for something to rise
as the other somethings did—
you imagine His surprise

bellowing through the general noise
Where is Effie who was dead?
—to God in a tiny voice,
I am may the first crumb said

whereupon its fellow five
crumbs chuckled as if they were alive
and number two took up the song,
might i'm called and did no wrong

cried the third crumb, I am should
and this is my little sister could
with our big brother who is would
don't punish us for we were good;

and the last crumb, with some shame
whispered unto God, my name
is must and with the others i've
been Effie who isn't alive

just imagine it I say
God amid a monstrous din
watch your step and follow me
stooping by Effie's little, in

(want a match or can you see?)
which the six subjunctive crumbs
twitch like mutilated thumbs:
picture His peering biggest whey

coloured face on which a frown
puzzles, but I know the way—
(nervously Whose eyes approve
the blessed while His ears are
crammed

with the strenuous music of
the innumerable capering damned)
—staring wildly up and down
the here we are now judgment day

cross the threshold have no dread
lift the sheet back in this way.
here is little Effie's head
whose brains are made of gingerbread.

E. E. CUMMINGS
(1894–1962)

One of the most gifted and independent poets of his era, American poet e. e. cummings wrote lyrical poems, humorous character sketches, and bitter satires on the foibles and institutions of his time.

To appreciate e. e. cummings fully, it helps to know that the energy of his poetry derived from his extremely strong iconoclastic sense of individualism. He was a student of Ralph Waldo Emerson's strong dissertation against established authority, "Self-Reliance." While serving in Europe during World War I he was interned in a detention camp by his own army because of his friendship with an American who was critical of the war effort. The French censor deemed him potentially dangerous because he had a mind of his own. He even went so far as to legally change his name to lowercase letters only, and he mostly used lowercase in his poetry, also using eccentric punctuation and phrasing. He spent thirty-six days touring Russia, confirming his distaste for collectivism and further strengthening his already firm resolve about the importance of thinking for oneself and resisting authority, particularly when it demands conformity.

This poem, the story of God greeting Effie on Judgment Day, has long been a particular favorite of mine. It speaks directly to cummings's steadfast belief in New England dissent and self-sufficiency. I love the image of God stooping by the coffin lid and being surprised when there is no Effie. Her brainless self has been supplanted by the poet's six symbols of empty-headedness, which cummings calls six crumbs. These crumbs of gingerbread are what Effie has left for a brain, and he asks us all to look at how often we employ these crumbs of conformity in place of our individuality.

The first crumb's name is "may," one of "the innumerable capering damned," as cummings calls his six symbols of being dead in the head. "May" needs to seek permission of others to act, as in "May I please have your blessing as well as your indulgence in allowing me to be or do anything?" This word "may" symbolizes self-doubt and the tendency to seek validation in the approval and authority of others. To always use it, says cummings, is to substitute gingerbread for your brain.

Number two crumb's name is "might," whose way of life is "It might have been." "Might" also is synonymous with "may" asking, "Might I have permission?" of others. In either case, the tendency to behave in these obsequious ways symbolized by "may" and "might" are inclinations the poet asks us to challenge strenuously, otherwise be at peril of having no substance for God to greet on Judgment Day!

Crumbs three, four, and five are the rhyming triplets of a way of life that is vacant and barren of personal power. "Should" is the term we use when we refer to our past actions from a wishful perspective. Here we take an action and assess it not on the basis of what we did, but on how we should have done it. In our reality system, though, you can never "should have done" anything. "You cannot 'should have been' here last week, today it's impossible," I told a taxi driver after he said, "The weather's beautiful here this week, but you should have been here last week." Those who live exclusively with their "shoulds" are living an impossibly empty life, using up present moments commiserating over what they should or shouldn't have done.

Little sister "could," and big brother "would" are indications that a vacancy sign is displayed because the brain's owner is unavailable. These three siblings' way of life involves despair as they hope and debate decisions and actions. "I would do it, if only I could" has both siblings making excuses in the same sentence, explaining away a lack of initiative and action. When they are used in an interrogatory fashion, such as, "Would it be all right?" or "Could I please have permission?" they are gingerbread substituting for a clear decisive mind. When they are used as explanations for why something didn't work out, they are still the stuff of empty-headedness.

The last, with some shame, gives his name as "must," the final symbol of a bare cupboard. This is the crumb that is used to explain all the obligations you have to live up to, the demands and expectations of others. "I must do this, because *they* will be disappointed if I don't." "I must do as I am programmed to do or I'll collapse." My friend and teacher Albert Ellis refers to this impulse as "musterbating."

There we have the six indices of a head that is so unoccupied that God stoops in surprise as He waits for something to rise. Here instead is a personal inventory of excuses that we employ far more frequently than we are aware. It often seems natural to seek permission and ask to be authorized rather than to take control of one's life. When we say, "May I?" we are really saying, "I don't trust myself to take the necessary steps, so I'll just turn my life over to someone else." To cummings, this is the same as having no brain, or at best to be brain-dead, and instead have gingerbread crumbs where God intended there to be a thinking person.

When we discuss what we should have done, or what we could have done, or what we would have done, we are not tuned into our reality system. No one could have done anything differently than they did. Period! No one can "should have done" anything any different, and no one ever would have done it differently regardless of any and all circumstances. We did it!

Period. You can learn from all that you have done, but "woulding," "coulding," and "shoulding" are clearly impossible in this moment.

Using the three rhyming triplets is like substituting gingerbread crumbs for your own thinking process.

You don't have to "musterbate," you are free to direct your own life, in your own fashion, irrespective of all of those who have laid "musts" on you in the past.

Don't let yourself be an Effie, whom God won't be able to find when you depart this world. You have been given a brain and a capacity to think and act based on your use of that remarkable organ. Don't let it deteriorate into a few crumbs by employing those six symbols of empty-headedness. To put the thoughts of this acerbic and strongly individualistic poet to work in your life, begin the process with these ideas:

- Catch yourself as you are about to use any of the six crumbs by first becoming aware of your use of these terms. You will then be able to remove them not only from your vocabulary, but from your life as well.

- Do not be a permission seeker when it comes to the important dealings of your life. Rather than saying, "May I attend that seminar?" or "Would it be all right if I went to this luncheon?" state your intentions in declarative sentences. Say, "I will be attending this meeting," or, "I have scheduled this luncheon on my calendar. Would you care to join me?"

- Let go of your attachment to responsibilities that others have given you without your consent. You and only you are the one to be making the choices about your own responsibilities, and you have no shoulds to live up to unless they are your decisions. Turn your shoulds and musts into your own personal options and carry them out with a strong sense of your own character, strength, and, most important, aliveness. No gingerbread for you!

✦ INDEPENDENCE ✦

THE ROAD NOT TAKEN

Two roads diverged in a yellow wood,
And sorry I could not travel both
And be one traveler, long I stood
And looked down one as far as I could
To where it bent in the undergrowth;

Then took the other, as just as fair,
And having perhaps the better claim,
Because it was grassy and wanted wear;
Though as for that the passing there
Had worn them really about the same,

And both that morning equally lay
In leaves no step had trodden black.
Oh, I kept the first for another day!
Yet knowing how way leads on to way,
I doubted if I should ever come back.

I shall be telling this with a sigh
Somewhere ages and ages hence:
Two roads diverged in a wood, and I—
I took the one less traveled by,
And that has made all the difference.

ROBERT FROST
(1874–1963)

The recipient of many Pulitzer Prizes, Robert Frost is reknowned for his poetic landscapes of rural America and of the human soul.

When Frost writes of taking the road "less traveled by," he speaks to something far more transcendent than merely picking the less busy byway at a fork in the road. The two roads diverging in the woods, and Frost's contemplation, "I doubted if I should ever come back," say in effect, "I only have one chance here. I can't take one road and when it doesn't work out, come back to try the second." He knows that he has a choice, and the criterion he uses to make his decision is his instinct, which prompts him to take the less-traveled road.

I read in this poem advice that applies in all areas of our lives. To me, Frost says be wary of following the pack, and don't do anything simply because everyone else is doing it. Also, do what you do in the manner that you perceive it, regardless of how everyone is doing it, or has always done it. In the last stanza of this, perhaps the most enduring of Robert Frost's poems, this valuable life lesson about living our lives by choosing our own path is underscored with the poetic conclusion that a life lived in this manner makes all the difference.

My wife and I are the parents of eight wonderful children. Our chief concern is to help them to develop their own sense of purpose in life, while doing all that we can to keep them out of harm's way. Each day we hear stories of young people who have become victims of such horrors as drunken driving accidents, drug overdoses, criminal activities, and sexually transmitted diseases that are often death sentences. In discussing those kinds of issues with our children, and their friends, we often hear the words, "Everybody does it." We hear terms like "peer pressure" and how it is only normal for young people to want to feel accepted by their peers. No one, we are frequently told, wants to look like a "dork" by not fitting in. And I always remind them of this poem, "The Road Not Taken." Given that you simply cannot decide which path to take, and they both look inviting, then go with the poet's advice and take the one less traveled by, it will make all the difference in your life.

If everyone seems to think that it is cool to drink and use drugs, and you are undecided, take a different path. Choose the road that you and only you are going to traverse, and it will make all the difference. One reason peer pressure has such a powerful effect on young people is that we adults are victims of the same group-think mentality. We often excuse youngsters because we have difficulty making a difference in our own lives.

Producing this collection of essays based on the creative offerings of so many great souls over the course of recorded history has been an eye-opener for me. Before writing what I believe the poet or writer is saying to us today, I read all that I could find about their lives and the choices they made in their own times. Virtually all these people we revere took the road less traveled by, and that is why they were able to make a difference.

Frost himself was expected to be a farmer, lawyer, and then a teacher. He tried farming and left it. He entered law school to be the lawyer his grandfather wanted him to be, but departed almost immediately without notice. He left Harvard because of an illness, perhaps brought on by trying the road *most* traveled. But poetry was in his heart, and when he went down a road that few traveled with him, it made all the difference, and today we have his poetry because of that choice. Because of similar choices, we have the music of Mozart, the paintings of Michelangelo, and the sculptures of the ancient Greeks.

Frost's poem invites you to forget peer pressure and instead know that if you truly want to make a difference in your life, you cannot do so by doing things the way everyone else does, or even because everyone else is. If you choose to lead your life just like everyone else, then what exactly is it that you have to offer? The road most traveled by is one that will allow you to fit in, to feel accepted, even to become enculturated. But it will never allow you to make a difference. As you read all these enduring contributions from great thinkers over the centuries, you are absorbing the wisdom of those who most frequently chose the road less traveled. Their writing endured because they continued in spite of the criticism of those who chose the more common path.

In my own professional work I have been willing to speak and write about topics and ideas that were criticized by those on the more frequented road. In the beginning, the road I took was filled with potholes and gravel. Yet my work has always come from that place I trust most—my own heart—and so I persisted. As the years passed the road became paved and well-lit. Now many who once thought this was a preposterous path are walking with me. I often hear, "I used to think those ideas were insane, but now I really like what you were saying then." I am happy to have experienced what Robert Frost was writing about.

Frost wrote of the common man and the uncommon choices he can make when he follows his intuition rather than the pack. What a great lesson for you, for me, and particularly for all our children. I am one of those children, now telling my children to take the road less traveled. I encourage you to know the pleasure of choosing *your* path and "telling this with a sigh somewhere ages and ages hence." Then I hope there will be more children in the world who become adults who know that it's never crowded along the extra mile.

To put this message into your life begin today to:

- Let go of using the behavior or accomplishments of others as a means of validating your own life. Even if many others, even a majority, believe in one way, if you feel out of harmony with that group-think, validate yourself by taking the road your heart wants to follow.

- Work hard at not using comparisons in your relationships. Expecting anyone else to conform to the standards of others does not encourage self-esteem or individuality.

- Listen to your own heart concerning the path you wish to travel. Even if your entire life training has been in one direction, if it is not what you feel now, then begin the adventure of exploring a less-traveled road. The reward of self-sufficiency will far outweigh the practice of conformity.

- Remind yourself, as Robert Frost does in his poem, that it is most unlikely that you will get a second chance to come back and travel a path that you really wanted to try, but didn't because it was less traveled.

APPRECIATION

ON BEING A WOMAN

Why is it, when I am in Rome
I'd give an eye to be at home,
But when on native earth I be,
My soul is sick for Italy?

And why with you, my love, my lord,
Am I spectacularly bored,
Yet do you up and leave me—then
I scream to have you back again?

DOROTHY PARKER
(1893–1967)

American writer of short stories, verse, and criticism, Dorothy Parker was noted for her caustic wit.

This poem, in the witty and clever style that was the hallmark of Dorothy Parker's writing, reflects on a common neurotic trait that most of us are familiar with. She puzzles poetically about our peculiar tendency to want what we don't have until we have it, and then not to want it! One of the great mysteries of humanity! Why is it that we so often don't enjoy our moments and persistently neglect the here in favor of there? Dorothy Parker titles this "On Being a Woman," but based on my own observation of my fellow males, including myself, I would retitle this two-stanza poem "On Being a Person."

So many of us suffer from this malady of not being fully immersed in the present, yet the present is the only place we can fully immerse ourselves. Why do we use up the present moments of our lives, the very precious currency of life, consumed with a longing to be someplace else? Why do we use up our present moments in feeling guilty about the past or apprehensive about the future, or in anticipating being anywhere but here, as Dorothy Parker so aptly points out in this short poem?

My answer to those questions is that we do so because we are living our lives with an attitude of depreciation rather than appreciation. And the way to resolve this dilemma is so simple that it eludes almost everyone. That is, live your life in a state of appreciation rather than depreciation. It is nothing more than making a decision to become aware of how you are using up your present moments in the very private inner world of your thoughts. When you find yourself in Rome and you are thinking about being at home, or vice versa, give yourself a nudge and make a choice to stop depreciating Rome and instead make the effort to appreciate. This is a kind of self-talk that will rescue you from the trap of never being fully here in the present moment.

One of the traits I have observed in highly functioning people is their uncanny ability to shut out the past and the future as well. When you are in their presence they look you directly in the eye and you know you have their full attention. Worry is not a part of their life experience. One of those people explained it to me this way: "First, it makes no sense to worry about the things you have no control over, because if you have no control over them, it makes no sense to worry about them. Second, it makes no sense to worry about the things you do have control over, because if you have control, it makes no sense to worry." And there goes *everything* it is possible to worry about. I feel this message is important enough to repeat it again and again to ourselves.

Thus, if I'm in Rome, I have absolutely no control over home. So I have the choice to not depreciate Rome and appreciate home, when Rome is where I am. Similarly, when I am with anyone, and bored, it is because I have made the deliberate choice to depreciate who I am with, and to only appreciate that which is not here. Thus when the boring one leaves, I still maintain the same neurotic thought process. I appreciate what is not here, and depreciate my aloneness, which is what constitutes the present. By learning to practice appreciating what is here, and to depreciate nothing, the dilemma that the witty author presents in her poetry disappears. And it quite simply is a matter of making a conscious decision in the moment.

Often I find myself falling into the trap that Dorothy Parker presents here when I am in solitude for the exclusive purpose of writing. Away from the noise and constant interruptions of a large family, I find myself wanting to be with them. Then, when I am home, I find myself longing for the privacy and solitude of my writing location. The way out of this for me is to become aware of what I am doing and how I am using my thoughts and to bring myself immediately back to the present.

While writing I practice the habit of appreciation for everything around me. I look out at the scenery and say thank you for these surroundings and the opportunity to create here and now. And then the writing itself becomes a great source of joy. Similarly, when I am home and the children are running about and there seems to be no end to the confusion, I push out all thoughts of elsewhere and practice being in a state of appreciation. I watch my wife in our home and I think of how lucky I am to be here. I even feel appreciative of the most obvious things we often take for granted, such as the refrigerator, the pictures on the wall, and the barking dogs. It is all about shifting to appreciation and out of depreciation.

I recognize that Dorothy Parker was known most for her acerbic and biting wit; perhaps that is why I chose to include her in this book. I love satire and a good laugh as well. When she was told of the death of President Calvin Coolidge, she responded, "How can they tell?" And in a review of Katharine Hepburn's performance in a 1934 play, Parker said, "She ran the gamut of emotions from A to B." I am well aware that Dorothy Parker was speaking glibly and with some self-sarcasm in this poem titled "On Being a Woman," yet it addresses a chief factor in leading a fully functioning life.

Perhaps the single most predominant feature of mental wellness is the ability to be in the present moment, fully and with no thoughts of being elsewhere. To Henry David Thoreau's description: "He is blessed over all mortals who loses no moment of the passing life in remembering the past," I would add with deep respect, "In anticipating the future as well." There definitely is a past, but not now. And there definitely is a future, but not now.

Our present moment is a mystery that we are a part of; a dream if you will, of the moment. Here and now is where all the mystery lies hidden. And make no mistake about it, to strive to live completely in the present is to strive for what already is the case. You can either use up these precious present moments in a state of appreciation, which is to be here fully now, or in a state of depreciation, which is to wish to be anywhere but here. But when all is said and done, now is all there is, and all there ever has been.

Enjoy Dorothy Parker's clever little poem and gain from her observations by incorporating the following suggestions into your present moments:

- Notice when you are wishing you were somewhere else and bring yourself back to a state of appreciation for where you are. When you plan something, thoroughly enjoy the planning. Remember that not being fully immersed in the present is nothing more than a habit that you have the option of breaking right now, in this moment!

- Discard thoughts of depreciation. When you find yourself depreciating anyone or anything in your immediate present moment space, see if you can substitute a thought of appreciation. For example, rather than being bored by a conversation, shift your thoughts to, "I am going to spend the next few moments just loving this person for who he is, and nothing more." This removal of judgment brings you back to being fully in the present.

- Take time to meditate. Meditation is so difficult for many people because their thoughts are always on some distant object or place. One form of meditation is to label the thought as it appears and then choose to let it go. This practice helps you first become aware of your thoughts, which many of us need to do, so that we can return to the present moment.

- Practice enjoying each phase of a meal for itself, rather than having your thoughts on dessert while you are consuming the appetizers. This also goes for enjoying the sunrise in the morning, and being awake during the day, and not thinking of your bed while at work. The essence of the entire message here is to be here now. There is no other place to be.

FORGIVENESS

CROSS

My old man's a white old man
And my old mother's black.
If ever I cursed my white old man
I take my curses back.

If ever I cursed my black old mother
And wished she were in hell,
I'm sorry for that evil wish
And now I wish her well.

My old man died in a fine big house
My ma died in a shack.
I wonder where I'm gonna die,
Being neither white or black?

LANGSTON HUGHES
(1902–1967)

American poet Langston Hughes also wrote humorous newspaper sketches, a novel, and a short-story collection. He is most widely known for his poems, which use the rhythms of the blues and the ballad, are often documentary, and deal with the trials and joys of the black American.

*T*his brief poem, written in a quick witty style, by the man I consider the forefather to the American civil rights movement, is a tribute to the healing effect of forgiveness as well as a parody on the absurdity of labeling people on the basis of physical appearances, particularly the color of one's skin. The final line in each of the first two stanzas sends a powerful message to all of us. They sum up what true spirituality as well as socio-mental health truly is: "I take my curses back," and "And now I wish her well." What is Langston Hughes saying to us through these lines? I believe he is expressing that he is spiritually mature enough to say to his parents, "I forgive you and I'm sorry for any evil thoughts I've ever directed your way."

The freedom in a simple act of forgiveness saves the expense of anger and the high cost of hatred. Forgiveness can buy peace of mind. Think of everything that has ever been directed at you for which you bear grudges or hostility. Every hurt or sting is like being bitten by a snake. You rarely die from the injury, but once bitten, it is impossible to be unbitten, and the damage is done by the venom that continues to flow through your system. The venom is your bitterness and hatred that you hang on to, long after you've been hurt. It is this venom that will ultimately destroy your peace of mind.

The antidote is forgiveness, which is not as difficult as you may want to believe. If you believe that forgiveness is a challenging and conflict-ridden act that you have to struggle with for a lifetime, I suggest quite the opposite is true. Forgiveness is joyful, easy, and, most of all, exceedingly freeing. It relieves us of the burdens of resentment and past grievances and is just another word for simply letting go. I speak here from my own personal experience, and it is perhaps why I am so attracted to this poem.

My old man was a white old man who walked out of my life when I was an infant and never even bothered to make a phone call. Not once in his lifetime did he ever call to see how his three boys were faring. He spent some time in prison, drank excessively, was abusive to my mother and many other women, died of cirrhosis of the liver at the age of forty-nine, and was buried in a pauper's grave in Biloxi, Mississippi.

I carried the burden of resentment and hatred until I was in my early thirties, when I went to his grave and said essentially the same thing that Langston Hughes said, "I take my curses back," and in doing so I literally transformed my life. My writing began to click, my approach to my health improved significantly, my relationships shifted away from hostility and toward spiritual partnership, and most of all, I felt free from the burden of having that venom pumping through my veins. When we learn to pardon, we rise above those who have insulted or aggrieved us, and this act of forgiveness puts an end to the quarrel. The last stanza of Langston Hughes's poem speaks to the labeling process of identifying ourselves by our outward appearances.

Søren Kierkegaard, the famed Danish theologian, remarked, "Once you label me, you negate me." The process of putting ourselves and others into neat little compartments on the basis of any label and then making judgments about everyone on the basis of those labels is as nonspiritual and dehumanizing an experience as I can imagine. Yet it is done all the time. Our government asks us to fill out census reports and to neatly compartmentalize ourselves racially. Funding is allotted on the basis of these distinctions, and prejudices are rampant because we tend to identify one another on the basis of what we can see with our eyes, rather than feel with our hearts. We know that we can exchange our inner organs, and borrow each other's blood, and we know that our thoughts and our souls are colorless, yet we still need to put labels on ourselves on the basis of what is outside.

We have a close friend who lives on Maui. His father—who has long been separated from the family—is black and his mother is white. Like Langston Hughes, he has been raised by his mother and his grandmother. He once casually remarked to me, "Being neither white nor black, I really have no one to hate." There is much to learn from this observation.

I love Langston Hughes's final two lines. They sum up the absurdity of ever putting any label of any kind on any person. "I wonder where I'm gonna die, being neither white or black." Such a dilemma. We know what to do with his old man and his old mother, but how do we deal with him? This man, Langston Hughes, wrote his poetry in the 1920s and 1930s when racial hatred and tension were at an all-time high in America. And he spoke from his heart with great courage. Perhaps his most famous poem is "I, Too, Sing America." I reproduce it here for you to read as you consider these twin themes of forgiveness and labeling.

I, TOO, SING AMERICA

I am the darker brother.
They send me to eat in the kitchen
When company comes,
But I laugh,
And eat well,
And grow strong.

Tomorrow,
I'll sit at the table
When company comes.
Nobody'll dare
Say to me,
"Eat in the kitchen."
Then.
Besides,
They'll see how beautiful I am
And be ashamed—

I, too, am America.

He reminds us from a generation or two back that we act shamefully when we apply labels to anyone. And he was correct. "Tomorrow, . . . nobody'll dare say to me, 'Eat in the kitchen,'" and it is so because a man like Langston Hughes was able to laugh, and grow strong, and feel beautiful despite what anyone might say to the contrary. And, yes, was able to forgive. He reminds us that everyone is of equal value, as did William Blake, who also wrote of his disdain for prejudice and left this poetic reminder: "In Heaven the only art of living, is forgetting and forgiving."

To put these ideas of Langston Hughes to work now in your own life begin to:

- Take stock of everyone who has ever wronged you in any way, regardless of how severe or recent it may have been, and make the choice to let go. Forgiveness is an act of the heart.

Do it for yourself, to provide the antidote for the poison that you have allowed to circulate inside you.

- Be aware that your parents (and everyone else in your past) did what they knew how to do given the conditions of their lives. You can not ask any more of anyone. Perhaps you would not have done it that way, so learn from it. Forgiving is recognizing that deep injuries will not recover until you forgive. So make that choice and you will immediately feel freer than you've ever felt.

- Make every effort to remove the labeling process from your life experience. Look past the skin and bone structure to the unfolding of God in all people, and address them and yourself from that space of no labels. And remember always that everyone, without exclusion, has the right to say, "I, too, sing America."

❀ NONVIOLENCE ❀

The non-violent approach does not immediately change the
heart of the oppressor. It first does something to the hearts
and souls of those committed to it. It gives them a new self-
respect; it calls up resources of strength and courage that they
did not know they had. Finally it reaches the opponent and
so stirs his conscience that reconciliation becomes a reality.

MARTIN LUTHER KING, JR.
(1929–1968)

*Dr. Martin Luther King, Jr., was a Baptist minister and passion-
ate fighter for civil rights through nonviolent action. He was felled
by an assassin's bullet in 1968.*

This quote from Dr. Martin Luther King, Jr., reminds me of a
story about the Buddha. It seems that a man had heard of the
reputation that Buddha had for being peaceful and nonviolent
regardless of what he encountered in life. This man decided to
test the divine one, and he traveled a long distance to be in his
presence. For three days he was rude and obnoxious to the Buddha. He criticized and found fault with everything the Buddha
said or did. He verbally abused the Buddha, attempting to get
him to react angrily. Yet the Buddha never faltered. Each time he
responded with love and kindness. Finally the man could take it
no longer. "How could you be so peaceful and kind when all I've
ever said to you was antagonistic?" he asked. The Buddha's
response was in the form of a question to the man. "If someone
offers you a gift, and you do not accept that gift, to whom does
the gift belong?" the Buddha replied. The man had his answer.

If someone offers *you* a gift of anger or hostility and you do
not accept it, then it still belongs to the giver. Why choose to be
upset or angry over something that does not belong to you?

This is the essence of the message that Dr. Martin Luther King offers us. When you choose the nonviolent approach your first impact will be on yourself. You become less inclined to accept the gifts of ill-will that come your way. You will simply "pass" when others try to seduce you into arguments or conflict of any kind. Your initial objective will not be to change anyone, but rather to deliberately and lovingly work on being an instrument of grace and indulgence. The more peaceful you become within yourself, the less you will be affected by the enmity or disaffection of others.

When Dr. King speaks of something happening to the heart and soul of those who are committed to nonviolence, he is not speaking exclusively of the civil rights movement or class warfare. He is telling us that if we can commit ourselves to a peaceful heart we will behave more courageously and with a strength that we have never known before. As those around us attempt to draw us into their battles, our commitment to being peaceful allows us to have a different dialogue with ourselves before we even consider accepting of the "gifts" being offered. Our affirmation is, "I will choose peace rather than this." After a series of these dialogues, we react peacefully automatically.

My wife, Marcelene, is a very peaceful, meditative woman, and always has been in the two-plus decades that we have been together. In our earliest years I would attempt to draw her into arguments with my rather loud logic, but she simply didn't play the relationship game that way. Essentially she was telling me with her behavior, "I am not interested in fighting with you," and she displayed this by showing me a peaceful countenance and not joining in my attempts to argue. Before long I realized that I was not going to bulldoze this woman into thinking my way. I realized that it is very difficult to pick a fight with someone who has no interest in fighting. She wasn't trying to change me with her behavior. She was responding peacefully from *her* commitment to nonviolent behavior.

As you read and reread these beautiful words of Dr. King, remind yourself that your objective in choosing to be a nonviolent person is not to change anyone or to fix the world. Your objective is to give yourself the self-respect that you deserve as a divine creation of God, and to remove the pain associated with conflict and "dis-ease." You will then begin to effortlessly radiate that strength of self-respect and peace, and impact those around you simply by your presence.

It was said of Buddha and Jesus Christ that just their presence in a village, and nothing more, would raise the consciousness of those around them. You have probably experienced this when you were around highly evolved peaceful people. They seem to radiate pheromones of love that make you feel peaceful and more self-assured. It is my experience that we can literally change the energy of *any* environment by making the decision to implement an affirmation such as this one from *A Course in Miracles*. "I will be peaceful and nonviolent regardless of the offerings directed at me."

I have practiced sending out nonviolent pheromones of energy in many situations where I used to think I had no power whatsoever. In grocery stores, when I hear or see parents who are being abusive toward a child, I literally move into the energy field and allow my peaceful loving energy to impact the field. It sounds crazy, but it always seems to work, and as Dr. King puts it so eloquently; "It reaches the opponent and so stirs his [and her] conscience that reconciliation becomes a reality."

When children are the ones being abusive and wanting to argue, let them see a real live example of a person who is unwilling to be so engaged. In your relationships with family or other adults, let them see a heart and soul first and foremost who is at peace. It is always a choice to participate in malevolence or benevolence, even if you feel you are being baited. Recall the words of the Buddha and the gift, and know that the nonviolence that Dr. King preached and lived is an example that applies to each of our lives, every day.

To become a part of this nonviolent movement try these suggestions:

- Catch yourself before reacting to violence of any kind with more violence, and vow to be an instrument of peace, as all our spiritual teachers have encouraged us to be.

- Work on yourself each day to bring a more peaceful stance into your life. Take time to meditate, practice yoga, read poetry, go for solitary walks, play with children and animals, or do anything that will give you a feeling of loving and being loved.

- Make a specific effort to remove violent input from your life. The newspapers and news reports that attempt to titillate your curiosity about hostility and malignant hatred by filling you with endless reports take you away from your peace. Turn away from these sources and each time you hear these reports, remember that for every act of inhumanity to man, there are a thousand acts of kindness.

- Remember this ancient Chinese proverb: "The sage does not talk, the talented ones talk, and the stupid ones argue."

COMPARISON

SO THAT'S WHO I REMIND ME OF

When I consider men of golden talents,
I'm delighted, in my introverted way,
To discover, as I'm drawing up the balance,
How much we have in common, I and they.

Like Burns, I have a weakness for the bottle,
Like Shakespeare, little Latin and less Greek;
I bite my fingernails like Aristotle;
Like Thackeray, I have a snobbish streak.

I'm afflicted with the vanity of Byron,
I've inherited the spitefulness of Pope;
Like Petrarch, I'm a sucker for a siren,
Like Milton, I've a tendency to mope.

My spelling is suggestive of a Chaucer;
Like Johnson, well, I do not wish to die
(I also drink my coffee from the saucer);
And if Goldsmith was a parrot, so am I,

Like Villon, I have debits by the carload,
Like Swinburne, I'm afraid I need a nurse;
By my dicing is Christopher out-Marlowed,
And I dream as much as Coleridge, only worse.

In comparison with men of golden talents,
I am all a man of talent ought to be;
I resemble every genius in his vice, however heinous—
Yet I write so much like me.

OGDEN NASH
(1902–1971)

American writer of light verse, Ogden Nash is known for his sophisticated whimsy and satire.

Ogden Nash was known for his great sense of humor and his audacious verse, which was often ragged and highly varied, from one-word sentences to lines that meandered for a full paragraph. He won a large following during his lifetime, particularly for poetry that satirized everyday foibles. In this selection he pokes fun at himself by justifying his weaknesses as they line up with "men of golden talents," who are some of the world's best poets. While this poem was obviously written with tongue in cheek, nevertheless it highlights the tendency that many of us have to compare ourselves to others.

It seems easier to look at our behavior in comparison to others to judge where we stand in life. Virtually all our upbringing at home and in school used the comparison method, and most of us were groomed to fit somewhere in the middle, depending on how everyone else stacked up. For purposes of evaluation, the standardized curve was applied to determine just where we fit, be it in geography, mathematics, what to wear, and what curfew to obey. Whatever everyone else was doing was consistently used as a barometer to determine what we should be doing. There were school transcripts and social report cards as well. Comparison as a means of assessment was so prevalent that it is most likely the means you employ for assessing your adult life as well as managing the lives of your family members.

Yet comparing one person to another negates each person's uniqueness and is often insulting to each person individually, and comparisons will never lead you to self-knowledge. It is comfortable to search outside oneself for validation if that is what others do. And if approximately sixty-eight percent of the people are doing it, we might be tempted to interpret that as the right way. We repeat the conditioning of the past in a search out there somewhere, for that which resides in here, when we continually compare our lives with others. I like this statement by Lao-tzu, the founder of Taoism: "He who knows others is wise. He who knows himself is enlightened."

When we resort to comparisons of any kind the most we can hope for is some wisdom. But to become enlightened we must know and honor the unique creation that each of us is. This is the genius that is never found near the median.

Ceaselessly striving toward the highest and widest point on the "normal" curve, and avoiding the narrow ends representing the extremes, is, as I am sure you are aware, not the path I think anyone need follow. Why? Because the creative genius is found in those more distant positions away from the median.

Jean Piaget is a famous Swiss psychiatrist who researched the ways in which students could best achieve in school. He provided me with an important insight which I have never forgotten, when I was a young doctoral student many years ago. His experiments with school children confirmed that learning and levels of achievement are different for different individuals. In any classroom in which one method of instruction, say lecturing, was the sole means of presenting the material, after an exam was given at the end of the instruction period, the levels of achievement resemble a standardized curve with approximately two-thirds in the C or average range; one-fourth divided in half in the above and below average (D and B grades); six percent divided equally as failures and high achievers (F and A grades) with tiny fractions in what are called distant deviations from the center. That is, a tiny fraction are geniuses and a tiny fraction simply absorbed nothing.

But this is not what impressed me, nor is it what I always remembered. Piaget then said, if you were to change the method of delivery from, say lecturing, to drawings, then you get the same standardized distribution, a tiny fraction of geniuses and zeros, six percent A and F; twenty-five percent D and B; sixty-seven percent C+ to C-. But the startling thing is that you now have new people in the genius range and the zero ranges, and when you try another method of delivery, with the same group, say small group discussions, or video presentations, with each new method of instruction on the very same material, you find new geniuses, new zeros, and a whole new grouping of average.

For me, Piaget's profound conclusion was unforgettable. There is a genius in every single person, and all we as educators, or parents, or directors of our own lives need to do, is find the method that will allow that genius to be revealed.

Ogden Nash's humorous and satirical poem "So That's Who I Remind Me Of" reminds you how absurd it is to compare yourself to anyone else at any time. His conclusion reveals the truth of this assertion, "Yet I write so much like me." And that is all he could ever do: be himself.

Often, in our efforts to fit in and be accepted, we ambush ourselves by looking to see how we compare to others. We have been conditioned since our first days in school and so it is easy to forget that our own individual genius may not have evolved. The idea of comparing yourself to anyone else seems absurd when you know you are a unique individual, and when you align yourself with the method, people, and circumstances that feel just right for you.

You know in your heart, as I do when I write, or speak, or run a marathon, or wash my car, or brush my teeth, I do not need to compare my actions with other people to decide how to do them. We are free when we can say, "This is my way, what is your way? *The* way does not exist!" I am free when I no longer need to see what I share in common with those men of golden talents. The conclusion is the same one that Ogden Nash reached: "Yet I write so much like me." Stop comparing and begin composing *your* life, your way.

To reduce the habit of comparing yourself with others begin to practice these suggestions:

• Use your own personal index for evaluating yourself and your performances. "Am I content with myself?" rather than "I'm not as good as my sister."

• When you find yourself in the old habit of comparison stop right in the moment and catch yourself. Becoming aware is the beginning of changing this habit. As you were about to say, "I guess I am about average in something," stop and rephrase to "This is how I perform and I'm fine with it."

• Don't use comparisons with your children unless you expect them in return. For every time you say, "All the other children at school are expected to do some household chores," expect to hear something like, "No other parents make their kids go to bed this early." The habit becomes insidious and will pass from generation to generation unless you stop using comparison as a standard. Change your directions to: "I expect you to do your housework and your chores, and it has nothing to do with your friends."

- If you are not as talented or expert as you want to be at a particular thing, remind yourself that it is not because you are deficient. It is the result of your unique reaction to and experience of this event. Your genius may reside elsewhere or it may require you to be exposed to another way of learning. Respect your individuality and uniqueness and resist speculating on how you compare. Comparison always puts the controls of your life in the hands of those to whom you compare yourself.

❀ ACTION/DOING ❀

There should be less talk; a preaching point is not a meeting point. What do you do then? Take a broom and clean
someone's house. That says enough.

MOTHER TERESA
(1910–1997)

*A nun who was a history and geography teacher and headmistress
in Calcutta, Mother Teresa was called to leave the convent to help
the poorest of the poor and live among them. In 1950 she and her
helpers established the Missionaries of Charity.*

*T*he most effective way to teach anyone what we would like
them to know is through behavior, not words. Often endless hours
are spent in conversation, expressing our frustration about what
we find objectionable, and verbally exchanging insults and examples of what is so exasperating. The desired change does not materialize and you still experience the anguish of being mistreated.

It may be true on some level that communication is the key to
successful relationships, but often it seems that the more words
are exchanged, the less successful the outcome. This can be true
with significant others, family members, employers and employ-
ees, even your own children.

Mother Teresa, the diminutive spiritual giant who worked
daily in the streets of Calcutta, seeing "Jesus Christ in all of his
distressing disguises," as she put it, offers us some profound wisdom in her briefly spoken advice. "There should be less talk,"
there should be more action on your part. Words that are not
backed by action become simply a "preaching point" and nothing
more. If you want to make a point, you may need to create a
"meeting point" with new and effective behavior. The old apho-
rism, "I hear, I forget; I see, I remember; I do, I understand,"

applies not only to what you want to learn, but also to how you wish to be treated. Obviously you cannot learn how to swim by simply listening to the words of others, or watching other people in the water. You must do it in order to know it. And this same concise logic applies to the folly of endlessly exchanging words as your only means of communication.

Behavior is the most effective way to communicate with others in your life. My wife and I have always told our children about kindness to all creatures. Yet the most effective way of communicating this message is our own behavior. Perhaps the most telling example of this occurred on Maui when Marcelene and one of our daughters discovered a tiny bird who had fallen from its nest. I recall my wife, who had many important family matters to attend to that day, taking that tiny bird in a shoebox and driving halfway around the island to a shelter that she had called, spending four hours in traffic and giving up her day for a little baby bird. She delivered the tiny creature to helping hands, and in so doing she created a meeting point rather than a preaching point. Our children and I saw love for all creatures in action that day, and the lesson had more impact than any tirade on the subject.

When you find yourself embroiled in the futility of word games that just address the surface of an issue, stop and remind yourself of the great wisdom in Mother Teresa's suggestion. Ask yourself, "What can I do here?" instead of continuing to try to make your point. If someone is disrespectful in language, by all means state your case in words, and then if the disrespect continues to surface, shift into the action stage, or the meeting point as Mother Teresa describes it. Remove yourself immediately from the scene. If you are dealing with an adult, do everything possible to convey your seriousness. Stay away for a week at least. If you are dealing with drunken behavior, don't be an enabler by using more words as your only means of communication. Rather demand that the person seek help or you will no longer be a part of his life. With children, remove privileges and stick to it when basic rules of decency and harmony are violated. By all means talk it out, but eventually you must take the broom and clean the house of another if you are truly going to be of help.

Mother Teresa was not a person you could call cruel or uncaring. Her life was devoted to charity and helping the less fortunate among us to have humane treatment. She seemed to know that the way to make this a reality was not to tell others about the importance of virtuous action, but to actually live it. It is not cruel to show, with behavior, that you will not condone those things you find objectionable. It may be the only way to effect change. Your words, while important, risk being forgotten if they are not followed by action.

We all seem to suffer from the inclination to discuss our problems endlessly. We put together committees to study problems and go to the committee meeting to talk about all the reasons that something probably cannot be done. People of action are not inclined to join committees and listen to ad hoc reports. I recall reading about Lee Iacocca, the automotive executive known for his impatience with excuses, whose leadership brought two of the largest automobile companies in the world to places of preeminence. When he asked his engineers to build him a prototype convertible car, which hadn't been done for many decades, he kept hearing reasons in the form of words about why this wasn't feasible to produce, and what all of the engineering problems were. Finally, in exasperation, he ordered them to "just take a car and cut the damn top off of it, and let me see it."

People of action, those who make a difference in life, those whom we most admire, all seem to know the truth of the ancient wisdom, "What you do speaks so loud, I can't hear what you say." Be a doer. And in the process you will do more to teach others and to bring fulfillment into your life than all the words in the dictionary could ever convey.

To implement the advice of Mother Teresa try the following:

- Keep in mind that you get treated in life the way you teach people to treat you. Ask yourself if your behavior is inviting any maltreatment that keeps coming your way.

- When you feel that your words are no longer making an impact, and they are leading you into long tiresome tales that end up with the same results, resolve to be creative in shifting from a preaching point to a meeting point. Write down new ways of action that will convey your point, and vow to follow through on these points, even though your temptation is to revert back to the word games.

- Let your family members, particularly your children, observe you living your philosophy. Regardless of what they might say, they will respect you for your actions, even if they appear to be critical. If you refuse to stoop to a level of argumentation and defensiveness and simply, with determination, demonstrate your life philosophy, you will come to know the value of that meeting point.

AWE

BRISBANE

Brisbane

Where God was revealed to us.

Only the two of us know the magic and awe
of that presence.

Against impossible odds . . .

Our connection to eternity further reinforced,
strengthened.

Yet the paradox always lingers . . .

We are in control/we are not in control,
doomed to make choices.

All I am certain of is our love imbedded in
forever.

WAYNE W. DYER
(1940-   )

*An infinite soul disguised as a husband, father of eight, writer, and
lecturer, Wayne Dyer is the author of this and sixteen other books,
including three textbooks.*

This book is not about appreciating poetry and philosophy as
much as it is about applying the wisdom of these writers to our
everyday lives. All the selections in this book convey messages from

sensitive, highly creative, and productive individuals who were alive here on Planet Earth at one time, just as you and I are today.

I feel a bit presumptuous including a selection of my very own in this assemblage of splendor from so many supreme poets, artists, and philosophers of the past. But I have chosen to welcome my discomfort and self-consciousness because I want to include "Brisbane" in this book, which has been an enlightening labor of love for me, as an example of a piece of poetic writing that is from the heart of a regular, everyday guy, written to his wife in a moment of pure awe and inspiration. And also because I want you to know the story behind the poetic effort, from someone who is still here to share his reasons for writing it.

So I conclude this compilation with a poem I wrote for my wife, Marcelene, and hope that you too will take pen in hand and toss aside fear of embarrassment, ridicule, or unfair comparisons to the great poets, and express your innermost feelings to those you love.

This selection is titled "Brisbane" because that is the city in northern Australia where, back in 1989, I felt and knew absolutely, beyond any doubt, that there was a force at work in the universe that I call God. It was my introduction to *knowing* God, whereas until that day, I had only known *about* God.

My wife, Marcelene, and two of our children, who were one and a half and three and a half at the time, were with me on a speaking tour of Australia in February of 1989. I spoke to a large gathering of people during the day, and we returned, exhausted, to our hotel in Brisbane and retired for the evening. I had one of the children in my bed, while Marcelene slept and nursed the baby in the adjoining bed.

At 4:05 A.M. something that had never happened before, or since, occurred to startle me beyond anything I could describe here. My wife awakened from a deep sleep and began to rearrange the room. She took our three-and-a-half-year-old out of my bed and put her with our little one-and-a-half-year-old boy. She proceeded to get into my bed and to snuggle up next to me. This was uncharacteristic of Marcelene, particularly because she was nursing our son full-time. I was in a semiconscious state of shock, thinking I was having a dream.

My wife had been either nursing or pregnant for the previous eight years, and consequently had completely halted her menstrual cycle. Furthermore she had been assured that she would not get pregnant again because of a surgical procedure in which one ovary had been removed. But to be certain we practiced birth control, and I withdrew at the critical moment to put an exclamation point on our precaution. Yet, despite all this, at 4:05 A.M. in Brisbane, Australia, our youngest daughter, Saje Eykis Dyer, was conceived, and was brought into our world on November 16, 1989.

What awoke my wife at that instant? What caused this strange behavior by a woman who is always in control, to appear to be almost obsessed? What force was operating that night? Who was in charge here?

Saje has been a uniting force of love in our marriage, yet when I discovered that my wife was pregnant from that wonderfully bizarre middle-of-the-night obsession, I knew, as did Marcelene, that there were forces working to bring that little angel into the material world through us that went way beyond our decision to not have any more children. Surgery, birth control, withdrawal, an absence of a female cycle with which to keep track of ovulation, and being sound asleep in a foreign land are all insignificant minor obstacles to a life force that strives to manifest into our material world!

On Mother's Day 1989 I wrote the "Brisbane" poem for my wife and put it in a framed collage of our Australia trip. But no matter how many words I write, and how desperately I attempt to convey the specialness of that experience, as I wrote: "Only the two of us know the magic and awe of that presence." From that time until now I have never experienced one moment of doubt about the presence of God in my life. I do not engage in long arguments with disbelievers, nor do I feel any particular need to convince anyone of what I know. I simply express it, in my writing, in my lectures. And yes, in my own little poetic expression written to and for my wife. I go back to that moment, and my connection to that divine awakening, all-pervasive omnipresent force is reinforced and strengthened. I also know through this experience that every soul which manifests into a human being is also a part of this divine drama.

We like to think that we are the ones in charge of such matters, yet a big part of me knows that nothing can stop a determined soul, and the paradox of the statement, "doomed to make choices," is evident at all times. That is, we are in control, and we are not in control, all at the same time, and learning to live with this enigma is a big part of what *knowing* God is all about.

You arrived here through a similar miraculous scenario. Your heart started beating inside your mother's womb a few weeks after conception, and it is a total mystery to everyone on our planet. How does something come from no-thing? Where was that life before conception? What happens in the instant of creation? We are all walking, breathing, talking paradoxes, and perhaps we do best to let go of the intellectual struggle and accept with a loving heart while being certain of our love embedded in forever.

By all means hang on to the awe, and appreciate every moment of life and every molecule of creation. But somewhere, deep down inside you, in a tiny corner of your awareness, know for certain that there is one divine presence at work in you and in the entire universe as well, and that it never makes a mistake, despite what you may have come to believe over the years. This is an intelligent system that we are all a part of, and we make our entrances and exits precisely on time.

This last selection is my message to you as well as my tribute to that all-revealing moment back in early 1989. Be certain of one thing as it is expressed in *A Course in Miracles*, and as I have attempted to convey to you here in this final chapter. It is the one and only suggestion I personally want to offer you and leave with you as you close this book. "If you knew Who walks beside you on the way that you have chosen, fear would be impossible."

Namaste! (I honor the place in you where we are all one.)